'This is a marvelous collection: the essays show Roger Cotterrell at his best: incisive but also open-minded, offering valuable lessons to both established scholars and beginning law students.'

Professor Brian Bix, Frederick W. Thomas Professor of Law and Philosophy, University of Minnesota, USA

JURISPRUDENCE AND SOCIO-LEGAL STUDIES

This book presents a set of related studies aimed at showing key points of intersection and common interest between jurisprudence and socio-legal studies, which are otherwise typically considered distinct fields. It reflects and draws on the author's work in these areas over more than four decades.

The first half of the book explores theoretical issues surrounding the enterprise of socio-legal research, its current scope, and its historical traditions. Some chapters directly compare juristic theory and socio-legal inquiry. Chapters in Part II profile a selection of European jurists whose work offers important insights for socio-legal inquiry. Other chapters frame these studies, explore the history of interactions between jurisprudence and socio-legal research, and show points of convergence between these fields that are increasingly important today. A main aim of the book is to show the current urgency of linking and broadening juristic and social scientific interests in law.

Internationally oriented, the book will be of interest to students and researchers in the areas of jurisprudence, legal philosophy, sociology of law, socio-legal studies, and comparative law. It is suitable as supplementary reading for courses in any of these subjects.

Roger Cotterrell is Anniversary Professor of Legal Theory at Queen Mary University of London. Educated as both a lawyer and a sociologist, he has written widely on jurisprudence, sociology of law, and comparative law, and has devoted much of his career to building conversations between the contrasting traditions of jurisprudence and sociology of law. He is a Fellow of the British Academy and of the UK Academy of Social Sciences. His book *Sociological Jurisprudence*, published by Routledge in 2018, won the international Dennis Mahoney Prize for Legal Theory in 2022.

JURISPRUDENCE AND SOCIO-LEGAL STUDIES

Intersecting Fields

Roger Cotterrell

Routledge
Taylor & Francis Group
LONDON AND NEW YORK

First published 2024
by Routledge
4 Park Square, Milton Park, Abingdon, Oxon OX14 4RN

and by Routledge
605 Third Avenue, New York, NY 10158

Routledge is an imprint of the Taylor & Francis Group, an informa business

British Library Cataloguing-in-Publication Data
A catalogue record for this book is available from the British Library

Library of Congress Cataloging-in-Publication Data
Names: Cotterrell, Roger (Roger B. M.), author.
Title: Jurisprudence and socio-legal studies : intersecting fields / Roger Cotterrell.
Description: Abingdon, Oxon [UK] ; New York, NY : Routledge, 2024. | Includes bibliographical references and index.
Identifiers: LCCN 2023047579 (print) | LCCN 2023047580 (ebook) | ISBN 9781032374642 (hardback) | ISBN 9781032374635 (paperback) | ISBN 9781003340324 (ebook)
Subjects: LCSH: Sociological jurisprudence. | Law—Social aspects. | Welfare state—Social aspects. | Lawyers.
Classification: LCC K370 .C6825 2024 (print) | LCC K370 (ebook) | DDC 340/.115—dc23/eng/20231012
LC record available at https://lccn.loc.gov/2023047579
LC ebook record available at https://lccn.loc.gov/2023047580

ISBN: 978-1-032-37464-2 (hbk)
ISBN: 978-1-032-37463-5 (pbk)
ISBN: 978-1-003-34032-4 (ebk)

DOI: 10.4324/9781003340324

Typeset in Galliard
by Apex CoVantage, LLC

For Ann

CONTENTS

PREFACE

Great changes are occurring in law and society in many Western countries. They necessitate new kinds of study, and new relations between existing fields of research. This book is intended to contribute towards building new research relations across one large area – the important but neglected region of overlap in theory between jurisprudence and social science. Law can be studied theoretically from many standpoints, but the most instructive contrast may be between, on the one hand, juristic inquiries and, on the other, the social scientific inquiries about law that are called sociology of law or, more generally, socio-legal studies.

Juristic inquiries, reflecting lawyers' perspectives, almost inevitably emphasise and explore the normative character of law – the idea that law is primarily a matter not of facts but of norms: that is, 'ought propositions', prescribing what citizens, organisations, or governments *ought or ought not* to do, or are *authorised* and *empowered* to do, judged in legal terms. More broadly, law as a normative phenomenon may also be understood as, in part, a repository of values to be reflected by lawyers in practice and interpreted by philosophers in theory.

By contrast, in a standard conception of social science, social life is to be understood in terms of empirical fact – the experienced reality that social relations exist, that social change occurs, and that social institutions endure or are transformed. Sociology, within the social sciences, advocates many methods of empirically studying social reality, and recognises that the nature of this reality and its interpretation can be approached in many ways. But the juristic point of view, with its focus on normative interpretation of law and recognition of legal values, has usually been seen as fundamentally different from social scientific study of legal phenomena.

Beyond that, the juristic standpoint can be and perhaps should be seen as one of commitment, a standpoint that assumes a concerned engagement with law, an ambition to make law work better, to defend and promote values that law is supposed to serve in an ideal legal system. The sociologist of law, by contrast, is not professionally required to have any such commitment to law's wellbeing but is required only to observe and explain legal phenomena; to treat them as a disinterested scientist, exploring, describing, and interpreting part of the social world.

These stereotypes of juristic and social scientific outlooks can be challenged when judged against the possible variety of ways of thinking about law and society. For example, realist jurisprudence edges towards sociological outlooks; social science often reflects researchers' value-informed commitments. Nevertheless, there have often seemed to be powerful barriers to productive interaction between juristic ideas and social scientific approaches to law. This book aims to explore past, present, and possible future linkages and interactions between jurisprudence – understood mainly as an enterprise of theorising about law for practical, committed juristic purposes – and social scientific studies of law.

My motive for this inquiry is that I have long been equally committed to studying both jurisprudence and sociology of law and have admired and appreciated the great theoretical traditions to which they have given rise. But these traditions remain largely distinct. Theoretical inquiry about the nature of law will surely benefit if the resources of jurisprudence and social scientific study of law can be put into productive conversation with each other.

The means of trying to promote that in this book is through a set of closely interrelated essays. Some chapters elaborate and analyse what I see as especially instructive theoretical dimensions in jurisprudence, on the one hand, and socio-legal studies and sociology of law, on the other. Building on this, other chapters compare aspects of the histories of these different fields of study. They also try to show how, while remaining very different in nature and function, these fields can complement each other in interesting and even surprising respects.

Some chapters are developed from previously published writings. But all material used in this way has been extensively rewritten and supplemented. I have freely elaborated and extended analyses from previously published papers, but the arguments originally expressed in them remain. Chapter 5 originates from a talk I gave at the Oxford Centre for Socio-Legal Studies in 2012. The introductory chapter and Chapters 6, 11, and 13 are entirely new. Part of the book extends, reworks, and applies in new contexts, ideas from my *Sociological Jurisprudence* (2018).

Permission to adapt content from the following journals and books is gratefully acknowledged: *Kobe University Law Review* (Kobe University Repository) vol 49 (2015) 242–60 (Chapter 1); H. Hydén, R. Cotterrell, D. Nelken, and U. Schultz eds, *Combining the Legal and the Social in Sociology of Law: An Homage to Reza Banakar* (Hart/Bloomsbury, 2023) 47–58 (Chapter 2); *Journal of Law and Society* (Wiley) vol 44, issue S1 (2017), S19-S36 (Chapter 3); *Retfærd: Nordisk Juridisk Tidsskrift* vol 31(4), no 123 (2008) 23–36 (Chapter 4); *International Journal of Law in Context* (Cambridge University Press) vol 11 (2015) 1–16 (Chapter 7); M. Hertogh ed, *Living Law: Reconsidering Eugen Ehrlich* (Hart/Bloomsbury, 2008) 75–94 (Chapter 8); *Law & Social Inquiry* (Cambridge University Press) vol 45 (2020) 539–58 (Chapter 9); M. Del Mar and M. Lobban eds, *Law in Theory and History: New Essays on a Neglected Dialogue* (Hart/Bloomsbury, 2016) 149–66 (Chapter 10); *Annual Review of Law and Social Science* (Annual Reviews) vol 17 (2021) 15–29 (Chapter 12).

I am grateful also to many friends and colleagues who gave me opportunities to write on the themes of this book, or in various ways encouraged the work presented in it. They include Mikhail Antonov, Karsten Åstrom, the late Reza Banakar, David S. Clark, Maks Del Mar, Howard S. Erlanger, Edoardo Fittipaldi, Gregor Fitzi, Werner Gephart, Ralph Henham, Marc Hertogh, Håkan Hydén, Michael Lobban, Rob MacCoun, Nicola Marcucci, Valsamis Mitsilegas, Krzysztof Motyka, David Nelken, the late Sverker Oredsson, Amanda Perry-Kessaris, Hanne Petersen, Fernanda Pirie, Jiří Přibáň, the late Per Stjernquist, Hiroshi Takahashi, Phil Thomas, and Mauro Zamboni. My main debt, as ever, is to Ann Cotterrell for her constant support, on which I rely for all my work. This book is dedicated to her.

August 2023

INTRODUCTION

Mapping Inquiries about Law

Jurisprudence and socio-legal studies are distinct – even contrasting – teaching and research fields. The relation between them is typically left unclear, or simply unexplored. This book examines that relationship. It does so through a diverse but interrelated set of studies. Some of these explore general aspects of socio-legal inquiry. Some examine contributions of particular scholars to the literature of jurisprudence, contextualising these contributions in relation to general themes in social inquiries about law. Others consider contemporary points of contact between juristic and sociological studies of law, a history of cautious engagement between these fields, and a tentative prospectus for the future. To juxtapose jurisprudence and socio-legal inquiry, and to consider their actual and potential interconnections, is this book's aim.

Why might this project be important? Because each of these enterprises of scholarship can be shown to be inadequate today without substantial input from the other. At present, this input is rarely offered. Most present conceptions of jurisprudence see it as not needing systematic input from the social sciences, including the kinds of social scientific inquiries about legal phenomena that are now often called socio-legal studies or 'law and society' studies. Correspondingly, socio-legal studies as a research field typically underestimates the significance of jurists' theoretical inquiries about law.

About Jurisprudence

One difficulty in making comparisons and developing links between jurisprudence and socio-legal studies is the uncertain, sometimes controversial meaning of these terms. Jurisprudence is often, especially in continental European countries but also sometimes in the Anglophone world, seen as jurists'

DOI: 10.4324/9781003340324-1

ongoing commentary on and interpretation of legal doctrine – primarily the rules, concepts, and principles of established law. Seen in this way jurisprudence is an auxiliary component in expounding and developing law alongside legislation and judicial practice.

However, in the English-speaking legal world jurisprudence is more often seen as a wider theoretical enterprise. As the legal theory created or used by jurists, it seeks to theorise the nature of law as a general idea, rather than to study specific laws, legal fields, or legal problems. Jurisprudence supplements lawyers' practical study and application of laws by theoretically considering wider themes attached to the idea of law, such as law's logical structures and typical forms of reasoning, and its relation to morality, authority, and the state.

Sometimes, jurisprudence has been seen, especially during the past half century in the Anglophone world and beyond, as a sub-field within the self-consciously professionalised academic discipline of philosophy. But a subsidiary aim of this book is to show that, while jurisprudence must draw on ideas from many fields of knowledge including philosophy, it should be seen – and evaluated – as a resource of *jurists* created specifically for the purposes of their practical work. It needs no validation from philosophy as a discipline. Its validity comes solely from its utility in aiding the jurist's understanding of what is required to advance the wellbeing of the idea of law as a regulatory practice tailored to its time and place.

In Part II, detailed profiles are presented of four remarkable – but often-neglected – scholars of law who as jurists contributed to jurisprudence in this practice-focused way. They are discussed in depth in terms of the projects which they set for themselves. Since each of them aimed to present a comprehensive view of law as they saw it, each of their individual theories should be seen as a unity to be judged for its coherence and its range of insight. So, a separate chapter is devoted to each of these scholars. They are not presented as part of a story of the historical development of jurisprudence, but as each offering a powerfully original and contrasting view of law, explored as a juristic idea. To consider them fairly they are presented in their own terms, each inhabiting a personal universe of thought arising in a certain historical and social context.

This is surely the way that all ambitious systems of jurisprudential theory should be studied. Each should be presented, as far as possible, sympathetically in its strongest form, with a real effort to understand not only its arguments but the motivation behind them and the conditions in which they arose. It is important to understand why particular jurists choose to portray law in a certain way, and what colours their choices in setting the directions of their thought. As Chapter 10 argues, no major theorist's work should be treated *merely* as an expression of the writer's time and place. It should not be *explained away* by its context, as if it can have no significance beyond its original local and temporal setting. Nevertheless, a great jurist's ideas, however original and distinctive, cannot be fully understood independently of context. This is part of jurisprudence's socio-legal dimension.

None of the profiles in Part II treats jurisprudence as abstract, self-contained legal philosophy justified only by the coherence or logical elegance of its thought. Each assumes that the profiled writer aimed to say something concrete about the social world, not just about the logic of legal doctrine. Certainly, these scholars looked through a legal prism, but in elaborating their view of law, they recognised (as all jurists should) that law is a part of social experience. Adopting such an approach makes it possible to see jurisprudence – at least a certain kind of jurisprudence presented in a certain way – as inviting and reaching out to socio-legal inquiry.

About Socio-Legal Studies

What then should be made of the obviously vague term 'socio-legal studies' (hereafter SLS)? The term became increasingly familiar in the English-speaking common law world from the early 1960s. It reflected a felt need, especially among legal scholars, to broaden legal studies, especially so that they could draw consciously on ideas from the social sciences. The insistence that law must learn from social science reflected, as discussed further in Chapter 1, a sense that in the second half of the twentieth century much more was being asked of law in Western countries than in earlier times. It was being required to intervene more deeply into socio-economic life, and new social and economic (as well as political) challenges faced it.

Orthodox methods of legal thought were inadequate. Fresh resources were needed – in particular, a better-informed appreciation of the changing social and political world in which legal regulation had to operate. In the United States, which took the lead in this period in providing financial support and incentives for empirical socio-legal research, the term most often used to refer to this kind of research was, and has remained, 'law and society' studies.

SLS can be seen in this historical context as primarily a remedial innovation to supplement, but also perhaps eventually to transform, orthodox doctrinal legal studies and to inform policy debates around law reform. Like earlier sociologically influenced movements in the world of legal studies, SLS appears, at least in most of the countries where it has flourished, as having an important base in the law school world. This aspect is discussed especially in Chapter 5. SLS has quite rapidly become an established aspect of legal research and teaching in UK law schools, as in several other common law countries.

The situation in the United States is somewhat different. There, as 'law and society' studies, empirical social research on law has found homes in social science university departments and liberal arts colleges. Its links to specific social science disciplines seem often stronger and more explicit than is the case with SLS in the UK and elsewhere. Perhaps this is especially because of the stronger institutional links of many law and society researchers to distinct social science disciplines, such as sociology, anthropology, and political science, and to criminal justice programmes, rather than to law school legal studies. However, certainly in the UK, SLS attracts numerous legal scholars because, in general, it is now widely accepted in the intellectual environment of the best law schools. It is assumed to be practically useful, just as traditional forms of legal scholarship are assumed to be. So, it currently offers a recognised research career trajectory for imaginative and ambitious legal scholars.

A consequence of this situation is that SLS does not need to pledge allegiance to any *particular* social science discipline. Its intellectual 'centre of gravity' is, at the present time, clearly in law and legal studies. There are exceptions, and certainly there are many researchers who see themselves primarily as social scientists rather than legal scholars, but the main orientation of SLS seems to be to the law school world, and as argued in Chapter 5 it is in this world that its greatest intellectual and institutional security for the future is likely to lie.

Several chapters, mainly in Part I, explore the nature of SLS as a broadly social science-oriented field of legal inquiry, and the scope of the terrain of research. Taking account of the overall aim of this book, juristically relevant themes tend to emerge in most of these chapters. For example, the place of ultimate values in SLS is discussed in Chapter 3, not least because the question of how values are to be addressed in legal inquiry is always an important one.

And questions of the complex relations of law to culture are discussed in a sociological context also in Chapter 4, not least because for legal scholars the question of the unity of society under a single unified legal system is becoming an increasingly important topic. Cultural pluralism, especially in the form of religious or ethnic multiculturalism, has long been discussed by politicians, moral and political philosophers, cultural studies scholars, and sociologists. It is now firmly on the agenda for lawyers too, as regards its legal implications. This raises difficult questions for jurisprudence (and for socio-legal inquiry) about the concept of legal pluralism, extensively discussed in the context of Santi Romano's ideas in Chapter 9.

Not all work in SLS appeals to general theory – whether legal theory or social theory. The focus is often on practically focused empirical research and on policy-relevant debates, informed by an awareness of changing social conditions or by a desire to research them systematically. Many SLS scholars are indeed much concerned with theoretical questions. Often, however, when this is so, interest is not in general juristic theory. Nor is it typically in empirically oriented social theory – that is, theory aiming to provide general perspective on the nature of social change, social relations, and social institutions. More often it is in theories bearing directly on the specific topics of empirical or policy-oriented research that concern the SLS scholar or the precise empirical project at hand. Feminist theory may be the only kind of general theory that is ubiquitous in much SLS research – a development much to be welcomed. And very recently, postcolonial theory is becoming more important in this overarching way.

Something else that may be lacking in much SLS work, despite all its achievements and ongoing promise, is an adequate historical perspective on the field. The importance of refocusing attention on the great classics of socio-legal thought is a topic in Chapter 5. It is understandable that intellectual history often gets pushed to the side-lines and left to the attentions of specialist historians. The contemporary problems of examining and assessing law's place in the socio-economic world are pressing enough, and they properly dominate the concerns of most socio-legal researchers. But a long view of the intellectual development of a research field can give vital perspective on present problems. And wise insights of method and theory developed by some of the great scholars of the past who have tried to study law empirically and theoretically as a social phenomenon in its time and place can remain valuable, even if the time and place of the classic writers is far removed from our own.

About Sociology of Law

Before SLS (and 'law and society' studies) became established early in the second half of the twentieth century, a great wealth of literature of social scientific inquiry about law had already long existed. Some had been produced by anthropologists, with the Polish scholar Bronislaw Malinowski (1926) and some of the followers of the great French promoter of sociology Émile Durkheim (Vogt 1982) as prominent twentieth-century pioneers in Europe. But it is now often forgotten that it was *well over a century ago* that an autonomous enterprise of systematic social scientific research on law emerged, with empirical interests and theoretical ambition, and gradually became firmly established in several continental European countries. Almost from its first emergence it was labelled sociology of law (or legal sociology). Some of this century-long evolution of the international field of sociology of law is discussed in Chapter 1.

By its very name, sociology of law appears to pledge allegiance to or see itself as a sub-branch of sociology, now a well-established distinct academic discipline. The subsequent history of sociology of law as an intellectual enterprise, often sharply distinguishing itself from the legal studies of lawyers and law schools, has demonstrated how it has drawn extensively over the decades on the methods, traditions, interests, and theories of academic sociology. However, sociology of law, as an avowed social science discipline distinct from juristic studies and from the law school as an institution, has often struggled to find an obvious institutional home in Western universities. This is a matter discussed in Chapter 2.

The great strength of sociology of law is that, like sociology, it has never been afraid of or uninterested in *theoretical* inquiry. Historically, its intellectual ambition has often been great. It has contributed theoretical insights that can inform not only the understanding of law's place in society, but also broader, more imaginative understandings of the nature of law itself. So, sociology of law has the potential to engage directly with jurisprudential understandings and analyses of the nature of law.

The most celebrated direct historical confrontation between juristic theory and theoretical sociology of law was the debate early in the twentieth century between the great Austrian lawyer-philosopher Hans Kelsen and his compatriot the jurist and pioneer legal sociologist Eugen Ehrlich (Van Klink 2008; Hopman 2022; Fillafer 2022, 431–3). Ehrlich's ideas are referenced throughout this book and are the specific focus of Chapter 8. Kelsen (1945, 177, 178) claimed that sociology of law had no unifying concept (of law) unless it relied on juristic knowledge of the nature of law. For Ehrlich this misunderstood the aims of sociology of law to study the regulation of social life in ways that should *change* jurists' understanding of the nature of law.

Who won in the debate between Kelsen and Ehrlich? In the view of most orthodox jurists and legal philosophers, Kelsen did so, by exposing what he saw as the naivete of Ehrlich's imprecise sociological concept of law and his apparent failure to take adequate account of law's distinctive normative character. But, for sociologists of law, Ehrlich's imaginative, socially aware insights remain of great importance, broadening an understanding of law by considering the varying empirical conditions that determine its character and consequences, matters of limited concern to Kelsen.

Kelsen was right to insist that sociologists of law should recognise the importance of adequately theorising the nature of law, not least because law is the ostensible focus of their attention. But Ehrlich was right to assume that conceptualising law does not have to rely on the methods of orthodox jurisprudence. Social scientific approaches to legal inquiry can theorise the nature of law *for their own purposes*, which may be wider than, or at least different from those of jurisprudence. This is a matter to be discussed further, especially in Chapter 9.

The primary importance of sociology of law – if treated as distinct from SLS – is, indeed, its long tradition of theory. Treated *solely* as a field of empirical inquiry using social scientific methods it need not be distinguished from SLS or law and society research. But social theories about the character of law as ideas and practices, developed over more than a century in sociology of law, are of enduring importance. The great pioneers of sociology, especially Durkheim and the German polymath Max Weber, devoted much attention to examining the nature of law as a social phenomenon to be studied in social scientific perspective.

Durkheim's and Weber's work in the first years of the twentieth century shows that early sociology of law grew up contemporaneously with the then new discipline of sociology. Sociology of law was not an offshoot of sociology dependent on a parent discipline but a distinct field of inquiry that could aspire to contribute to sociology and other social sciences as well as to learn from them. So, sociology of law can claim a place of its own in the firmament of academic inquiry. In fact, it is a transdisciplinary enterprise drawing on all the social sciences, but perhaps inevitably and very properly drawing most from the heritage of Western sociology – potentially the most general and all-embracing of the social sciences (cf. Delanty 2023, 411–2).

This conclusion about the transdisciplinary nature of sociology of law draws it close to SLS, despite differences noted before. For many purposes there is no need to distinguish SLS and sociology of law. But sociology of law could develop as a theoretical field of social science long before empirical research on specific legal institutions (police, courts, lawyers, legislatures, etc.) using social science methods became commonplace. So, as stressed previously, it has a far longer history than SLS and much of its historical heritage consists of social theory about the nature of law in society, sometimes called socio-legal theory. A more sustained attention to social theory is what most obviously distinguishes much work over more than a century in sociology of law from that which is most typical of modern SLS.

So, where on a map of inquiries about law should the various scholarly enterprises considered in this introductory chapter be placed? There is, first, jurisprudence, with an unclear relation to philosophy but a clear link to the world of the jurist, the jurist being taken to be a lawyer with a sustained interest in the wellbeing of the idea of law as practised and experienced in the conditions of its time and place. And then there is SLS, which I have suggested is, however indirectly, linked to the law school world and to orthodox doctrinal and institutional legal studies. Seen in this way SLS should have a secure mooring in the intellectual world, in legal studies, whatever its relation to social scientific or other academic disciplines.

What then of sociology of law? Sociology of law might have a destiny to exist under the umbrella of the established discipline of sociology, as part of that discipline. In some countries this is its position. But given its general institutional marginality in sociology in many countries this is unlikely as a general prospect. Also, this prospect entirely belies the history of sociology of law as having, from its beginnings, developed in parallel with sociology and other social sciences, rather than as dependent on them.

Chapter 2 notes that sociology of law has been called a stepchild, unclaimed among the disciplines. Consequently, that chapter sketches what I think is a far more satisfactory characterisation of sociology of law, not by reference to any possible disciplinary allegiances but in terms of unique and essential functions, which it can perform as a distinct field of practice mediating conflicts and tensions between other such fields – political, juridical, and social. Sociology of law has its own place, based on the tasks it can take on. The intellectual world can be portrayed in ways other than by disciplinary links and boundaries. Sociology of law, seen in this way, is an *objectively necessary enterprise* of social scientific inquiry, even if the conditions of its institutional existence may sometimes remain unstable and controversial.

Part I of this book addresses key issues about the nature and scope of SLS and sociology of law. It claims no comprehensiveness in its overview of this terrain, but it highlights topics that are important in considering how far SLS can raise issues of interest to jurists, and conversely how far jurisprudence might suggest theoretical insights useful for SLS.

Profiles in Pre-Hart Jurisprudence

The first chapter in Part II further emphasises some of these jurisprudential themes lurking in the interstices of SLS and sociology of law. But it also serves to introduce the profiles of jurists in the following four chapters. Any reader already having some knowledge of the literature of contemporary jurisprudence will be aware that the jurists chosen for presentation in these chapters are hardly in the mainstream of current jurisprudential thought. If they are known at all by jurisprudence students and scholars it is as mavericks, theorists who have either been largely written out of the consciousness of jurists, at least in the Anglophone world, or have never had a place in that consciousness. Their work seems like isolated intellectual islands.

So, why choose them? More will be said about this in Chapter 6 but, for the moment, some similarities among these four otherwise very different legal scholars can be noted. The most important similarities are that all four wrote in the first half of the twentieth century, and all did so not in the Anglophone common law world but in continental Europe. Thus, they wrote in a significantly different context from that of contemporary English-speaking jurisprudence scholars and SLS researchers. Certainly, as regards their relations to, or relevance for, the concerns of contemporary Anglophone jurisprudence, it is obvious that they are inhabitants of a different intellectual world. To take careful account of their ideas, universalising them but also relating them to their diverse contexts of creation, is to begin to take a distance from the parochialism that so often today afflicts legal thought, trapped as it still so often is, inside the territorial or cultural boundaries of national jurisdictions.

The concerns of these juristic scholars seem remote in many respects from those of twenty-first-century legal philosophy. Indeed, they are not philosophers, at least in terms of the protocols of contemporary professionalised, academic Anglophone philosophy. In most cases, they identified themselves explicitly as jurists and made no claim to be professional philosophers. However wide-ranging their inquiries, each has a concern to write in a way that primarily serves the interests of jurists and juristic practice – a practice of making law work better in its time and place, the environment in which they wrote.

Except perhaps for Leon Petrażycki, the subject of Chapter 7, they do not seek philosophical elegance in any modern sense. Yet each seeks to observe empirical social reality. As jurists they focus on law as a field of knowledge and practice oriented to addressing the socio-economic, cultural, and political issues of their time. Each of these jurists wrote before the influence of H. L. A. Hart (1994), which imported ideas and protocols of linguistic philosophy into jurisprudence, and which has dominated much Anglophone writing in legal theory since the 1960s. Hart's pervasive influence in the world of jurisprudence has inspired its most prominent theorists to model themselves on the intellectual interests of philosophy rather than the practical (and even prosaic) needs of making law work in its time and place.

As noted previously, in the early 1960s SLS was becoming established, and empirical social scientific research on legal institutions and legal experience was beginning to proliferate in many countries, so that through SLS the legal imagination was turning very clearly *outwards*. It is an interesting, thought-provoking coincidence that, at precisely the same time, the influence of Hart-inspired legal philosophy was beginning to turn theoretical studies in jurisprudence clearly *inwards*, towards the armchair abstractions of the philosopher's study, towards a conscious legal introversion and away from juristic curiosity about the empirical complexity of law's changing social environments. It is as though, at a certain historical moment, legal studies arrived at a fork in the road. Part of it moved in one direction while the other part took the opposite route.

Certainly, this does not mean that pre-Hart jurisprudence in general was concerned with systematic empirical studies of the social world. But there was perhaps often a relative open-mindedness about the kinds of social knowledge that could usefully inform studies of the nature of law. Indeed, for the purposes of presenting jurisprudential profiles in Part II, many jurists, especially in continental Europe, who wrote in the period before Hart's theoretical innovations, might have been chosen.[1] Most of these theorists are ignored today in an Anglophone jurisprudential consciousness that, under the tutelage of contemporary legal philosophy, has become narrow, introverted, and uninterested in patterns of variation in the social world.

So, Petrażycki, Ehrlich, Romano and Vilhelm Lundstedt, profiled in Part II, provide case studies from a different jurisprudential world. I chose to write about these scholars at various times because I thought their ideas were intriguing, very unusual when set against the conformity of much current juristic thought, and (most importantly) acutely aware of the distinctiveness of their times, and the forces of change operating in their societies. These case studies illustrate what is possible in a jurisprudence unconcerned for precise disciplinary boundaries, constraining research protocols, or particular intellectual fashions.

The work of the theorists profiled in Part II might be seen as reaching out through time and beyond place to meet socio-legal ideas considered in Part I. These juristic writings and others referred to elsewhere in this book can, if read

1 See further Chapter 11 and Cotterrell 2023b, 12–3.

with an awareness of their aims and contexts, offer historical and comparative perspectives on current socio-legal concerns. They should be recognised alongside classic works of socio-legal theory by such as Weber, Durkheim, Karl Marx, and Georges Gurvitch; part of a single great repertoire of theory from the past – still rich, often still only partly explored – that is available today to SLS and sociology of law.

How to Build Bridges

The chapters in Part III are intended to make more explicit the range of links possible across the jurisprudential and socio-legal terrain. Chapter 11 presents aspects of the histories of modern jurisprudence and sociology of law as parallel records of theoretical inquiry about law across more than a century. To juxtapose and compare these histories shows that juristic and social theoretical studies of law have sometimes interacted, or competed, or worked in parallel in mutual ignorance. Sometimes they have influenced each other and sometimes merely run alongside each other. Mutual learning has occurred, but more could have been done.

Chapter 12 takes stock of common themes and topics in contemporary legal theory and social theory, focusing on five clusters of issues that have attracted the attention of contemporary jurists and social theorists alike. The chapter could be seen as a partial checklist of available contact points today between these fields of research.

Finally, Chapter 13 looks to the future and tries to address the question that underlies all the contents of this book. Does the legal imagination, in parallel with the sociological imagination (Mills 1959), need to expand so that the full responsibilities of law in a changing world can be realised? Can jurists see law as something whose place in the empirically observable social world must be continually renegotiated? If so, can they also see that the insights of empirical and theoretical social scientific research are absolutely indispensable in this endeavour? Chapter 13 ends by selecting three areas of fundamental challenge for law which arise from social changes that are now becoming central topics for social theory. So, it suggests commonalities between the concerns of jurisprudence and social science that should be increasingly obvious in future if current challenges are to be addressed.

The tasks of jurists and social scientists must not be conflated. The jurist's concerns are explicitly normative and committed to attempting to realise values that they can associate with law as an idea. Social scientists, if they take seriously the aspiration to advance an empirically grounded explanatory science of social life, cannot have any professional commitment except to that advancement. Yet there can be many as yet unrealised intersections between these distinct professional realms.

PART I

A Terrain of Socio-Legal Inquiry

1

THE DEVELOPMENT OF SOCIOLOGY OF LAW

Modern sociology of law is now more than a century old. The publication in German in 1913 of Eugen Ehrlich's *Fundamental Principles of the Sociology of Law* (Ehrlich 1936) was an early intellectual landmark for this research field – still a source of some of its basic concepts and methods. In some sense, it has been a foundation of all subsequent thinking in it. Yet Ehrlich's work has never been seen as uniquely central to Western socio-legal inquiry. Theoretical and methodological resources have come from many sources.

Among classic social theorists, it is Max Weber who has had the most powerful and enduring impact since Marx's insights fell into wide neglect from the 1980s. Weber's influence has been very important in shaping socio-legal ideas about law and economic development, the legal structures of capitalism, the character of modern formal legal rationality and the nature of the modern bureaucratic *Rechtsstaat*. Weber, writing in early twentieth-century Germany, appears as the dominant classical socio-legal theorist of the highly developed capitalist state; a state structured by law, governing socio-economic relations through law, and entirely monopolising the production, interpretation, and enforcement of law.

When Weber (1968) wrote, the state in the West appeared to have triumphed over all potentially competing sources of law: law would mean, for the foreseeable future, *state law*. The state's claim to monopolise the legitimate use of force seemed fulfilled. State law was the obvious technical means of harnessing that force to the purposes of government.

Weber's thinking reflects the fact that he worked in an increasingly powerful Germany: a nation still celebrating its new-found political unity (from 1871) and its emergence as a great capitalist power; possessing a vast state apparatus and confident in its regulatory capacity and directive powers. Among all the

DOI: 10.4324/9781003340324-3

classic social theorists, Weber most strongly conveys a sense of the inevitable domination of society and culture by the powerful state and its law.

In this context, Ehrlich's insistence on the fundamental regulatory importance of what he called 'living law'[1] – authoritative *social* norms as contrasted with the legal norms by which state agencies decide disputes – was an act of *constructive subversion*. It was a challenge to the state's omniscience in regulatory matters and specifically to that of jurists serving the state. Living law arose in the everyday social practices of communities, not in the directives of the state. But the reason why the idea of living law had limited resonance during the twentieth century in the leading Western nations was that their jurists tended to assume that state law was well integrated with national socio-economic and cultural conditions. State officials and lawyers could assume that legal-political development and socio-economic development followed broadly parallel paths. State and society were not inevitably in tension.

So, in France, at the dawn of the twentieth century, Émile Durkheim (1957, 30) could see the state as a 'brain' responsible for 'thinking' on behalf of society as a whole, providing powerful guidance for socio-economic life but also expressing and reflecting the moral conditions of social solidarity. And for Weber (1968, 895) the progress of the modern idea of law as a 'rational technical apparatus' seemed to parallel the ongoing rationalisation of most other aspects of Western life.

Ehrlich's sociology of law, by contrast, suggests a potentially serious divorce between state law and social norms, or between politics and culture. It is surely no accident that he developed his ideas in what was, at the beginning of the twentieth century, one of the most *unstable* of Western political societies, the vast but crumbling Austro-Hungarian Empire. In it, the political structure of the unwieldy and disunified imperial state, experimenting cautiously with liberal pluralist ideas, was unable to embrace all the diverse local cultures of the regulated populations. In many cases they existed in remote provinces far from the seat of imperial power.

As a loyal jurist, Ehrlich intended his sociology of law largely as a *warning* to the state and to his fellow state jurists, a warning that state law could be seriously incompatible with the cultural expectations and experience of the populations it sought to regulate, and that this situation posed the risk of state law being ignorant, irrelevant, ineffective, oppressive, or unpredictable in its operation.

1 Ehrlich's concept refers to social norms widely operative and accepted in a particular population, treated within it as authoritative in governing social relations and culturally validated, whether or not they are recognised by state authorities as law. Ehrlich's work is discussed in detail in Chapter 8.

Where the idea of living law or similar ideas did have significant influence in the early development of sociology of law, this was because living law was presented as an inevitable or necessary *control* on what state law could (or should) do – a counter to the hubris of the all-powerful modern state. In contrast to Weber's sociology of state law, Ehrlich's emphasis on the importance of living law suggests an embryonic sociology of legal cultures aimed at subverting the idea of the state's unlimited regulatory capabilities.

How have these contrasting models of law related to each other over the past century and more, and what is their relation today? It can be said that the career of the living law concept has paralleled the career of the state as lawmaker. When the state has seemed supremely strong the idea of living law has had little purchase except among those who resent this strength; when regulatory capacities of the state, or their use, have been put in doubt the idea of living law (or some related idea) has been practically important.

Yet the concepts that underpin both the state law focus and the living law focus are becoming unstable. On the one hand, the growth of new types of law – international, transnational and intra-national – not tied securely to the state undermines any equation of law with state law. And, on the other, the growth of transnational socio-economic networks producing their own regulation, as well as diverse multicultural populations, shows a need for more precise concepts than living law. These new concepts are needed to distinguish the variety of social contexts in which regulation arises, and in which it claims authority and seeks acceptance (Cotterrell 2018, 103–55). Sociology of law needs new ways to conceptualise the diversity of social and legal life.

Living Law: A Problem for State Law?

Ehrlich saw living law as a practical and inevitable control on what the law of the state could be expected to achieve. What lay behind this vision was the idea that society's self-regulation is fundamental, but the state is only *a derivative regulator*, parasitic for its regulatory success on the conditions that society provides for state regulation to operate. Hence, Ehrlich (1936, 71) made the striking, anarchistic claim that one 'might reasonably maintain that society would not go to pieces even if the state should exercise no coercion whatever'.

Such a view was unlikely to be taken seriously by Western jurists. They were generally happy to let sociologists study social norms and saw no reason to take an interest themselves in such studies. They could assume that the main problem for the law of powerful Western states was not to defend it from seemingly bizarre charges of social irrelevance but to make it as technically sophisticated, doctrinally consistent, and convincingly rational as possible, and to shape it to express social values recognised by the jurists themselves. All of these were matters that jurists could address without seeking any help from social scientists.

Empirical research in sociology of law did not develop significantly in Western countries until the 1960s. Until then sociology of law remained a largely *theoretical* subject – perhaps the most enduring contributions coming from radical imaginative scholars such as the French sociologist Georges Gurvitch (1935, 1947) who combined a focus on social theory with an extensive background in philosophy. Until empirical evidence began to be collected systematically, about the 'gap' between the aims of state law and its actual effects in society, sociology of law could be treated as *speculative* social science, with little attention given to it by lawmakers or jurists.

It was in the United States that Western *empirical* sociology of law – as 'law and society' research – began to establish itself most notably from the mid-point of the twentieth century. As this empirical focus became prominent, theoretical efforts to develop a sociological concept of law declined. These theoretical efforts had characterised not only the work of the pioneers such as Weber, Durkheim, Ehrlich, and Petrażycki but also that of major contributors influenced by them.[2]

The changed balance away from theory and towards empirical research is important. Before that change, juristic assumptions about the power and effectiveness of state law were little troubled by theoretical arguments about the significance of living law because hardly any empirical research had been done to show this significance. So, juristic legal theory (focused on state law) and socio-legal theory (derived from the work of scholars such as those mentioned before) could exist in entirely separate intellectual worlds. Hardly any influence of sociology of law on juristic thought occurred.

Far from ideas of living law exerting some control on state law-making or judicial practice, as Ehrlich must have hoped would occur, his sociology of law could be dismissed as 'megalomaniac jurisprudence' (Allen 1964, 32) – a futile, impractical attempt to study all human social life and present it as an undifferentiated pile of data for juristic consideration.[3]

In the second half of the twentieth century, as empirical sociology of law developed in leading Western countries and elsewhere, understandings of the relationship between state law and living law changed greatly. Comparisons between 'law in the books' (the precepts of state law) and 'law in action' (the social effects or consequences of this law) were made easier through expanding programmes of empirical research. Such developments were influenced by (and to some extent influenced) new ambitions to use state law to steer and shape society and to respond to political imperatives to engineer essential socio-economic change.

2 Petrażycki and his Russian followers Gurvitch, Nicholas Timasheff and Pitirim Sorokin are discussed in Chapter 7. Some of Durkheim's close associates in sociology of law are discussed in Cotterrell 2008, chs6 and 7; Cotterrell 1999; and Vogt 1982.

3 See Chapter 8, p. 122.

From the 1960s and 1970s, state law was used (differently in various Western countries) to attack racial and sex discrimination (and, later, many other forms of discrimination), to build welfare structures and shape welfare rights, to steer economies, to attack poverty and the social causes of crime, to uproot traditional restrictive practices and privileges, and to protect and promote aspects of national culture. In this context, one might well see living law (entrenched social norms) as presenting a set of *problems* for state law to solve. Living law might be seen as an object of state intervention, sometimes a *target for attack* through state law. The aim might be to change popular normative assumptions and social expectations.

In this perspective the idea of living law as a control on the operation of state law is turned on its head. The state is assumed to have the power to regulate. The issue is how this should be done. What are required are techniques to make it possible to recognise and overcome obstacles to law's effectiveness. Much socio-legal research was directed to discovering and addressing such obstacles. The era of the activist state (especially from the 1960s to the 1980s) promoted, in Western socio-legal studies, a wealth of research about the mechanisms of state law – on police, administrative and enforcement agencies, legal professions, judicial decision-making, citizens' access to justice, and legislative processes.

This could be called the period of *state optimism*, a brief phase in the second half of the twentieth century animated by a sense that, if the right techniques could be devised, and used with adequate knowledge of socio-economic conditions, significant social change (and a greater realisation of desirable social values such as equality, democracy, and liberty) could be achieved through law. However, one of the most important effects of the proliferation of empirical socio-legal research was quickly to encourage a deepening disillusionment about the state's capabilities. Research reporting regulatory failure or unintended consequences of law accumulated, and critiques of juridification (excessive legalisation) of social spheres (Teubner 1987) became widely influential. The claim was: too much misguided use of law; too much misuse of law for purposes for which it is unfitted.[4]

Some of the most powerful of these critiques have been informed by the most sophisticated theory in contemporary sociology of law – Niklas Luhmann's (2004) theory of self-reproducing and self-regulating communication systems. This theory in no way denies law's important contribution to the specific character of complex, functionally differentiated modern societies, but its thrust is to warn incessantly of the dangers of over-extension of law as a distinct communication system in society, and it does so in ways that encourage a politically conservative view of law's social tasks.

4 But for more recent nuanced assessments of juridification see Aasen et al. 2014 (effects of juridification on social citizenship); Croce 2021 (its effects on the practice of politics).

The perceived danger of over-extension is not seen as arising from recalcitrant living law. It is seen as resulting from limitations *built into law itself* as a communication system or discourse. While early sociology of law, such as that of Gurvitch, sometimes developed new sociologically informed concepts of law to show law's regulatory potential *far beyond* what jurists recognised, Luhmannian sociology of law conceptualises law in a way that defends a strictly limited (although vital) place for it in society, more or less consistent with conservative juristic understandings of law's practical scope. The essential modern function of law, on this view, is to stabilise normative expectations, not to reshape them.

Alongside this resurgence of theory, it is easy to point to general socio-legal developments that indicate great challenges for the state in governing through law. The rest of this chapter focuses on these developments and suggests that they also pose a challenge to ways of thinking that have been familiar in sociology of law from its beginnings – about 'society' as the object of legal regulation, and about the state as monopolistic creator of law.

Escaping the Limits of Living Law

In many European countries much debate centres on the challenges that multiculturalism, or cultural pluralism, poses for state law.[5] When a UK government inquiry into the application of *Shari'a* law in England and Wales was announced in 2015, the official reason given for the inquiry was that

> we know enough to know we have a problem, but . . . not . . . the full extent of the problem. For example, there is evidence of women being "divorced" under *Shari'a* law and left in penury, wives who are forced to return to abusive relationships because *Shari'a* councils say a husband has a right to "chastise", and *Shari'a* councils giving the testimony of a woman only half the weight of the testimony of a man.
>
> *(May 2015)*

In fact, much empirical research has been done on the operation of *Shari'a* law principles among Muslim minorities in Britain and other European countries, but not enough systematic data exists to give an entirely clear picture. This is an area in which research on living law in Ehrlich's sense, rooted in the culture (especially traditions and beliefs) of minority populations, is now seen as urgently required, and is being actively pursued.

It is likely that in important respects dispute resolution in *Shari'a* councils works well and is widely accepted because it responds to the cultural

5 On sociological concepts of multiculturalism see Cotterrell 2023a, 66–8.

expectations and understandings of the populations it serves. For them, the norms applied may fully deserve respect as law and may sometimes be more meaningful and relevant in everyday life than much state law. But *Shari'a*-influenced living law may also sometimes appear inconsistent with assumed underlying values of state law; it may seem to undermine this law insofar as state law purports to represent these values as universally defended in its jurisdiction. Controversy centres on the jurisdiction of *Shari'a* councils over religious marriages and divorces and associated property matters – making decisions lacking the binding force of state law but having popular acceptance among Muslim minority groups as living law.

Cultural pluralism is a normal condition of large, highly developed, contemporary political societies. As flows of population around the world continue and intensify, national cultures are changed and reinvigorated by newcomers bringing with them different, sometimes challenging cultural inheritances – imported varieties of living law. Ultimately state law's capacity to direct this importation of culture is limited. So, it can be asked: is this living law (i) a *control* on state law so that state law must accommodate it or (ii) a *problem* for state law to try to remove? In fact, it is neither, although attempts are made to think of it in both ways.

For example, as regards *accommodation* by state law to living law, the idea of cultural defences in criminal law and other legal fields has been invoked in some Western legal systems (Foblets and Renteln 2009). According to this idea, it could be appropriate in certain cases for evidence of features of the minority culture of an offender to be admitted in court to help to explain the motivation of acts done; these cultural factors might then sometimes be considered as *mitigation* in the court's sentence. In any case they might help the court to understand the case better (Ruggiu 2019). However, the risk of uncontrolled subjectivity in cultural defences and their potential incompatibility with orthodox conceptions of the rule of law make it unlikely that they could ever be free of controversy.

As regards the second approach (treating the living law of cultural pluralism as *a problem to be solved* by appropriate state law techniques), this can be seen in efforts to make cultural pluralism invisible in the public realm by determined enforcement of apparent cultural uniformity. Hence the attack by state law in several continental European countries on symbols of cultural pluralism such as the Muslim female veil, prohibiting the wearing of it in public places (Ferrari and Pastorelli 2013). But some such efforts to use state law seem to have been forgetful of decades of research on the resilience of culture – especially aspects of it deeply rooted in basic beliefs, traditions, and sentiments.[6]

6 Early studies include Levy 1950 and Massell 1968.

How should sociology of law address cultural pluralism? How, in these conditions, is the relationship between state law and living law to be worked out? As noted, it seems that one approach would be to accommodate state law to living law; the opposite one would be to force living law to yield to state law. Neither seems satisfactory. Neither recognises the complexity and subtlety of the interactions involved between state law and social norms. The difficulty here is caused by the dualistic, confrontational, either/or way in which the issues are presented, and this dualism is a legacy of Ehrlich's sociology of law.

In this scenario, on one side are all the norms (treated as an undifferentiated category) by which state courts and other authorities decide disputes. On the other side is living law, a conceptually undifferentiated mass of norms existing in social associations of innumerable kinds. But the 'social' – the social environment in which state law operates – needs to be understood with more conceptual subtlety: the idea of cultural pluralism implies *many* ways in which the social is differentiated – for example, by religious belief, by customs and traditions, by language, by geographical factors, by shared history and collective memory, by emotional allegiances and rejections, and by economic conditions.[7]

A uniform concept of living law can hardly recognise these very varied criteria of distinction in the social; nor does it suggest the contrasting kinds of attitudes to regulation and problems of regulation that may be associated with them. State law may face different problems in regulating social relationships founded on traditions and customs, as compared with those centred on fundamental values or beliefs, or on emotional attachments or rejections, or on shared economic necessities or opportunities.

This analysis indicates some reasons why the concept of living law is no longer very useful to sociology of law. Sociology of law can make progress by replacing this concept with that of law rooted in *different types* of communal relations. It should then carefully distinguish these as Weberian ideal or pure types and ask what general regulatory problems and needs each of the types might present. So, it would be necessary to distinguish:

- relations of community based on shared *ultimate values or beliefs* (which might be religious beliefs, but could equally be fundamental secular values such as human rights or human dignity),
- those based on shared or convergent economic or other *instrumental projects*,

7 *Shari'a* issues in Britain are typically addressed in popular and public debate almost entirely in terms of a dualistic state-law/living law dichotomy, instead of with a focus on the complexity and variety of cultural relations – a focus that would distinguish variables relating to belief and ultimate values, economic situation, affective (national, ethnic, etc.) allegiances, and the experience of co-existence in established environments. For this latter approach see Cotterrell 2006a, 97–108; and Chapter 4.

- those grounded in tradition and custom or the mere fact of co-existence in an established *shared environment* (whether a geographical environment, a linguistic one, or one historically shaped by shared experience or collective memory), and
- those based on shared *affective ties or resistances* (love, hatred of others; emotional attraction or rejection).

Evidence from research in sociology of law and comparative legal studies might then suggest that each of these ideal (pure) types of communal relations presents significantly different general regulatory problems and possibilities.[8] Because they are very different kinds of social bonds, regulating them will involve different general considerations. But in reality, these types will not exist in isolation but will be combined in complex ways; these combinations make networks of community, or communal networks. And communal networks can be big or small: as small as the relationship between two contracting parties; as large as a nation, or transnational networks such as the membership of the world-wide Catholic Church.

This idea of communal networks based on ideal typical communal relations has been developed elsewhere (Cotterrell 2006a, 2008). It offers concepts more precise than the all-embracing idea of living law. Using such an approach makes it possible to avoid the unreal either/or conundrum of a confrontation between state law and living law in cultural pluralism. Applying the concept of communal networks, all law *including state law* can be seen as arising in such networks, because the national political society is itself a (complex) example of such a network. Law emerges in communal networks and can structure and regulate them.

The problem for sociology of law is not to work out the relationship between state law and living law, but to analyse how law is produced in different kinds of communal networks and how these networks interact. So, the national political society as a communal network is composed of, but also must integrate and co-ordinate, other communal networks within it. State law as the law of the national political society must *respect and draw sustenance from* forms of regulation produced in communal networks within this society; but it must also *guide and co-ordinate* the regulation of these networks to ensure the overall integrity of the national political society.

When state law interacts with the legal structures, expectations, and aspirations of minority groups, what legal sociologists should see is the interaction (and potential conflict) between different communal networks, each producing

8 For example, instrumental (e.g. contract, commercial) relations have often been said to be easier in general to shape through state law than social relations based on ultimate values or beliefs; purely emotional relations may, for a range of reasons, be hard to regulate. In Chapter 3, the four pure types of communal relations are further discussed as components of culture.

its own regulation and its own legal expectations and demands. What really exists is not the dualism of state law versus living law, but a *regulatory pluralism* that mirrors cultural pluralism. This is surely the pluralistic condition – not to be regretted but to be welcomed as a challenge for legal sociologists – that now exists generally in most – perhaps all – large, developed, modern societies.

All of this may suggest that the formula 'law and society' which has long defined the focus of sociology of law should generally be avoided. It is misleading insofar as it seems to set 'law' and 'society' against each other, as two distinct monolithic phenomena. Much of sociology of law has tried to study the impact of law on society, or the gap between law and society, or the influence of society on law. But a view of law as existing in and created in communal networks avoids these crude oppositions. It suggests, indeed, that even the concept of society might now be of limited use[9] for sociology of law; a concept of social relations of *community* might be more useful – because this latter concept can recognise explicitly the diversity of types of these communal relations and how law reflects and grows out of them.

An approach that views law as located and created in communal networks would reject the idea of society as an entity to which law must relate. Instead, it would emphasise different kinds of social relations that are relations of community insofar as they rely on a degree of mutual trust and have some stability and endurance. This approach would see law regulating innumerable communal networks varying in size and scope (intra-national, national, transnational).

Legal Pluralism and the State

If the concept of society is problematic for sociology of law, perhaps the concept of law is, as well! Sociology of law has long assumed that law means state law. When Ehrlich introduced the concept of living law, he failed to indicate clearly in what sense it should be thought of specifically as law. As has often been noted, his concept of law remains very unclear.[10]

Sociology of law has to recognise that state law is not the only kind of law that it must address, and that the normal condition in the contemporary world is one of *legal pluralism* – the co-existence or conflict of distinct legal regimes purporting to regulate the same social space.[11] The concept of legal pluralism has been present in sociology of law from its earliest phases, emphasising the existence of many forms of law other than state law. Sometimes it has been

9 Cf. Bauman 2002, 41: 'Among many conceptual keys once deployed by sociology . . . but now falling out of use . . . "society" is the first term of the sociological vocabulary to go . . . '.

10 See Chapter 8.

11 See Chapter 9.

emphasised that state law itself is not a single legal regime.[12] Indeed, legal plurality very often exists in some form, even in what lawyers would recognise as highly integrated legal systems and is usually dealt with by normal juristic methods (Cotterrell 2018, ch6).

However, relations between, for example, European Union law and EU Member States' law or between EU law and World Trade Organisation law are not always routine interpretive matters but can often provoke debate about the nature of the legal regimes involved. And the question of how to handle the relations of state and international legal systems operating in the same social spaces has become more acute. This is because international law (i) has sought greater independent authority, less easily subsumed into state authority, for example via assertions of *ius cogens*, (ii) has become more prominent in the regulatory landscape by developing in many new or newly significant doctrinal fields (such as human rights, trade and finance, environment, and intellectual property), and (iii) now sometimes (as with international criminal law) directly addresses the citizens of states as individuals. Further, international law has been seen as breaking up into diverse legal regimes whose relations are sometimes unclear.

Beyond all of this, many further dimensions of regulatory plurality are now widely recognised. Regulation created in (often transnational) networks of interaction – such as merchant communities, corporate groups, industries, financial systems, internet developers, private NGO movements, religious communities, or sports organisations – has been shown empirically to be at least as practically powerful as much juristically recognised law, and no less authoritative for those subject to it. Much of it is characterised by unions of primary and secondary rules (cf. Hart 1994). The term transnational private law is widely used to include at least some regulation created wholly or partly in these kinds of communal networks.

The result of these developments is to challenge any idea that law can be conclusively equated with state law. So, for sociology of law, as for juristic thought, the question of the concept of law becomes significant. What should be taken to be law for the purposes of sociology of law? The contemporary legal landscape is now often referred to as one of global legal pluralism (Berman 2012). The issue is not merely to decide what is to be recognised as law for research purposes; it is also to assess the authority of the different kinds of regulation that now address individuals, organisations, corporations, and states in an era of transnational operation of law.

12 Different parts of the state apparatus may create regulation independently, and interpret state law differentially: see Dalberg-Larsen 2000, 103–14. This plurality may remain unless mechanisms are available, and steps taken, to identify it and select a final 'official' legal position.

If the state's practical monopoly of law is being challenged by global legal pluralism, it is important also to note other considerations that alter perceptions of the state's capacity to legally regulate. Even in many strong, stable, representative democracies this capacity is greatly weakened (Cotterrell 2018, 132–4). For example, private forces (corporate interests, mass media pressure, corruption) sometimes shape or constrain the practical exercise of state authority. Tax evasion and avoidance, and misuse of public finances, can diminish financial resources available to make the exercise of state authority effective. And resources of expertise in parts of the private sector may be superior to those on which public regulatory agencies can draw.

Equally significant is the point that a state's practical regulatory capacity often depends on its external strength in the world, that is, its strength relative to other states. Globalisation pressures limit freedom of action for all but the most powerful states, often directly affecting the content of legislation, for example in areas of economic policy. Official or unofficial extraterritorial law enforcement by some states affects the practical legal authority of others over their citizens. Extradition provisions can sometimes have similar effects, in effect handing over the exercise of legal authority in particular cases to another state.

Some states are able even to exercise punitive force in others without permission, including the power (for example through clandestine raids or use of remote technology) to execute or seize residents of weaker states in the territory of those states. In this way they undermine weaker states' capacity to assert their own authority within their borders. And as is well known, disparities of power between states are reflected in the shape, use, and effects of international law (Krisch 2005), so that its legitimacy as an extension of the political authority of states, founded on their consent as an international community, is often doubted.

In the light of these conditions any idea that sociology of law can treat the state as a given – as a law-making agency that does not, itself, require much analysis – cannot be sustained. Economic and financial globalisation has encouraged the growth of new kinds of regulation outside the effective control of states as autonomous lawmakers. It highlights the diverse conditions of existence of states as regulators and the fact that their law-making and law-enforcing capacities are powerfully shaped by both internal and external pressures.

Rethinking 'Law' and 'Society'

If sociology of law's time-honoured focus has been 'law and society', it is necessary to recognise that both elements in this focus (both law and society) have been destabilised and sociology of law can no longer operate with assumptions that have underpinned much of its research in past decades. The concept of society seems less useful than it has been in the past because it is becoming harder to think of law as relating to a single national political society in which culture can be assumed to be uniform. Insofar as large movements of population around the world become familiar, an intensification of cultural communication is occurring. National political societies that formerly seemed to be relatively homogeneous are forced to recognise the extensive cultural diversity existing within them, as well as between them.

This cultural diversity can be represented theoretically in sociology of law by using ideal types of social relations of community and by emphasising the many ways in which these types of community can be combined. This approach highlights the variety of ways in which cultural bonds are maintained – through beliefs and ultimate values, economic interests and projects, co-existence in a common environment, and emotional attachment and allegiance.

The concept of law – the other pole of 'law and society' – can also no longer be taken for granted in sociology of law. Law is no longer just the law of the state, and there is a need to devote attention to the way internal and external factors affect the state's capacities as a regulator. There is also a need for a sophisticated sociology of international law (Hirsch 2015) and a sociological focus on the many forms of regulation that address the relations of individuals, groups, and corporations across national boundaries. The term transnational law now references these latter kinds of regulation, which seem inevitable despite resistance to them (Michaels 2016, 60). Suffice it to say that they inform important agendas for Western sociology of law, as for jurists.

Empirical studies in sociology of law will be increasingly needed by jurists to map out the emerging new forms of regulation and to study the communal networks in which these forms of regulation are created or which they purport to address. At the same time, sociology of law will need to pay more attention than it has in past decades to the concept of law. It is no longer possible to leave the question 'what is law?' to the theorising of legal philosophers; it has become a practical matter.

2

THE IDENTITY AND FUNCTION OF SOCIOLOGY OF LAW

Chapter 1 considered sociology of law in terms of an evolution of ideas. But the comparative history of the development of sociology of law as an international institutionalised enterprise is not yet written. There are studies of the development of the field in particular countries, as well as pioneer cross-national collaborative surveys (Ferrari 1990; Treves and Van Loon 1968). But it remains to show why a self-identifying *collective and institutionalised* enterprise of social research on law emerged as a prominent focus of activity in a significant number of highly developed and politically and culturally diverse countries around the same time, generally in the 1950s and 1960s – a research enterprise focused on studying legal phenomena, using modern methods of empirical social research, aiming to be systematic and scientific, and linked to the progress of the social sciences. Where did this flowering of collective activity come from?

What needs did it respond to? Did important common factors operate in different countries? If these questions could be conclusively answered to show distinct historical causes and conditions, other questions might receive answers. Within the established array of academic disciplines or fields of practice and inquiry relating to social life, how was it that a *space* became recognised, if sometimes reluctantly, for a distinctive focus on social scientific study of law? What defines that space and its borders? Specifically, what place does sociology of law occupy among the established academic disciplines and research fields that border it?

A Stepchild among the Disciplines

The legal sociologist Reza Banakar tried to clarify its methods, the kinds of theory that it could use, and above all its identity as a research field. Influentially, he called it an intellectual 'stepchild' set uneasily between law and

DOI: 10.4324/9781003340324-4

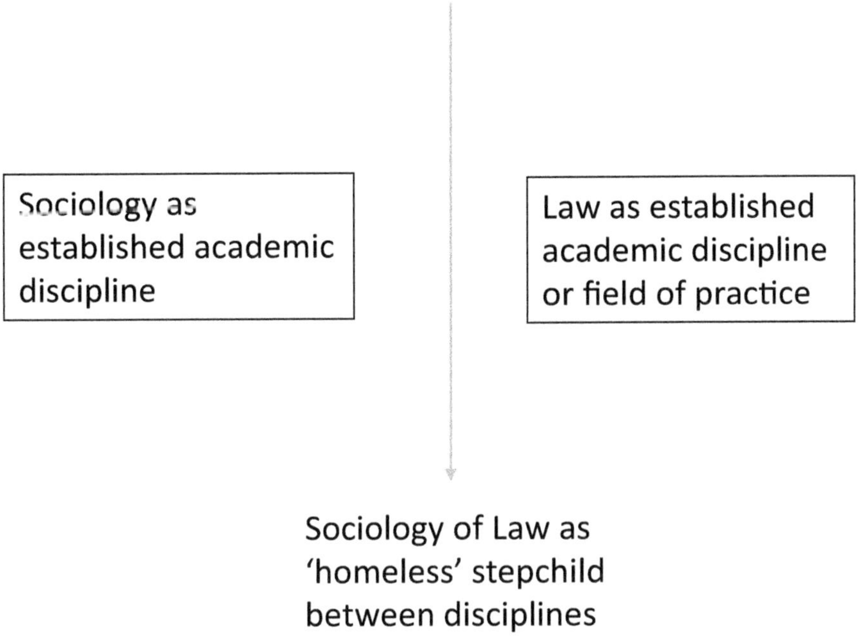

FIGURE 2.1 Sociology of law as a stepchild unclaimed by the disciplines

sociology (Banakar 1998). As such, sociology of law, largely unclaimed by either juristic studies or academic sociology (both of which have usually showed little interest in it), drifted insecurely in the open sea of social inquiries, lacking, Banakar thought, theoretical coherence and fundamental paradigms to organise it. He denied that sociology of law was a branch of either sociology or of jurisprudence and hoped it would 'limit its dependency' on both (1998, 5, 18). Eventually, he defined it as 'an interdisciplinary field of research placed somewhat precariously at the intersection of the disciplines of law and sociology' (2003, 1). It had to go its own way intellectually, not seeking 'to reproduce the basic assumptions and academic identities of the parent disciplines' (1998, 5).

Banakar rightly insisted that the question of the identity of sociology of law is not to be ignored, and he threw down a challenge to look inside the enterprises of socio-legal inquiry for their marks of intellectual pedigree and integrity. Probably most researchers on law as a social phenomenon, whether they call their inquiries sociology of law, socio-legal studies, or 'law and society' scholarship, are mainly concerned to ensure the coherence of their distinct research projects, not that of some much wider intellectual field. But Banakar was right to renew debate on the identity of sociology of law, not least because uncertainty about this has sometimes encouraged the idea of its marginality.

However, sociology of law is far from marginal when the conditions of its emergence and the nature of its significance are understood.

Can the nature of this research field be clarified in disciplinary terms? Ultimately, I shall argue, the search for disciplinary pedigree or a clear relationship of sociology of law to what are claimed as its 'parent disciplines' should not be a priority in solving what Banakar called its identity crisis. What constitutes an intellectual discipline can be controversial and the term is often used very loosely. More concretely, if the question of modern sociology of law's identity is considered in relation to its historical emergence – its 'rebirth as an independent science' which Vincenzo Ferrari (1990, xv) dated from the 1960s – it must be recognised that the main pioneers who worked then to establish it were very diverse in their acknowledged disciplinary allegiances.

Some were jurists (e.g. Jean Carbonnier in France), others were sociologists (e.g. Adam Podgórecki in Poland, in a direct line of influence from the lawyer-polymath Leon Petrażycki), or were influenced by diverse social science traditions (e.g. Per Stjernquist in Sweden, trained as a lawyer but strongly drawn to anthropology and socio-economic history).[1] In the United States, 'law and society' studies became a favoured term because of the wide range of disciplinary affiliations (not just sociology or law) contributing to socio-legal research. This is far from saying that disciplinary allegiances were unimportant, but it seems doubtful that they confined the vision that helped form a socio-legal field and facilitated diversity within what was quickly understood as a common transnational enterprise of sociology of law.

Many national studies of the emergence of this enterprise suggest that what is important to the identity of the socio-legal research field is not a jockeying for position among academic disciplines but the recognition of a new (complex, multifaceted) 'object of study' (Noreau and Arnaud 1998, 270); perhaps a set of problems unseen or neglected in the established disciplines, and perhaps incapable of being fully addressed in them. Sociology of law became a good label to refer to efforts to address these problems.

Sometimes, to confront them required much knowledge of law or legal institutions and processes, sometimes of socio-economic conditions. Sometimes, but certainly not always, it needed direct political imperatives from government policy or social control objectives to encourage the institutionalisation of socio-legal research and the teaching of sociology of law, for example in the education of state administrative officials. This is evident in the cases of countries mentioned earlier.

In Sweden, teaching in sociology of law, and later a chair in the subject, were established as a direct result of government initiative (Stjernquist 2000, 65–9). Correspondingly, early research initiatives in France were linked to the need for

1 See Andrini and Arnaud 1995 (on Carbonnier); Kojder 1999 and Wicenty 2018 (on Podgórecki); Cotterrell 1997, 2006b (on Stjernquist). On Petrażycki, see Chapter 7.

data to inform legislative policy (Andrini and Arnaud 1995, 34–5). And in communist Poland, for a time, research initiatives were promoted by government (Kurczewski 2001, 89), especially focused on a need to study popular understandings of and attitudes towards law. Many other instances might be mentioned.

Elsewhere, policy interests were sometimes much less direct and obvious in spurring the beginnings of socio-legal research. They provided merely a background, encouraging funding from the state, from within universities, or (especially in the United States) from private foundations aware of the need to adapt law to social change, or to address social issues. But in other cases, implicit policy or political understandings of legal sociologists ultimately ran counter to those of government and were rightly seen as in competition with them (Kojder 1999; Wicenty 2018).

The engagement of policy interests was often important to fund empirical research, the hallmark of the 1960s 'renaissance' of socio-legal inquiry (Ferrari 1990, xlvi) even when those interests made no effort to steer 'pure' research towards specific policy goals. But typically, the 'pull of the policy audience' (Sarat and Silbey 1988) is in the background – in the funding structure of universities, the interests of grant awarding bodies, or an atmosphere of national importance informing research. In the foreground is often the researchers' desire to research independently, with scientific credibility and peer respect.

Sociology of Law as a Field of Practice

The limits of generalisation are quickly reached but the observations outlined are intended only to suggest that the identity of sociology of law need not be analysed only in terms of the positioning of academic disciplines or intellectual fields. It can be considered more empirically in terms of the interrelation of and tensions between *different arenas of action*. Pierre Bourdieu's concept of field (*champ*) is useful here.[2] Banakar (2003, 168–9) used it in examining the internal organisation and conflicts of sociology of law as a scientific field, but it can be used also to consider tensions and potential conflicts between fields of action and experience. Sociology of law, as itself such a field, is located at the intersections of other fields: not only the heavily professionalised *juridical* field, and what might be called the field of social relations in *civil society* which sociology has assumed as a primary research focus. There is also a *political* field – a field of state action, governmental direction, and societal steering.[3]

2 See also Chapter 12, p. 189.

3 Bourdieu's idea of field can be very flexibly applied but he seems to see the juridical field (Bourdieu 1987) as conceptually distinct from but closely interrelated with state and governmental power. What this chapter calls the social field is not a concept adopted from Bourdieu but a device to characterise, for present purposes, the arena of citizens' societal experience that, in various ways, juridical and political practices address. In sociology various terms such as civil society, the societal community or the civil sphere attempt to characterise it.

Researchers have often resisted the pull of the policy audience, or not even consciously felt it; they have sought the objectivity and status of science. But my suggestion is that the identity of sociology of law, seen in the light of conditions of its emergence and the kind of tasks that those conditions have created for it, can usefully be understood in terms of the relations between these three fields – the juridical, the political[4] and the social (broadly, civil society).

Sociology of law has the strategic role of addressing tensions between these fields. Its relation to them varies in different contexts depending on the challenges of the time. The political, the juridical, and the social can be thought of in this approach as the points of a triangle with sociology of law at its centre. And it is a 'variable geometry' triangle. Sometimes one or another of the points is most prominent, encouraging certain emphases in sociology of law.

But in all cases, sociology of law is unified by a strategic mission, not by its disciplinary position or by any uniform intellectual sources of its theory or methods. Its mission is to be a transdisciplinary science (not beholden to government policy, specific juristic values and commitments, or populist social demands on law) occupying an *essential mediating position* between the political, the juridical, and the social, providing forms of knowledge necessary for their continually shifting interrelations as realms of action and experience.

Seen in this perspective, sociology of law could not be institutionalised until certain historical conditions, which have been analysed in social theory, were satisfied. A distinct realm of the *social* had to be recognised, as in the concept of civil society. Government and the state had to evolve to recognise a *political* responsibility for managing or steering society, and so to assume an interest in the social as such, evidenced, for example, by the emergence of the idea of a welfare state (Simon 1999). The *juridical*, too, had to become a developed professionalised field, somewhat autonomous from the policy imperatives of government and the moral or customary frameworks of everyday social life. The three points of the triangle had to become sufficiently distinct so that sociology of law could begin to find its place inside this structure.

A further question is then: if sociology of law finds its strategic task (and so its identity) in the mediation of tensions inside the triangle of the political, the juridical, and the social, what kinds of tensions are these, and when might they arise? I suggest that relevant tensions or conflicts necessarily involve *all three* fields, not just any two.

The isolation of the juridical, in the sense of professional lawyers' practice, from the social is perennial; it long predates the emergence of modern sociology of law. It becomes a catalyst for action usually when the political becomes

4 'Political', in this chapter, is taken in what George Orwell (2004, 5) called its 'widest possible sense. Desire to push the world in a certain direction, to alter other people's idea of the kind of society they should strive after.'

interested in it – for example when the 'gap' between juristic law and society provokes disquiet registered in government or policy arenas. A similar situation can arise when the juridical and political spheres seem at odds in their responses to pressing social demands and social change: then the social focuses the tension.

Again, sociology of law might become relevant when the state, seeking to control or steer society through legal instruments, needs to understand their possibilities, effects, and limits; or where the state needs to use law to address perceived problems or demands in the social that have become political or government policy issues (Banakar 2016). In democratic societies such matters increasingly arise; even in societies without effective representative democracy but where government seeks popular acquiescence, sociology of law might (as in Poland under communist rule) be officially supported to some degree as a 'searchlight' shone on the population to inform political powers about the society they seek to govern (Kurczewski 2001).

Are these generalisations too broad to be useful? As noted earlier, the comparative history of sociology of law remains unwritten.[5] It might be said that all hypotheses should be left aside until that distant future date when it is written. Nevertheless, this chapter's argument is that Banakar was right to argue that the identity of sociology of law needs clarification, not only to locate it intellectually on the map of social inquiry, but also to assess its ongoing significance as a research enterprise.

Banakar rightly saw the limitations of thinking about that identity in terms of academic disciplinary categories of legal and sociological knowledge which seem to leave no intellectual space between them. Thinking in terms of fields of action gives a way forward. The tensions in a triangle of fields – juridical, political, and social – map a space for sociology of law to occupy; at the same time, they suggest the strategic necessity of occupying it.

Significantly, socio-legal studies in the United States were established and have developed while avoiding the thickets of disciplinary identity. They grew in conditions where law had, as now in America, a remarkable centrality in the national culture, especially evidenced in the prominence in both cultural and political life of American courts. So, the juridical field evidenced special prominence in the triangle of fields.

The political, by contrast, was – as probably intended by the framers of the United States Constitution – far weaker in terms of its capacity to respond energetically to developments in the social. But, in the twentieth century, a behavioural case-law focus in legal studies encouraged progressive jurists

5 For detailed discussion of problems of cross-national comparison in sociology of law see Cotterrell 2012.

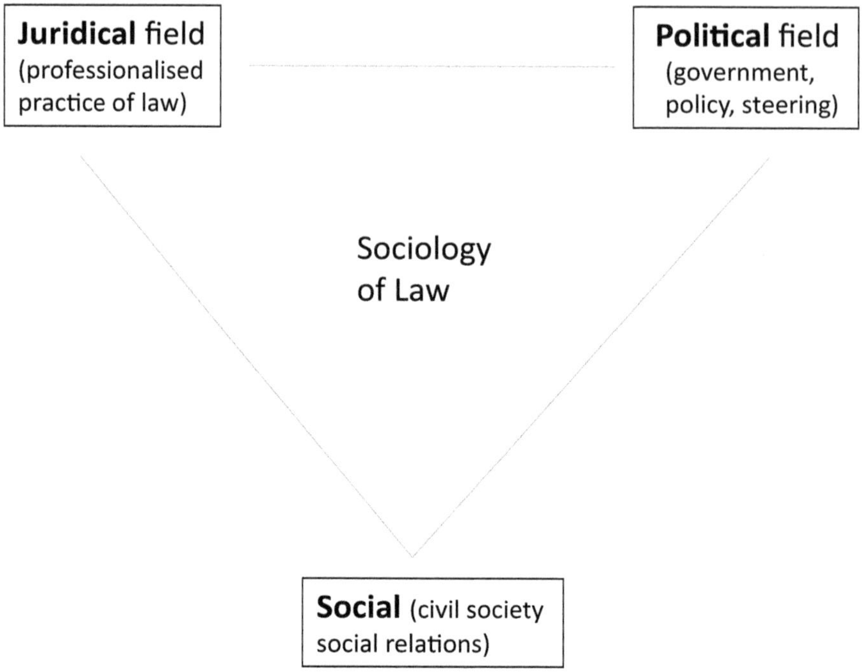

FIGURE 2.2 Sociology of law located in the tensions between different fields of action

to develop a significant sensitivity to sociological realities of law, especially through the American legal realist movement (Schlegel 1995).

Despite the rapid and intense twentieth-century professionalisation of sociology in the United States, the strength of the juridical and the relative limitations (and frequent distrust) of state governmental direction perhaps allowed the juridical field to dominate in the triangle of fields. Under the pressures of immense change in the social, and the many challenges faced by post-war American society, a flourishing growth of empirical socio-legal research occurred. But law (understood politically and juridically), rather than sociology, provided its unifying focus. So American sociology of law is explicitly transdisciplinary, and known as 'law and society' studies, even when its practitioners recognise allegiance to distinct social science disciplines. The focus of this social research enterprise is not sociology but *some idea of law*.

This national case is mentioned here because it has many lessons in considering the identity of sociology of law. In the United States (and, to some extent, in other common law countries) the term sociology of law, with its disciplinary connotations noted earlier in this book, is mainly avoided. Yet much of the work done as socio-legal studies or 'law and society' can hardly be differentiated in scientific character (except perhaps in its balance between empirical research and theory) from that done elsewhere as sociology of law.[6] What unites most inquiries, whatever their national provenance, is the strategic mission that they share through their location at the intersections of the political, the juridical and the social.

The Problem of the Concept of Law

Does this chapter's approach simply avoid issues of intellectual coherence and integrity? Does it suggest, at best, some conditions under which socio-legal research emerged in its modern forms, but not address its *epistemology* as a form of knowledge, or indicate a shared object of study that gives it *ontological* coherence? The answer is that the nature of the knowledge that characterises sociology of law must be understood outside disciplinary locations.

The experience of 'law and society', socio-legal studies, and transdisciplinary sociology of law in many countries suggests that ultimately what unites these research enterprises is their focus, in some way, on *law*. Very importantly, however, law for sociology of law cannot simply be law as jurists understand it. The idea of the triangle of fields with sociology of law at its centre, relating to all three of its points, implies that *there is no single concept of law* that sociology of law can take from any one of the points of the triangle of fields – juridical, political, and social. The nature of law may be understood differently at the different points.

Thus, law typically can appear somewhat differently in each of the three fields – the juridical, the political, and the social. Undoubtedly, none of them has any uniform, pervasive understanding of law – an understanding that might be seen, in Bourdieu's terms, as rooted in its habitus (cf. Bourdieu 1987, 833). Certainly, the social – an umbrella term here for a vast diversity of socio-economic and cultural relations – could hardly be a uniform locus as regards understandings of law. Nevertheless, it is possible to speculate about some contrasting commonplace assumptions in each of the three fields as to law's most obvious nature.

In the *political* sphere, law is very often seen mainly instrumentally as a tool of government and policy implementation. In the *juristic* sphere, lawyers like to see it as a (or perhaps the) cohesive, overall normative framework of human life, and the legitimating idea that structures their practice. In the *social* field, law is sometimes seen, from the 'receiving end', so to speak, as a structure of oppression, and sometimes as a promise (often frustrated) of rights or justice.

6 However, the relation between some kinds of socio-legal history, which have long been prominent in US law and society research, and sociology of law, as understood in many European contexts, might need further discussion. I am grateful to David Nelken for this point.

For this chapter what is important is only the very different emphases in thinking of law indicated by conceptions such as these.

The conclusion should be (i) that law is a necessary unifying idea for sociology of law but (ii) that sociology of law must find its own understanding of the nature of law, reflecting conflicts and convergences in ideas of law at each of the three points of the triangle. It needs understandings of law *for its own purposes* which are not those of the political, the juridical, or the social but which exist in the interaction and conflicts between these fields.

However, in practice, legal sociologists have tended, when they have expressed or assumed a concept of law for their work, to gravitate in their thinking towards one or other of the points of the triangle. Often a governmental, primarily instrumental, *political* understanding of law has been assumed (especially where the policy relevance of sociology of law has been stressed in research practice) – the pull of the policy audience has operated.[7] Sometimes, a *juristic* view centred on law as normative discourse or professional knowledge has been assumed or adopted. In such cases, where a juristic emphasis on legal values conflicts with the research quest for social scientific objectivity, sociology of law risks being seen only through the lens of sociological jurisprudence – that is, the importation of social science perspectives to serve juristic commitments to the wellbeing of law, understood in the lawyer's sense (Cotterrell 2018).

Sociology of law can also adopt various concepts of law present in the *social* field: popular understandings of the nature of law created in experience of law, but such understandings are not necessarily easily identifiable. When legal sociologists have sought to avoid the state's conceptualisations of law (as its governing mechanisms of regulation) or lawyers' concepts, they have sometimes found social concepts of law in classic social theory. Such theory is most useful for this purpose when it offers concepts not confined to state law or 'lawyers' law' but sees law embedded in social experience – as in the work of Weber, Petrażycki, Ehrlich, or Gurvitch.[8] As discussed in Chapter 1, effective law – experienced legal reality – can be something other than or more than the working of state regulation.

Sociology of law cannot do without efforts to conceptualise law because the idea of law must unify the field intellectually. But there is no need for (or possibility of) a single concept agreed on by all researchers. Even jurists do not have such a concept, and legal philosophers argue incessantly around the question 'What is law?' as they have for centuries. Sociology of law needs practical,

7 See Chapter 3, pp. 44–6.

8 Gurvitch (1947, 94) emphasised the importance of distinguishing 'the legal order of society and the legal order of the state', as he thought early social research on law had firmly done.

provisional models of what it will treat as law for its own research purposes in mediating between the political, the juridical and the social.

Nevertheless, an explicit statement of the model of law with which the researcher is working can help greatly in locating the research on a conceptual map of socio-legal inquiries. That is, it can contribute to an arrangement of understandings of law that makes the comparison and interrelations of law-focused research projects, both theoretical and empirical, potentially more systematic and intellectually integrated. Sociology of law should not neglect problems of conceptualising law, even though any conceptualisations will be provisional – useful models to organise thought.

The consequence of this approach to the nature of law is admittedly paradoxical. In sociology of law, law is an *essentially contested concept*, even though that concept, insofar as it informs action in different ways in different fields, is what intellectually unifies socio-legal research.[9] Part of the mission of sociology of law is to explore the variability of the idea of law – that is, legal understandings, practices and experience – a variability that reflects the very tensions between political, juridical, and social fields that justify sociology of law's existence.

The focus of sociology of law has rightly been on social action in legal contexts, the forms of consciousness informing such action, and the institutional frameworks in which this action occurs. Sociology of law is centrally concerned with action – meaningful social behaviour – but that does not mean it cannot say important things about law as *ideas*, in whatever fields of social action these ideas are found. Seen in this perspective, sociology of law seeks neither to replace jurisprudence nor to operate without reference to lawyers' concerns.

Part of its destiny is to develop a view of law recognising juristic understandings but *relativizing them*, contrasting them with other understandings of law in other fields of (political and social) experience. In this way sociology

9 This idea has been resisted by several legal sociologists, because of the difficulty in finding a conclusive definition of law. So, for example, John Griffiths (2006, 63) argues that the focus of sociology of law must be on types of *social control*. But this is to point the research field in a controversial direction – towards the study of authority structures rather than, for example, varieties of social interaction as in Ehrlich's (1936) early sociology of law. A converse approach is found in the attractive argument (in a direct line from Ehrlich) that sociology of law might be re-conceptualised in terms of a wide-ranging sociology of *norms*. But, if research is to avoid the dilemmas that Ehrlich's concept of living law raised a century ago, the question of which norms are to be accepted theoretically as legal needs to be faced by legal sociologists. The best approach, I suggest, is to treat ongoing exploration of the sociological nature of law (at the intersection of the juridical, the political and the social) as part of sociology of law's project. This need not be a disabling irresolution since, as suggested in the text, a variety of explicitly developed models of law can be the basis of fruitful empirical research; and comparing them contextually can promote important theoretical development in the field.

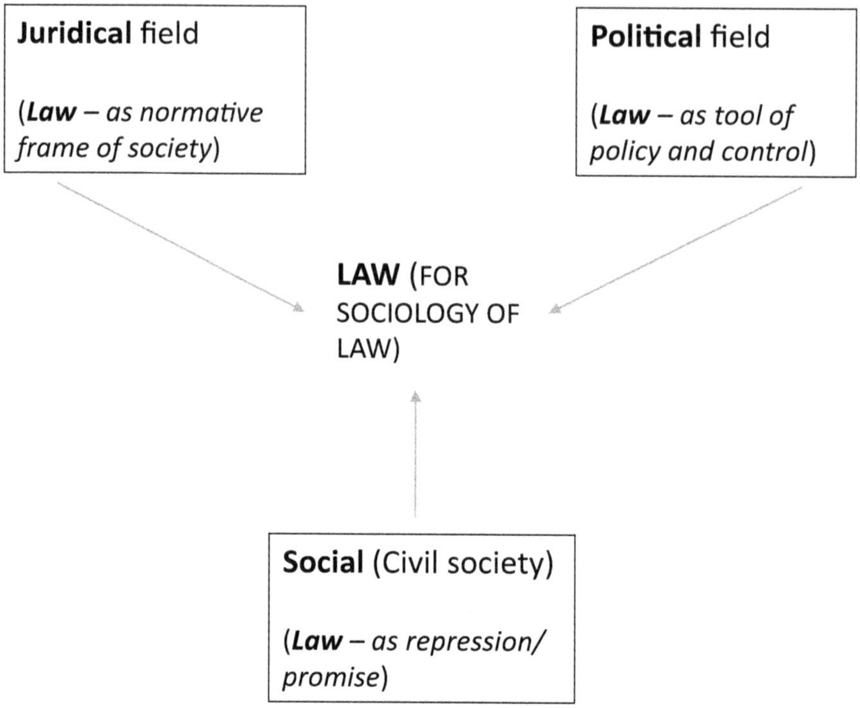

FIGURE 2.3 Conceptualising law in sociology of law and in its neighbouring fields

of law creates its *own* image of law as its unifying object. It will be an image that reflects the concerns and conclusions of ongoing social research.

Instability and Promise

Nothing in this chapter is intended to prescribe specific directions of socio-legal research. The chapter's focus is on the identity of the research enterprise, not its scope or research emphases. But a reader might well be dissatisfied with its apparent dismissal of distinct disciplinary criteria (methods, theories, or disciplinary traditions). Sociology of law as presented here might seem far too eclectic.

However, to maintain its independent position inside the triangle of fields, it must have an unshakeable commitment to social science – that is, to the methodologically systematic, empirically informed, theoretical study of social phenomena (Cotterrell 2006a, 54–8) – and, in this, the heritage of academic sociology (as well as other forms of inquiry in the human and social sciences) offers much as a resource of methods, theories, and research exemplars.

Sociology of law is probably fated to suffer from permanent instability. It is vulnerable to being co-opted – drawn too firmly towards one point or another in the triangle of fields. One tendency can be called *policy-science co-option*. Here social research becomes mainly a useful adjunct to government, a general aid in governmental tasks and policy formation and implementation.

Another tendency is co-option as support for the world of *legal practice*, processes, and institutions. Examples are some varieties of 'empirical legal studies' (Eisenberg 2011; Heise 2002), 'legal-empirical research' (Kurczewski 2001, 88) or 'fact research' (Rehbinder 1972) organised around legal professionals' agendas. A juristically oriented outlook might create a space for a sociology of law admittedly 'without rigour' (Carbonnier 2001) as regards social scientific theory, yet potentially enlightening for lawyers and law students.

Finally, sociology of law might become just a general study of *the social* – general sociology – if its concept of law seems too loose and unclear. We might say then that sociology of law has been co-opted by sociology! So, as noted in Chapter 1, Ehrlich's (1936) sociology of living law was once criticised as 'megalomaniac jurisprudence' embracing almost everything in social life (Allen 1964, 32). On this view, law just disappears into the social. And theories of legal pluralism, seeing law in many social contexts beyond the state and the lawyer's practice, are sometimes seen as potentially unlimited in scope: 'Where do we stop speaking of law and find ourselves simply describing social life?' (Merry 1988, 878).

It is wise just to accept this three-way instability – the risk of co-option or loss of identity within the triangle of fields – as inevitable, something that always needs to be guarded against. But the other face of it is the immense potential variety and scope of sociology of law, its openness, and above all, its natural *centrality as a field of inquiry* situated in the space of tensions between the political, the juridical and the social.

It is important not to be complacent. Sociology of law has usually needed extensive pre-conditions for its firm establishment:

(i) a well-established juridical field prepared to co-exist with it, amenable to it or at least not powerful enough to stop its development,
(ii) reliable sources of funding (public or private) for empirical research,
(iii) some institutional security (usually in a university, and often carrying risks of co-option),
(iv) political support or acquiescence,
(v) a recognised need (linked to social change or social problems) firmly rooted in civil society,
(vi) a sufficiently clear focus on law (even if the conceptualisation of law necessarily remains fluid); and
(vii) the availability of existing intellectual resources of theory and method in social science.

Even where all or most of these conditions have existed, sociology of law has not necessarily been established. Equally, some pioneer socio-legal work was developed largely in the absence of these conditions. Thus, another condition might be added to the earlier list:

(viii) intellectual leadership. To adapt Karl Marx, people (not fields of action) make history, but not under conditions of their own choosing.

Visionary individual pioneers of the 1950s and 1960s, especially in Europe and North America, scholars such as Renato Treves, Vilhelm Aubert, Jean Carbonnier, Adam Podgórecki, Philip Selznick, and Per Stjernquist, created pockets of socio-legal research and teaching on their own initiative, through their own energy, talent, imagination, and personality, and sometimes initially with few of the conditions for success as listed. And socio-legal research began, in isolated, farsighted work by other even earlier pioneers, long before what Ferrari saw as the modern 'rebirth' of sociology of law.

The case of Stjernquist in Sweden is an instructive case of individual leadership exerted at an opportune time when the need for sociology of law was recognised in the political field but not the juridical field (Stjernquist 2000; Cotterrell 2006b). Stjernquist, a member of a well-connected academic family with links to government in the nation's small political-cultural elite, became a professor of civil law at Lund University, one of Sweden's most prestigious centres of higher education, but found that his commitment to develop teaching in sociology of law was strongly opposed by the law faculty. As a result, the popular programme he introduced in 1963 (the first in Sweden) was designed for and taught to administrative sciences students, and only later opened to law students.

Eventually a chair of sociology of law was created for Stjernquist by government decision, but this chair was located outside the law faculty which continued to deny any need for the subject. Such a lonely, isolated development, entirely detached from the juristic world (and at first also from academic sociology) and directly inspired by governmental imperatives, with 'no supporters among influential [academic] social circles' and initially closely 'attached to the perspectives of legislators and administrators' (Stjernquist 2000, 66, 67), contrasts sharply with the broad grant-supported socio-legal movements in some other countries, and certainly with the vast US growth in this research area. It also illustrates how the orientation of teaching and research in sociology of law can be very strongly shaped, at least initially, by local conditions of its institutionalisation.

The comparative history of sociology of law deserves to be written and celebrated. To do so would encourage a proper recognition that, despite much variability and contingency in the conditions of its emergence, sociology of law is far from being a lost stepchild among the disciplines. It is an enterprise of great importance set strategically at the intersections of governmental imperatives and policies, professionalised legal scholarship and practice, and the ever-shifting challenges and demands thrown up by social change.

3

THE PLACE OF VALUES IN SOCIO-LEGAL STUDIES

The development of conceptual frameworks in sociology of law was considered in Chapter 1, and Chapter 2 sought to clarify the identity and functions of this research enterprise. Issues were noted in those chapters that are potentially significant also for jurisprudence. For example, how far is it important to conceptualise the nature of law in general and how might this be done? How should the meaning and significance of culture be judged in relation to law? These matters will reappear in different guises throughout this book since its overall aim is to compare jurisprudence and socio-legal studies. Jurisprudence is, I argue, best understood as a committed, value-oriented enterprise of jurists (Cotterrell 2018). In contrast, social science is a search for social knowledge using modern empirical scientific methods. If so, the place of *values* in inquiry in both research fields must be a crucially significant issue. This chapter addresses aspects of that issue as regards social scientific study of law.

How far then should socio-legal studies (SLS) be concerned with values? What place should the study of ultimate values or beliefs have in social scientific research? I mean, values or beliefs held, as Max Weber (1968, 25–6) put it, for their 'own sake'; that is, seen by those committed to them as *intrinsically worthy* and requiring no special justification. It is easy to think of many such beliefs or value commitments that closely relate to law and are supported by various constituencies – for example, commitments to human rights, human dignity, social equality, the sanctity of private property, liberty of contract, social welfare or wealth redistribution, religious freedom, religious beliefs that seek expression in law, democracy, and national sovereignty or national legal autonomy.

Can and should such relatively abstract ideas be studied directly in the empirically focused enterprise of SLS? Or should socio-legal scholars, as

DOI: 10.4324/9781003340324-5

hard-headed positivistic social scientists observing law, leave values to philosophers and jurists except when they are translated in some precise way into the provisions of positive law?

This chapter argues that SLS should concern itself with ultimate values insofar as these influence law and social action linked to law. Law is typically thought of as focused on governmental, citizens', and corporate *interests*, and much SLS work brings to light law's relations with these. But, as Weber (1948, 280) noted, ideas rooted in ultimate values and beliefs often determine 'the tracks along which action has been pushed by the dynamic of interest'. Values and interests, however conceptualised, sometimes intertwine in complex and sociologically significant ways.[1]

Because values inform action, at least to some extent, they inform the activity of socio-legal research itself. What values guide social research on law? Even Weber, who famously insisted that social science must be pursued in a value-free manner and not distracted by the value commitments of the researcher, recognised that the choice of topics for research is not likely to be neutral, but will be guided by the researcher's (or sponsor's) preferences or by considerations of cultural relevance; and usually these will be interconnected. Value commitments are part of culture. They influence directions of research even for those committed to 'pure science' – entirely disinterested inquiry (Weber 1949, ch2). And the very idea of commitment to science imports perhaps debatable values (Silbey 2013).

Many social researchers find it hard to be disinterested when they see society faced by urgent problems that raise pressing moral issues. A once-famous presidential address to the American Society for the Study of Social Problems was titled 'Whose Side Are We On?' (Becker 1967). But few professional researchers want to tie themselves very explicitly and uncompromisingly to the promotion of specific values, unless these can be assumed to be shared almost universally among the audience addressed. Fear of research being dismissed as 'biased' or 'unbalanced' goes with the felt need for scientific and thus professional respectability. Yet value questions haunt all social (including socio-legal) research.

Legal scholars of all kinds can also be asked: Whose – or what – side are you on? Legal scholarship in the Anglophone common law world does not usually claim to be 'science', but it has much the same need as social science for professional respectability. However, unlike most social scientists, conscientious lawyers can hardly avoid invoking ultimate values, and usually do so readily – for example, about justice (the realisation and administration of it, and access to it), doctrinal certainty and consistency, and equality before law. Perhaps, as these examples suggest, it is *process* values that lawyers are most comfortable

1 Miles 2015; Gecas 2008; Wuthnow 2008; Swedberg 2005; Spates 1983; Van Dyke 1962.

with and view as least controversial, often seeing them as inbuilt in their structures of professional expertise.

In some sense, therefore, law is always seen in terms of values. So, it is possible to ask: whose or what side is *law* on? It was the asking of this question that impelled many legal scholars to become the pioneers of SLS from the 1960s. But the impulse towards professionalisation and the realities of securing research support tend to marginalise efforts to pursue overt value critique, just as they did with radical criminology after it started to question the core value structures of societies in which crime arises (as in Quinney 1980).

In what follows I shall, first, discuss two topical illustrations to show how the meaning of ultimate values is sometimes raised in practice as an urgent legal issue, and should therefore be treated as part of the socio-legal reality that SLS studies. The chapter then sketches orientations in socio-legal theory that have tended to divert attention from a concern with ultimate values. It goes on to suggest a way of conceptualising values as part of culture. And it illustrates this by reference to the regulation of religious and ethnic minorities, on the one hand, and business and financial networks, on the other. Finally, it considers implications of SLS' own commitment to science in considering values and argues that theory can give guidance in judging the importance of ultimate values as a focus for the socio-legal enterprise and can even indicate values that SLS might emphasise.

Ultimate Values in Regulatory Practice

In May 2016, two unrelated and contrasting news stories about law and values appeared in the press at the same time. One was headlined 'Legal fears stall new laws to tackle extremism' (Travis 2016). It reported on 'an eight-month struggle to find a "legally robust" definition of extremism' that would 'not be immediately challenged in the courts'. This problem was said to explain 'the delay in bringing forward . . . flagship legislation to tackle Islamist extremism in Britain'. The problem was that the definition in the UK government's counter-extremism strategy, focusing on 'vocal or active opposition to fundamental British values', could be legally challenged as infringing rights to freedom of speech.

What is of special interest here is that the idea of extremism implies ultimate values *without conclusively delineating them*; it indicates the outer edge of a definitional vacuum; actions or attitudes beyond an unclear range of normative acceptability. An 'extreme' person, in one dictionary definition, is someone 'advocating severe or drastic measures; immoderate in opinion'[2] but the criteria against which to judge these measures or opinions are not necessarily

2 *Shorter Oxford English Dictionary*, 6th ed (2007).

specified and may be just assumed. A politician was quoted in the press reports as saying that the Home Office 'know what they dislike but they can't describe it'. What is implied in the effort at legal definition is a compendium of ultimate values seemingly *impossible to express in legal language*. 'Extreme' appears to mean – though it cannot be legally defined in these terms – outside a range of fundamental values that are to be assumed as universally shared and must be upheld as essential if co-existence is to be secured.[3]

Why was an effort being made legally to reach these values and police them? The reason is that they were sensed as actually or potentially destabilised because of forms of cultural diversity and associated attitudes and actions thought to be impossible to reconcile with them. Here, surely, is a situation in which socio-legal inquiry becomes essential. What social conditions is law being required to address – and what value commitments shape these conditions?

Law is required here to identify social problems, partly in terms of the values underlying them. Law and policy, built on a concept of extremism, are thereby presented as engaged, as a practical matter, directly in value conflict. So, the socio-legal study of how this law and policy operates would necessarily have to address the value commitments that drive it, and those that are thought to define the targets to which it is addressed. Crucially, it is the sense of a *dislocation of ultimate values* that leads to an effort to make these values explicit, and this sense links the lawmakers' conundrums here to a second news story dealing with wholly different matters.

On the same day as the 'extremism' story, media in several countries reported the quashing by the Italian Court of Cassation after three lower court trials of the conviction of a homeless Ukrainian immigrant for stealing a sausage and a piece of cheese from a Genoa supermarket. The court stated that the 'condition of the defendant and the circumstances in which the . . . theft took place' proved that he took 'that small amount of food in the face of the immediate and essential need for nourishment'. He acted 'in a state of need' and in such circumstances no crime had been committed. An Italian leader writer remarked: 'For the supreme judges, the right to survival has prevailed over the right to property. In America that would be blasphemy. And here as well, some conformists will talk about a legitimation of proletarian expropriation.'

In the absence of a full case report, only opinions reported in the press are available here; they refer to such matters as a new application of the necessity defence, a legal right to dignity, the non-violent nature of the theft, the failure

3 The UK government's *Revised Prevent Duty Guidance: for England and Wales*, 2015 (updated April 2021), para 7, gives examples of British values as 'democracy, the rule of law, individual liberty and mutual respect and tolerance of different faiths and beliefs'. This list, not further discussed in the Guidance, seems to be given as indicative.

of the legal system in requiring three sets of proceedings to decide the case, and corruption and the economic crisis (as the real issues). A commentator in the daily newspaper *Corriere della Sera* wrote, supporting the decision: 'As the law is nothing but the box where our living together takes shape, it was unthinkable that jurisprudence did not take reality into account.'[4]

Cases of small-scale thefts in tragic circumstances are hardly uncommon. In England, at Kidderminster Magistrates Court in 2015 a woman was fined for stealing a 75p pack of Mars bars although, the court was told, she had stolen 'the cheapest item she could find because she had not eaten in days since her benefits were sanctioned' (Mortimer 2015). While this is surely morally striking,[5] legally it may not be, as a simple application of positive law. But the Italian case directly raises the relation of law and ultimate values as an issue for the court (and society at large) to face. It brings the value of the sanctity of property to the fore, and not in terms of familiar debates around legally enshrined human rights (values expressly put in legal form) but as a fundamental questioning of a normally silently presupposed, implicit value that underpins law.

The fact that the Italian case attracted international media attention hints at its socio-legal interest, as symptomatic of an at least partial destabilisation of the fundamental, underlying value of private property, one of the crucial value pillars of private law. The thread of readers' comments after the *Guardian* report of the case reinforces this impression: 'Theft is theft . . . but the punishment should reflect the magnitude of the crime'; 'The man was homeless and broke. Should they have taken his sleeping bag? His jacket?'; 'In the UK steal [sic] £490 million from pensions – punished with a knighthood'; 'Leaving people to starve in the street is a crime'; 'the real offence was caused by the state because of its abandonment of the poor' (Kirchgaessner 2016). Reference is made to wider economic circumstances, disparities of wealth and the fragility of social support structures.

The case, from this point of view, highlights one aspect of a larger socio-legal reality also reflected in the mass media through reports of 'aggressive' tax avoidance or tax manipulation by those with access to the knowledge and resources to engage in it, the growth of vast disparities of wealth between the richest one per cent and the rest, and suspicions of widespread financial corruption – all of these being issues that presuppose and rely on, yet also contextualise and potentially subvert, the ultimate value of sanctity of property.

4 All quotes in this and the previous paragraph are from Pianingiani and Chan 2016; see also Kirchgaessner 2016.

5 Mortimer (2015) notes that the fine and costs imposed amounted to 438 times the value of the stolen property. A support campaign, described as 'a small gesture of solidarity' with the defendant, raised not only the money to discharge her liability but more than £13,000 in excess, which was to be given to charity.

As regards tax avoidance and related matters, issues for socio-legal attention may not be mainly about obtaining empirical evidence because much evidence is made readily available by means (including journalistic investigative reporting and the large-scale leaking of electronic files) that bypass the usual methods of academic socio-legal inquiry. Issues may centre instead significantly on law's relation to ultimate values (Prebble and Prebble 2010); for example, the influence of popular and official value-orientations on the operation of law.[6]

Tax avoidance as the legitimate protection of one's property is often called 'tax efficiency' or 'tax planning'.[7] From some viewpoints it is not only morally blameless but praiseworthy and linked directly to values of liberty, privacy, and security, as well as sanctity of property. Insofar as values, as Weber says, mark 'tracks along which action' is 'pushed by the dynamic of interest', the promotion of ultimate values may not only legitimise the behaviour of individuals and corporate actors but influence the attitudes of courts and enforcement agents in matters of regulatory policy.[8]

There is a role for socio-legal theory in areas such as this, to explore how powerfully defended structures of absolute values link with attitudes to law, and to practices of legal interpretation and application; as well as to perceptions of the nature of private and public interests and of how these interests may properly be pursued.

How Instrumentalism Marginalises Values

A concern with values as a specific focus for socio-legal research may seem strange, even eccentric, although a minority of scholars – for example, Philip Selznick among modern writers, and Émile Durkheim among the sociological classics – have adopted such a concern.[9] One danger in adopting it is that of forgetting that values are sociologically significant only insofar as people, individually or collectively, *actually recognise them* as important; so, their social salience is always relative to time and place. Although such values are often treated as absolutes, their relevance as social phenomena depends on the

6 Ordower 2010, 113, notes that 'tax avoidance in many developed economies is cultural. It embodies a free-standing set of beliefs, traditions, and practices.'

7 Prebble and Prebble 2010, 696, define it more critically as 'contriving transactions and structures that reduce tax in ways that are contrary to the policy or spirit of the legislation'. The question then becomes a difficult one of unambiguously specifying this policy or spirit.

8 See Martinez 1994, 547–67 on relationships between US tax enforcement and popular value-orientations; Ordower 2010 on avoidance culture as a powerful force of resistance to effective tax law.

9 A focus on the study of ultimate societal values and their evolution as an aspect of large-scale social change also typifies the distinctive sociology of Pitirim Sorokin (Johnston 1998, 34–8; Ford et al. 1996). On Durkheim's approach to values see Cotterrell 2018, ch12; on Selznick's approach see Cotterrell 2021.

contingencies of their acceptance and the ways in which they are defined and interpreted. The focus, therefore, must be on values having meaning in *specific social contexts*, not as timeless objects of philosophical analysis.

Long-established theoretical traditions militate, however, against a socio-legal focus on values. They reinforce a narrow view of the nature of law as techniques, practices, and norms – narrow because it underestimates law's potential cultural significance and its power to reinforce and help to constitute broad understandings of the nature of the social world. Powerful theoretical traditions and wider currents of common-sense understanding of the nature of law reinforce an *instrumental* view of it, and a view of social life as structured primarily around instrumental action, rather than giving due weight to the significance of action shaped by commitments to ultimate values or beliefs (Cotterrell 2018, ch14). In much socio-legal research, as in much legal practice and experience, law has been seen primarily as a tool of government and a resource by means of which actors (citizens, corporations, groups) pursue their private purposes or protect their interests (Tamanaha 2007; Cotterrell 2009).

If one dominant theoretical influence underpins this view of modern law and society, it is that of Max Weber. While he in no way denies the important place that value commitments play in influencing or giving meaning to action, or to law, he sees values in modern society as primarily a mass of normative inconsistency and mutually incompatible prescriptions. In this view, since the decline of natural law ideas, no consistent value-orientations can be attached to law. Values are limited to distinct spheres of experience (Brubaker 1984, ch3); projected outside these they become irreconcilable and confused; modern law incorporates values but in a piecemeal way depending on the specific fields being regulated. So, values may provide some of law's content but are typically subordinated to the formal rational qualities that dominate it. It seems that the only values expected to pervade modern law – to be inherent in it – will be process values of consistency, coherence, and predictability.

The everyday authority that supports modern law appears also to be largely free of any appeal to ultimate values. It is substantially free of what Weber (1968, 215–6) described as 'charismatic' or 'traditional' elements. The dominant basis of modern authority (legitimate domination) is, for Weber, 'the *belief in legality* . . . compliance with enactments which are formally correct and which have been made in the accustomed manner' (1968, 37, emphasis added). That is, it is based on systems of impersonal rules defining hierarchically organised official positions and their jurisdictions. But Weber seems only partly to support the idea of modern law as self-justifying through its formal rationality. A better interpretation is that, for him, modern law justifies itself by its *obvious usefulness* in the pursuit of governmental and private interests (Cotterrell 1995, ch7); it is merely 'the product or the technical means of a compromise between conflicting interests' (Weber 1968, 875).

Sociology of law has largely internalised the kind of perspective on law that Weber theorises. And in much legal scholarship it also dominates implicitly. Even human rights are often interpreted legally as categories of legitimate interests so that ultimate humanistic values are legally transformed into specific participation and membership rights (Cotterrell 2018, ch13). Economic analysis of law, emphasising market efficiency and purpose-rationality as drivers of law, has had only indirect relations with the mainstream of SLS. But sociology has been influenced by rational action theory influenced by rational choice economics (Goldthorpe 1996). Much sociology of law, too, has been bewitched by concerns with the instrumental effectiveness of legal action and its limits.

This is so even where (as often) scholars have critiqued law's instrumental use and its negative 'impact' on social life. There has been a tendency to leave aside inquiries about overarching ideologies driving law (at least since Marxist theories fell out of favour), or about cultural values pressed on law for recognition or assumed as underpinnings of law (such as those presupposed in the 'extremism' case, discussed earlier, or brought into contention in the Italian one). Admittedly with many exceptions, socio-legal research has tended to prefer to examine law as instrumental rather than expressive, and as 'externally' regulating projects rather than 'internally' inhabiting culture.

What would be entailed in seeing law as 'inhabiting culture'? This might involve attaching much more attention to the nature of law itself as not only an instrument of state regulation but also an *aspect of culture* (Mezey 2001; Saguy and Stuart 2008). State law's relation to culture does, indeed, include operating on it instrumentally; and there is no good reason to see instrumental (especially economic) social relations as outside the scope of culture in considering culture's relation to law. But culture includes much more that is legally relevant.

This chapter is especially concerned to emphasise law's implication with *values and beliefs*. But law can also be an embodiment or safeguard of *tradition*, taking this word in a broad sense to include any well-established frameworks of co-existence in a particular natural or social environment. So, law protects 'cultural heritage', natural and built environments (planning and conservation laws), national and minority languages, customs, and traditions – even history itself as collective memory (for example, in laws against Holocaust denial). In such ways it affirms and expresses tradition.

Finally, law may express *affective* elements of culture – emotional attachments, allegiances, resistances, and rejections. It can be seen as – and sometimes (as in the preambles of some national constitutions) proclaims itself to be – an expression of patriotism or national identity. Conversely, rejection of foreign elements in legal systems may sometimes be an expression of cultural xenophobia, of resistance to foreign influence simply because it is foreign.

Culture and Community

Ultimate values that inform law in particular social settings can be taken as distinct objects of research – and this has been done to some extent in comparative legal studies. For example, James Whitman has extensively explored what he sees as a dichotomy between a fundamental *value of liberty* characterising much American law and a contrasting *value of dignity* deeply embedded in continental European Law (Whitman 2000, 2004, 2005; Friedman and Whitman 2003). But this research is controversial and, although based on intricate comparative studies of legal doctrine, necessarily results in very broad generalisations.[10]

A more familiar way to include the study of values in socio-legal research is to treat them as one component of culture, analytically distinguishable but almost invariably implicated in empirically observable social conditions with culture's other elements. The most feasible way to do this involves first conceptualising culture along different dimensions – (i) instrumental or material aspects especially focused on economic relations; (ii) aspects relating to shared ultimate values or beliefs; (iii) elements of tradition (in the wide sense indicated earlier) focused on conditions of co-existence in a shared environment – such as common language, experience, history, or geographical location; and (iv) affective elements – emotional attachments and identities not necessarily explicable in terms of any of the other aspects of culture, although they may arise from or colour them. One might, for example, simply feel 'British' or 'European' in the sense of identifying emotionally with a certain society or communal network or fixing a cultural identity by emotionally rejecting or separating from some other group or nation.

Conceptualising these different dimensions of culture is a means to an end. It is a methodological device to help make intellectually manageable the myriad kinds of social relations that law must regulate and the different kinds of communal relations that give rise to, seek, or support regulation. Such a 'community lens' is a way of classifying the radically different types of bonds that stabilise social relations, so as to highlight contrasting features of these types; features that are likely to be significant in considering how these types can be regulated by state law, and how they will relate to law. The idea of

10 See further Finkin 2010 (doubting a sharp US-Europe divide in ultimate values underlying employee privacy law). An extreme example of the difficulties of providing empirical grounding for broad characterisations of values claimed as dominating societies or cultures is found in Pitirim Sorokin's sociology, mentioned earlier. Sorokin made strenuous efforts to gather quantitative data (often presented in graphs and tables) to support claims about the shifting values of civilisations but the vastness of his generalisations almost guaranteed that the data would seem inadequate. On Sorokin as a socio-legal theorist see Deflem 2008, 87–9; and Chapter 7.

thinking of 'community' as communal relations in this way has already been discussed in Chapter 1.

The differences between these types from a regulatory perspective are complex and present a large agenda for research. But it is not hard to recognise that, in general, relations between law and emotion, law and beliefs or ultimate values, law and instrumental (especially economic) relations, and law and tradition are likely to be different in kind. Indeed, the insights of sociology of law, on the one hand, and long juristic experience, on the other, have already illuminated the contrasting character of these relations (Cotterrell 2006a, ch7).

These different elements of culture point to the four contrasting 'pure' types of communal relations discussed earlier in Chapter 1 – shared instrumental projects, beliefs or values, traditions, and emotional orientations. They can be separated for analytical purposes especially because they are likely to give rise to different kinds of regulatory problems, but they are almost invariably combined in complex ways in social life. So, as suggested, we should speak of *communal networks* or groups made up of often very complex combinations of these different, distinguishable types of social bonds.

Values seen in this way are just part of a complex mix, and it is the complex mixes making up communal networks that carry what can be called culture. So, culture is an ever-shifting pattern of values, beliefs, traditions, projects, and allegiances holding these communal networks together. Law addresses culture in this sense and draws its meaning and relevance from it. Most importantly, culture seen in this way is not necessarily bounded by the territory and legal jurisdiction of the state. The society inhabiting such a state territory is indeed a communal network, but so are numerous more local groupings and minority populations within it, as well as numerous transnational networks that extend beyond it.

Such a perspective shows law interwoven in the social in many ways – influenced in its operation from different cultural sources and facing different kinds of challenges presented by diverse elements of culture. Such a perspective is obviously different from a 'linear' instrumental or causal approach that sees law (a unified entity) as *acting on* 'society' (another unified entity) or, in a reverse formulation, as passively *mirroring* society. Law and culture are best seen as mutually constitutive (Mezey 2001). A major part of state law's activity is devoted to regulating instrumental (especially economic) relations. But even where communal networks are dominated by instrumental relations and law seeks directly to address these, other matters are likely to be implicated: values and beliefs (e.g. shaping understandings of and attitudes to economic activity and state regulation); practices and customs arising from working together in a common business environment; and emotional allegiances or rejections touching on business decisions (e.g. regarding choices of clients or trading partners, or dealings in certain nations).

Such possible cultural variables suggest why culture should be an important consideration in judging the likely success and optimal strategies of state legal regulation. Indeed, this has been seen in important socio-legal research, for example on formal organisations and business regulation (Chappe et al. 2013; Awrey et al. 2013; Moorhead and Hinchly 2015). It is now widely recognised that problems of regulating corporate structures are often not readily solvable by regulators designing law, however expertly, as an *external* control on corporate activity – in other words by maximising law's effect as an instrument applied from 'outside' on the 'internal' activities of business entities.

The reality is, it seems, often much more one of getting inside the culture of communal networks (such as banking and financial systems, corporations and corporate groups, transnational industries, and commercial networks) so that law – or other regulation that it encourages – becomes absorbed, interpreted, and often transformed in internal business culture rather than appearing (and being resisted) as an invading instrument (Gilad 2014; Edelman and Stryker 2005).

Tendencies towards Cultural Closure

Culture, then, does not indicate an integrated entity ('a culture' or distinct 'cultures') but a contingent mix of elements. Culture does not usually have clear boundaries because its instrumental, affective, traditional, and beliefs/values aspects may, at least to some extent, exist independently of each other, informing different patterns of social relations, uniting different groups. People are usually involved in many different relations of community at any given time and so they experience aspects of culture in many ways.

However, it is reasonable to talk of distinct *cultures* when the four elements of culture identified in this chapter appear *superimposed on each other* in a particular population or network of social relations: when, for example, the integration of instrumental economic relations is strongly reinforced by (i) the participants' shared beliefs, (ii) the emotional attachments that unite them, and (iii) shared traditions that have grown up through constant interaction.

These conditions may arise when communal networks create their own regulation, and in the process resistance to or suspicion of 'external' regulation, especially perhaps state law, may develop. Their bounded character, relatively self-contained along all four dimensions of culture, can mean that it is hard for state law to penetrate or influence them when cultural characteristics sharply mark out social limits separating a communal network from others.[11]

11 For an excellent recent study of one such relatively self-contained communal network in Britain, see Tas 2014. For an early study of communal networks becoming less self-contained, see Doo 1973.

It might be possible in theory to observe entirely 'closed communities' or groups *absolutely* culturally separated from others. But it is very unlikely that, in modern liberal societies with a highly developed division of labour and widespread networks of social interdependence, such total isolation of cultures will exist. But a practical issue for socio-legal research is how far *pressures* towards such isolation can create problems for state legal regulation.[12]

In relation to powerful communal networks primarily organised for economic or financial activity these problems of cultural separation have been widely recognised. 'Banking culture' is often cited as a matter for examination and reform, which may or may not significantly involve (state or international) law. In some business networks seen as having distinct 'cultures' in some sense, value commitments may be an important part of the cultural mix – for example, to individual liberty (inspiring hostility to state regulation and commitment to contractual freedom), sanctity of property, security and privacy, and the social importance of markets.

The socio-legal issue then becomes whether or how state law or other forms of regulation can engage with such ultimate values if they inform and influence kinds of economic action that law is expected to oversee. How can the significance of such values be judged and what are the limits of legal action in engaging with this aspect of culture?

In popular debate such issues about law and culture are much more frequently raised in an entirely different context – that of the cultural pluralism associated with religious or ethnic minority populations. In banking and commercial networks, the dominant relations of community integrating these networks culturally can be seen as instrumental – focused on common or convergent economic projects – with other aspects of culture perhaps arranged around these. But in some other communal networks, such as those of Muslim minorities in Western societies, the dominant relations of community are often, more obviously, those of tradition (customs, established or inherited practices of co-existence) or values and beliefs (e.g. rooted in Islamic religious doctrines). Again, there is the possibility that all aspects of culture may converge and be superimposed on each other.

Thus, economic relations may become significantly co-extensive with bonds of belief or custom (perhaps partly because of discrimination from *outside* the communal network, or the relative ease of establishing understandings *within* it). Again, affective allegiances to the group and affective rejections of its external environment may sometimes be correspondingly strengthened.

12 One reason they may do so is that history shows that minority 'closed communities', whether they have drifted into cultural isolation or had it forced on them, often become highly vulnerable to external attack.

But minority networks do not inevitably become significantly 'closed' through such processes of cultural overlay. Very often they do not.

Bonds based on belief or values may be diverse and sometimes conflicting because of religious differences; customary practices may vary greatly, especially because of different ethnic group origins and different ongoing transnational ties; economic relations are unlikely as a practical matter to be exclusively limited within a network of religious believers or an ethnic group; and emotional allegiances may be complex and variable in such communal networks, even when (and, perhaps, sometimes because) outsiders imagine them as having strong group identity and uniformity.

Where there are tendencies to drift – or be pushed by outside pressures – towards cultural homogeneity, self-regulation often flourishes in well-defined communal networks. Also, these networks tend to resist, reinterpret in their own ways, or distance themselves from state law. The communal network that is the politically organised society of a state produces its own law in a fully juridical sense as state law. Other communal networks produce regulation that may or may not be recognised or labelled as law. Sometimes this internally generated regulation exists in accommodation with state law, sometimes in recognised subordination to it, or without reference to it, or in effective competition with it. Sometimes it is explicitly promulgated, and sometimes merely implicit, understood by insiders but substantially hidden from the world outside the communal network in which it arises.

In relatively closed communal networks it is often difficult for outsiders to study this implicit regulation. It may be merely normative understandings shaped by members' shared projects, by their value commitments and affective orientations, or their settled common practices. It can be very hard to penetrate the sheer complexity and density of combinations of cultural elements that shape the internal regulatory structures of communal networks. Perhaps then it is unsurprising that, although some communal networks are of great contemporary significance, they do not become popular foci for socio-legal inquiry.

This is the case (despite important research by a relatively small number of specialist socio-legal scholars) with powerful transnational business and financial networks, some of which may seem to have clearly defined and relatively self-contained cultures.[13] Where extensive research has been done it is often by 'insiders' – people with inside, first-hand experience or specialist knowledge of these networks. Similarly, Islamic communal networks in Britain are also of

13 See e.g. Ailon 2019 (culture of 'atomistic indifference' among financial traders); Van den Steen 2010 (beliefs and values as component of corporate culture); Simpson 2019 (City of London finance market culture).

great socio-legal importance but the study of them seems surprisingly marginal alongside the mainstream topics of SLS research.

Among major reasons that can be suggested are their cultural complexity and diversity and the difficulty sometimes posed for outsiders in gaining adequate conditions of entry into them. So, it is not easy to study these networks by 'cultural immersion' (Curran 1998) – the term favoured by some comparative lawyers – aimed at 'thick description' of culture. Muslim and other minority communal networks have attracted much socio-legal research in many countries (e.g. Bano 2012; Tas 2014; Bowen 2016; Ahmed and Krayem 2021). But this has often been done by scholars outside the SLS mainstream who are members of these networks or have special experience of them, and findings are often not strongly linked to any wider themes in the socio-legal literature.

Values in Socio-Legal Theory

Studying values in culture empirically is difficult. Cultural immersion is a time-consuming activity requiring great sensitivity and perception from the researcher. The conditions for undertaking it may often be hard to secure. Although legal scholars have advocated this kind of research, it is professional anthropologists who have been its main practitioners in socio-legal inquiries (Geertz 1983, 167–234). But can socio-legal *theory* help to clarify the position of ultimate values among the range of cultural research concerns that SLS should recognise? In this final section I shall suggest that it can.

If the regulation of communal networks is accepted as an important focus for socio-legal inquiry, it can be recognised that much of this regulation often arises internally, produced in the networks themselves. This was emphasised from the very beginnings of modern sociology of law in Ehrlich's idea of living law.[14] Some regulation *internal* to communal networks is readily recognised as law, especially when the network's regulation is guaranteed by the state. But many communal networks are also regulated *from 'outside'* to co-ordinate their relations with others. Thus, the law of modern liberal states is assumed to have the task of establishing peaceful, productive relations between communal networks in its jurisdiction, and limiting the reach of their regulatory power.

Liberal law does this primarily by guaranteeing equal citizenship and uniform individual rights; that is, rights not dependent on individuals' status in any specific communal network within the state. And it polices, to some extent, rights of entry and exit from communal networks (for example, setting itself against racial, sexual, religious, and other kinds of discrimination). It is assumed that complex modern societies need to ensure freedom for people

14 See Chapter 1 and Chapter 8.

to move in and between as many communal networks as they wish. This is a value-judgment underlying much of modern law. But can anything be said about this value-judgment from a socio-legal perspective?

Socio-legal research surely cannot, as *science*, prescribe any ultimate values to guide law. But where value choices are to be made it should be possible to advise about the likely social effects of these choices. Social research can also potentially explain the social conditions in which certain value choices are likely to seem meaningful or even obvious to people; it can explain conditions that define what are likely to be seen as the parameters of meaningful debate around values – that is, what value commitments will be seen as reasonable or at least matters for legitimate discussion and which will be seen as 'off the wall' and unlikely to be seriously entertained in a given time and place. When and why, for example, do the rights and wrongs of slavery, abortion, or capital punishment become live issues?

Durkheim seemed to go very far in suggesting that sociology could clarify and inform value debates. He wrote that 'science can help in finding the direction in which our conduct ought to go, assisting us to determine the ideal that gropingly we seek' and 'having observed reality . . . we shall distil the ideal from it' (1984, xxvi). On this view, sociology can indicate the possible consequences of adherence to certain values, and so it can suggest their appropriateness or otherwise depending on whether the indicated consequences are desired.

Durkheim thought that social solidarity – the relatively harmonious integration of society – was a desirable value and, at the same time, a social fact produced by ties of interdependence without which complex modern societies could not function. But this apparent eliding of value and fact is something that many social scientists would properly reject. A similar problem affects Philip Selznick's sociology of law when it seems to assume that a value of legality is inherent in law as an empirically observable social phenomenon (Cotterrell 2018, 62–5). In fact, a choice to pursue the co-ordination and integration of communal networks through law – and to select which networks to support and which to repress or ignore – involves value commitments. So, solidarity is a value that *may or may not be pursued*. Social research can do no more than try to show the consequences of pursuing it or not.

The strongest part of Durkheim's claims about solidarity is his argument that complex modern societies need elaborate co-ordination and functional integration of their diverse elements if they are to be most fully productive, peaceful, and liberating environments for all their members. So, the value of solidarity *in such contexts* is likely to become a meaningful one; societies can ignore this value but there are crucial reasons not to. Then many questions remain to be asked as to how law can relate to this chosen value, how law expresses it, and how law undermines possibilities of acting on it. And these are issues that fall directly within the capacities of socio-legal research. To the extent that social co-ordination and integration seem pressing issues, the socio-legal conditions of solidarity become important for the agenda of research.

Some co-ordination between communal networks and among individuals irrespective of the networks to which they belong could presumably be structured by any of the four types of cultural bonds discussed earlier. Bonds of solidarity could arise (i) from 'tradition' – common traditions of co-existence and experience that transcend the boundaries of specific communal networks, (ii) instrumental ties of common or convergent economic relations crossing these boundaries, (iii) shared values or beliefs, or (iv) affective ties that transcend groups or networks. But tradition can isolate as much as integrate, emotional ties can be strong but volatile, and instrumental ties of common interest can be transient, ephemeral, and changeable. Especially where communal networks tend towards relative 'closure', as considered earlier, none of these means of co-ordination with the social world beyond the network may be sufficiently strong and reliable (Cotterrell 2018, 164–7).

Durkheim's answer was that only a society-wide commitment to a *value system* of moral individualism was consistent with the needs of integration in complex modern societies. Individuals may have many different, shifting group allegiances; different structures of economic relations; different ethnic identifications, customary ways, and well-rooted traditions. In such circumstances all that can unite people morally across these numerous social divides is a humanistic insistence on the universal worth of every individual simply by virtue of that individual's equal humanity alongside all others. This is moral individualism.[15]

As societies become increasingly complex, the co-ordination and stable integration of social life seems not only more elusive, contingent, and fragile but also more essential. These conditions suggest the relevance of a humanistic value system enshrined in law and actively promoted in government policy and perhaps educational practice. Sociological analysis does not *mandate* ultimate values, it cannot do so. But it can indicate conditions in which such values seem meaningful and pertinent, and social research can suggest how to act on them.

It is unsurprising that concerns with human rights and dignity dominate so much contemporary legal thinking in complex modern societies. They directly reflect the value system of moral individualism (Cotterrell 2018, ch13) but are only the most general and explicit legal expression of it; other aspects of law are at least partially informed by it. Moral individualism demands respect for individuals in certain crucial ways across all boundaries of communal relations. It also suggests reasons for state legal concern with communal networks that become so isolated through tendencies towards cultural closure that they

15 See generally Cotterrell 1999, 103–18.

threaten to undermine wider conditions of solidarity within the state's claimed jurisdiction.

The values of moral individualism are obviously not the only ultimate values that underpin contemporary law, and they compete with others; they are often undermined by law at the same time as they inform it. Their relevance for many areas of international and transnational law remains currently largely unexplored. The most important point about them, however, for the purposes of this chapter is that their significance under specific conditions can be analysed sociologically. As in the case of other values, their relation to law can be a topic for socio-legal research.

4

LEGAL CULTURE AND CULTURAL DIVERSITY

This chapter extends the discussion in the previous one by asking how the idea of *legal culture* should be conceptualised in socio-legal perspective. More generally, it tries to illustrate further how relationships between law and culture should be addressed. These topics are surely among the most pressing for socio-legal scholarship today. No one who reads newspapers or watches television can doubt that culture – in some sense – has become a vitally significant issue for law.

In Britain, aspects of this issue were brought into wide public debate initially by statements in an extensively reported speech in 2008 by Rowan Williams, the then Archbishop of Canterbury and head of the established Church of England (Williams 2008). Williams indicated that he thought it inevitable that some aspects of Islamic *Shari'a* law would eventually be recognised in United Kingdom law. They would enter British legal culture. His comments produced furious condemnation in the popular press and led to calls for his resignation (Brown 2008). The speech became an enduring reference point in discussion of law and culture, at least in its religious aspects, in the British context. The central issues are the commitments and sensibilities of religious minorities and the extent to which the law of the nation state should express these commitments and sensibilities.

At the same time, in Denmark and beyond, controversy was reignited around the so-called 'Danish cartoons' case, involving portrayals of the Prophet Mohammed, widely seen by Muslims as offensive and derogatory. The republication of the cartoons in Danish newspapers, almost contemporaneously with Williams' speech, but entirely unconnected with it, produced further fury (Tait 2008; Olsen 2008).

The fundamental controversy is about how law should reflect or even control an aspect of culture. The issue attracts intense passions. 'Law and culture'

DOI: 10.4324/9781003340324-6

is a topic that makes people angry. It has become prominent, as highlighted by Williams' speech, because of a recognition that culture can no longer be taken for granted by law; it can no longer be treated as uniform and unproblematic but must be seen sociologically and legally as a plurality of not necessarily harmoniously co-existing forms.

Contemporary Western societies are multicultural. No doubt they never were mono-cultural. But in times when population movements between nations were more limited it was easier for legal analysis to assume cultural homogeneity – even while recognising social diversity as regards class, social mobility, and levels of wealth. The assumption was that culture in the sense of beliefs and values, allegiances, national sentiments, and customs and traditions, could be treated as relatively uniform (Citrin and Sides 2008). When such an assumption exists, culture can seem largely *invisible* to law, not a concept that legal analysis must address. But this myopia is no longer possible.

Components of Culture

What does 'culture' mean? The sense of culture 'invading' law, made vivid by Williams' speech, reflects the existence of diverse fundamental beliefs in the same society. In Britain it was a religious leader who advocated official recognition of practices reflecting minority religious convictions. Opposition came from those who saw a threat to national legal culture. The conflict was about *beliefs and values.* Similarly, in Denmark, the main stated justification for re-publishing the Mohammed cartoons was, according to press reports, to defend freedom of speech. The value system of liberalism was set up on one side; on the other were precepts of a comprehensive religious belief system.

But any legally relevant concept of culture must cover more than beliefs and values. At the same time as the Williams speech and the republication of the Danish cartoons, came news from Turkey that the *hadith*, the reported sayings and traditions of the prophet Mohammed, were being officially re-edited to remove accretions reflecting not the fundamental beliefs of Islam but the local understandings and practices of the particular communities and times in which the *hadith* were assembled (Piggott 2008; Traynor 2008). The aim was to separate core beliefs from matters of contingent custom and tradition.

In practice, beliefs and tradition are often closely intertwined but as argued in Chapter 3 analytically they are separable, and it is often important in a socio-legal context to distinguish them. Law's capacity to respond to matters of belief and values – to interact with or regulate them appropriately – may be very different from its capacity in relation to custom and tradition (Cotterrell 2006a, 123–4, 155–6).

As discussed in Chapter 3, 'tradition' can be taken to include many kinds of inheritance – for example, common language, common historical experience, collective memory, and shared geographical environment. Law has important challenges to face in regulating everyday conditions arising from the mere fact of living together in the same language group, the same neighbourhood or the same environment of custom. Its task will often involve defining *arenas of co-existence*; that is, relevant environments and their boundaries. It must prevent friction across those boundaries, and between people who have to co-exist inside them.

A further 'cultural' concern for law is technological development and economic interaction. 'European culture', for example, can be a meaningful idea. It can refer to a sense of 'European values', however ambiguous and contested these may be; or to a common European territory and history, although the experience of that history has differed across Europe and may divide as well as unify Europe's populations. It can refer to kinds of technological development and economic cooperation, development, and integration typical in Europe but less so in other parts of the world. Yet these economic and technological patterns are diverse and not always unifying.

Culture can also be a matter of affective relations, loves and hatreds not necessarily reducible to differences of tradition, belief, values, or shared conditions of economic interaction. So, when people think of their cultural attachments, they sometimes find that these are not entirely explicable in terms of beliefs/values, traditions, or material interests (though efforts may be made to rationalise them in those terms). Also involved may be feelings of allegiance or belonging, or of differentiation from what are seen as alien cultures. As noted earlier, one can, for example, simply feel 'European' or not – or to varying degrees at different times and different circumstances.[1]

There is no single relationship between law and culture because culture is not a single thing – not a 'thing' at all. It is a central socio-legal task to examine how, as a technical and policy matter, law can address each of the four general components of culture – beliefs/values, tradition (in the wide sense indicated), instrumental economic/technological matters, and matters of affect (emotion). What differences are there in law's resources and capabilities when it addresses each of these components?

As indicated in Chapter 3, networks of community life (communal networks or groups) are built on complex combinations of these four components of culture, which are themselves expressed in innumerable forms. Nevertheless, precision in juristic thought requires that at least these basic components should be analytically separated in terms of their challenges for law. Otherwise, to try to relate law to a concept of 'culture' that defies precise definition is like trying to nail jelly to a wall.

1 Chapter 3, p. 47.

A Politics of Legal Culture

What of *legal* culture? This has become an important idea in legal scholarship. It has tended to replace the old comparative law concept of legal families. That concept distinguished, in Zweigert's and Kötz's (1998) authoritative modern formulation, between 'Romanistic' (primarily French-influenced), 'Germanic', 'Anglo-American', and 'Nordic' families of legal systems, and between these collectively and their exotic 'others' – 'Law in the Far East' and 'Religious Legal Systems'.[2] Merely listing these crude classifications is enough to signal the abject failure of the 'legal families' concept to recognise the cultural complexity of today's legal world.

If the primary focus of the legal families approach in practice was to highlight broad differences and points of comparison between European legal systems, much literature on legal culture adopts a similar focus. But it has aimed to do more. The legal families approach focused on formal legal institutions and official legal doctrine – in Lawrence Friedman's phrase, on 'mandarin materials of legal scholarship' (Friedman 1997, 38). Legal culture literature, however, is concerned also with differences in the assumptions, perceptions, feelings, and expectations about law and legal practice that exist in different contexts. Contributions to it by jurists still tend to show a 'mandarin' orientation, but socio-legal research often adopts a much broader focus (Nelken 2020), revealing different patterns of popular and governmental attitudes to law and its use and of social effects and experiences of law in different cultural environments.

Something more than the needs of disinterested scholarship has inspired juristic invocations of the concept of legal culture. The idea was used, for example, to claim that there are fundamental cultural differences (essentially in terms of legal professional outlook) between continental European civil law and English common law; and these differences would make it impossible or undesirable to harmonise European private law (Legrand 1996, 2006).

Sometimes, legal culture was invoked to support opposite arguments. Thus, claims that a European legal culture was already in existence (Wieacker 1990), that its traditions could be reinvigorated (Zimmermann 1996, 600–1), or that European lawyers inhabit a common culture[3] were used to argue for increasing European legal harmonisation. So, culture could be seen either as a barrier entrenching legal divisions or as a potentially unifying background. The latter view has tended to suggest that divergences at the level of rules can

2 Cf. Siems 2022, ch4, reviewing and critiquing legal families approaches.

3 See Lando 1997, 529–30: 'The peoples of Europe share the legal values of a Christian society and of a market economy which is under governmental control.' Among numerous other efforts to explore the idea of European legal culture see e.g. Helleringer and Purnhagen 2014. For a nuanced empirical study across several European countries see Grødeland and Miller 2015.

be less significant than they superficially appear.[4] Unsurprisingly since Brexit, arguments around the harmonisation of common law and civil law have lost momentum. But the idea of legal culture has remained important.

Juristic concepts of legal culture have tended to emphasise *lawyers'* legal culture. This has been seen as a matter of (largely) legal professional values and ways of thought (*mentalités*) that are said to inform all aspects of legal practice, often in hard-to-define ways. The claim made by some writers is that lawyers think in a fundamentally different way in France, for example, as compared with England (Legrand 2006, 30–2). But it is not clear that there is any single monolithic national legal culture in these or other countries (Samuel 2003, 50, n.141), given the diversity of kinds of law and of legal practice and experience. Again, those who assert that differences in legal culture present fundamental barriers to ongoing legal integration have yet to show that legal cultures are necessarily impenetrable, rather than porous.

Why should these differences not be understood (like culture, more generally) in terms of diverse, often contradictory experiences of shared beliefs, values, traditions, allegiances, and interests? Why deny that elements of culture can be modified, and are probably being modified continuously, not least because of their impact on each other? Why not assume that some parts of culture change as other parts stay constant?

On the other hand, those who have seen culture as no obstacle to processes of legal harmonisation take a no less unsatisfactory view of legal culture. The needs that promote legal harmonisation have been thought of largely as those of business networks built on the instrumental relations of the market (Von Bar and Lando 2002, 198–9). In so far as the general interests (e.g. in profitable, efficient commerce) of these networks are uniform, and harmonised law relates only to them, culture may seem *irrelevant*. Harmonisation can appear self-evidently economically useful – simplifying transactions for business actors who readily see the point; trade is trade.

But non-instrumental aspects of culture cannot be ignored. Harmonisation debates should address more than instrumental (economic) considerations because law's relation to culture is a relation to *all* its potentially intertwined components.[5] The question is: how do instrumental and non-instrumental aspects of culture interrelate, especially when the likely effects of legal regulation are to be considered?

4 The legal sociologist Lawrence Friedman (1994) claimed that what he called 'modern legal culture' was producing a gradual convergence of legal solutions in 'modern, industrial, "advanced" societies', despite national doctrinal differences.

5 Cf. Banakas 2002, 185, noting resistance to harmonisation on the grounds that private law 'is more than competition in the market or corporate and commercial transactions. It is also about intimate, very personal aspects of personal life, that judges are convinced are better dealt with in the environment of the local culture and tradition.'

Debates about the viability or desirability of harmonising law across national boundaries clearly occupy a very different intellectual terrain from the debates with which this chapter began, relating to legal recognition of minority religious concerns. Discussions of legal integration can be impassioned. But they do not show the intensity of feelings that have made some controversies about law's relation to religious beliefs and to ultimate values not really debates at all, but more a matter of anguished protestations and unleashed fury on all sides.

Legal Culture in the Conference Room

Could it be said that discussions of legal culture, as reflected in legal harmonisation debates, involve an entirely different understanding of culture from that involved with, for example, the Danish cartoons case, or arguments about the possibility of a European *Shari'a* law?

If legal culture is specifically lawyers' legal culture, then what it embraces in terms of the four components of culture that I have been discussing are the constraints and possibilities arising from common interests, traditions, beliefs, values, and allegiances *of lawyers* – legal professional groups – rather than those existing in the wider society. On this view, legal culture might seem potentially a narrower, quieter, less fundamental topic for inquiry than relations between law and culture in a larger sense.

Thus, it was possible for someone such as Professor Ole Lando of the Copenhagen Business School, a leading figure in the Commission on European Contract Law over more than two decades, and in other harmonisation projects, to see shared values and a 'common attitude' among lawyers from different European countries (including pre-Brexit Britain) as the key to achieving legal harmonisation.

Lando wrote:

> Several factors have caused this common attitude. The similar economic and political structure of the [EU] Member States is one. Another is their common cultural heritage. All Europeans share the Christian ethic and have been influenced by Roman law and the great moralists. The milieu in which both judges and law professors are raised and live is also a factor. Most of the guardians and preachers of our law and justice grew up in well-to-do bourgeois homes with moral traditions. In Europe, the middle class has been the guardian of ethics, and so have the parents of the judges and professors. . . . Thus, the legal values of the European brotherhood of lawyers are very similar.
>
> *(Lando 1999, 20, 21, 22)*

The image is striking. Inside the harmonisers' conference room, the quiet processes of legal professional negotiation and agreement go on. The clamour from an increasingly noisy multicultural population outside does not disrupt this calm. Nor should it, necessarily: the wider constituency for which the effort to harmonise contract law in Europe has been relevant is primarily the constituency of business – a network of mainly economic, instrumental social relations of community that might be assumed to be not very directly linked to matters of belief or ultimate values, tradition or affect.

But if this network of social relations is well delineated (a matter that would require empirical study) it, nevertheless, extends beyond any professional network of lawyers and it might be dangerous to see legal culture as purely legal professional culture, rather than one that always relates to constituencies in society beyond the lawyers' professional sphere. Indeed, it might be reasonable to think that this professional sphere itself will change to reflect better the cultural diversity of the wider society.

In sociology of law, the best research on legal culture has tried sensitively to consider variations in both professional and popular legal experience, holding in focus the *widest possible range* of components of culture and considering how these interrelate in specific contexts. It has been most effective when it illustrates the sheer complexity of cultural variation and the problems of interpreting this (Nelken 2003, 2010, 48–55).

Otherwise, scholarship on law and culture is often particularly rewarding when it focuses on *distinct juristic foci* of cultural difference – such as conflicts or contrasts of values or beliefs,[6] or questions of how far elements of tradition (including, for example, minority languages) should be protected by law, or of how far law can sustain legitimacy and attract allegiance in culturally diverse societies. Juristic tasks of interpreting culture will be most manageable when culture is broken down into its components. The effect will be to show relations of law and culture as complex, often contradictory but pervasive features of contemporary regulation.

So, why not avoid referring to culture and merely focus on its juristically distinct components – beliefs/values, tradition, instrumental (especially economic) relations, and emotional allegiances and resistances? After all, it is conflicts around *these* matters that cause problems that law needs to address. Culture, as such, is too vague an idea for law to address as a unity. Nevertheless, culture and legal culture remain useful ideas to suggest that variable *linkages* exist between the elements that have been separated out, and that these linkages can be explored in specific contexts.

6 See James Whitman's controversial but imaginative comparative studies of fundamental legal values, cited in Chapter 3, p. 47.

Cultural Self-Sufficiency

Also, to think of all four basic aspects of culture together is especially important when conditions arise in which the four aspects *tend to mirror each other*. A social group may come to be divided from other social groups not only by different *beliefs* and *customs*, but also by distinct, self-contained *economic networks*, and perhaps by *emotional hostility* to other groups or by becoming the focus of such hostility. Different aspects of culture may then reinforce each other strongly, not necessarily because the group in which this occurs chooses a relatively pervasive cultural separation but because circumstances of interaction with other groups promote this. The result could be that different social groups tend to inhabit self-sufficient cultures of their own. Culture becomes something with definable boundaries, and cultural difference becomes a matter of invisible walls. Indeed, this may lead, if all productive communication becomes impossible, to real walls built to keep populations apart.[7]

In Chapter 3, the terms 'cultural closure' and 'closed communities' were used to point to such a hypothetical self-sufficiency, and to tendencies towards its realisation. It is important to emphasise that complete cultural self-sufficiency may be impossible in complex, intricately networked contemporary societies. Nevertheless, it is one of the major tasks of law to try to avoid moves towards this kind of development[8] in a national political society which, at the extreme, could lead to a fracturing of society and the decay of crucial supports of solidarity across it. Cultural pluralism is wholly beneficial where it presents a diversity of beliefs, traditions, allegiances, and interests linked together and relatively integrated through the interactions of numerous networks of community. But tendencies towards absolute cultural divisions reify culture to create social groups isolated from others.

This issue is very far from relating only to conditions of multiculturalism. In fact, it arises from all cultural polarisations that locate populations in social silos in which communication from and to other populations outside becomes attenuated or even largely ceases.[9]

To take one example from many, commercial enterprises can, in certain conditions, become culturally isolated from the social world around them. In large, powerful corporations, corporate groups, or merchant communities, means can exist to defend the cultural autonomy of the entity from perhaps very different cultural conditions of the world beyond it. Attitudes

7 See Turner 2007, 133–6, on the creation of 'social enclaves' in contemporary societies.

8 See Cotterrell 2023a, 76–82, on techniques available to state law to do this.

9 Thus, 'culture wars' (Gitlin 1995; Nash et al. 1997) – bitter, seemingly irreconcilable cultural conflicts often played out in national political arenas, as well as in educational settings and in print and broadcast media and social media – have a very close affinity with the ideas of cultural closure and closed communities discussed here.

and motivations of those working inside an enterprise or corporate group (a communal network structured around primarily instrumental, profit-seeking collective objectives) can be strongly reinforced and controlled partly by the self-interest, ambition, or peer pressure of the members of the communal network, and their shared commitment to their work. A corporation may also be strongly focused on developing and sustaining a shared culture within it – a variable amalgam of values, beliefs, sense of tradition, instrumental focus on the corporation's objectives and policies, and sense of allegiance to and identity with the collective.[10]

It might be reasonable to suggest that steps towards (partial) cultural closure may be much more feasible and attractive for powerful, primarily economically focused communal networks such as some large corporations, corporate groups, or trading networks than for communal networks where ethnic or religious identity is a key unifying element. And they may also be more pernicious for society at large.[11] Dominant corporate entities may have more power to resist external influences or incursions on their autonomy, and to hide aspects of their internal culture from public view, more capacity to present their regulatory autonomy as necessary for the wellbeing of the wider society, and a stronger public and political voice to insist on the importance of being free of external interference with their ways of operating. They can sometimes get aid in shielding their internal culture from view through legal protections of commercial secrecy and confidentiality. Yet these possibilities for corporate cultural closure[12] are much less often a focus of popular attention than are compatible possibilities in religious or ethnic populations.[13]

Law's primary strategies in dealing with all tendencies towards cultural closure must be to foster *cross-cultural communication*. It needs, in every way possible, to promote social interaction across cultural divides, mutual learning and transparency across difference, consciousness of interdependence, and awareness of the many kinds of vulnerability and risk that often ultimately follow from isolation.

Law should communicate and, where appropriate, enforce ultimate values of respect for individual autonomy and dignity that encourage and protect social interaction and participation by all individuals in the national political society (Cotterrell 2018, 167–71). What Durkheim understood as moral

10 See Chapter 3, p. 51.

11 But relatively 'self-sufficient' culture can also be powerful (and sometimes repressive) inside small to medium-sized business organisations (Brannan 2015), just as it can sometimes be in primarily ethnically or religiously structured communal networks.

12 Weber (1968, 341–3) long ago recognised them, but discussed them only in economic terms. For a wider discussion of 'social closure' see Murphy 1988.

13 Typically discussed in terms of problems of 'social inclusion' as in Young 2002.

individualism[14] – universal respect for the equal humanity of all other individuals – is the necessary ultimate basis for respecting (and communicating across) cultural differences, within a framework of complex solidarities appropriate to contemporary societies.

Law and Culture across State Boundaries

There is another important reason for holding on to the idea of culture in relation to law and for making it, if understood in socio-legal perspective, a focus for juristic study. The concept of culture marks out, even if only provisionally, a terrain which legal scholarship can occupy that takes it beyond any narrow limitation to the legal categories established by the law of national political societies.

In two ways this chapter has already attempted to illustrate this. First, in considering the relations of law and culture in multicultural societies, legal scholarship is led to recognise a diversity of legal aspirations *inside* the nation state. It is no longer just a matter of formally equal citizens before the law. Instead, legal inquiry has to consider the variety of forms of group life in the national political society and their impact on the situation and expectations of individuals. A focus on law and culture does not displace other approaches of legal study, but it can strongly supplement them.

Second, debates about legal culture in connection with legal harmonisation or integration projects suggest a different kind of extension of the legal imagination. Here culture is invoked to suggest what can be similar and what can be different in legal thought and experience *across national boundaries*. The focus is not on cultural similarities and differences inside the nation state in their relation to law, but on these kinds of similarity and difference in relation to cultural networks not necessarily limited by the borders of specific nation states.

A focus on relations of law and culture allows an escape from the limitations of seeing law solely in terms of nation state jurisdictions. Culture, appropriately conceptualised, is an idea that points to new emphases in juristic study of diversity in national societies. But it also points to conditions that juristic scholarship should study in relation to newly significant kinds of transnational law.[15]

These varied kinds of law (for example, international human rights law, international commercial and financial law, European Union law, internet law, and many less clearly definable forms of transnational regulation) need cultural foundations. In other words, they need support from networks and groups

14 See Chapter 3, pp. 54–5.
15 See Chapter 7, pp. 107–10.

linked together by aspects of culture – shared beliefs or values, tradition in various forms, common or convergent interests uniting people instrumentally, or more diffuse allegiances and attachments.

So, it is possible to speak of business cultures, legal and other professional cultures, human rights cultures and so on. All of these can exist on a transnational basis,[16] and all are potentially carriers of law – in the sense that cultural groups or communal networks can foster or inspire the regulation they require. They may be important in giving (or refusing) legitimacy to law – confirming (or denying) its moral authority and its practical meaning and significance. Insofar as communal networks recognise the binding force of transnational regulation, invoke it, and rely upon it, they enable it to develop.

The main obstacle to invoking culture usefully in these kinds of contexts is that comparative lawyers, legal sociologists, and other scholars of law still often try to use the concept of culture as if it designates a phenomenon – a bounded, unified entity – that law can address directly. When comparative lawyers claim that differences in legal culture obstruct the harmonisation of law across national borders (or conversely that the existence of a European culture will ultimately make a pan-European law feasible) they rarely define what they mean by culture – how one culture is to be distinguished from another, and how culture causes or hinders legal developments.

Culture as an Umbrella Concept

The problem, long recognised by anthropologists and sociologists, is that culture, because of its conceptual imprecision, cannot identify causes of or constraints on social and legal developments. The solution is not to discard the concept but to use it to highlight provisionally a range of social phenomena awaiting analysis and comparison – phenomena that can be conceptualised in terms of social relations that unite or divide people in groups and networks. Thus, the portmanteau concept of culture should be ***disaggregated*** to reveal the diverse types of social relations of community that it implies. It is law's relation to each of these types of community that should be theorised when the links between law and culture are being studied.

Because, as noted in the previous chapter, law's instrumental uses and its relevance for instrumental (especially economic) social relations are always prominently recognised in contemporary legal and socio-legal scholarship, a focus on 'culture' has most significance in putting back into the centre of attention law's links to tradition, affect, belief, and ultimate values. In doing so it suggests not only that these matters are as important for legal analysis as

16 Cf. Lando 2001, 1023: 'international business is more and more becoming a cultural circle of its own where the commercial practices have been influenced by the great trade nations.'

instrumental economic considerations, but that the latter should be understood in the light of their interrelation with the former.

So, the idea of culture usefully focuses attention on the phenomena that shape and reinforce social relations of community in different forms. Culture is best thought of as inhabiting communal networks that are flexibly structured through bonds of social relations of community. The more these communal networks are stable, the more meaningful will 'culture' seem, as it refers to social life in them. So, law, in so far as it supports and protects social relations of community, helps to build culture. Yet culture remains an ever-changing aggregate of diverse networks of social relations.

Studies of law and culture designate not a special field of legal scholarship but an *approach* to legal scholarship in general. It is a socio-legal approach that emphasises law's place in and contribution to communal networks. The study of law and culture focuses on law's contribution to sustaining and integrating communal networks that, if relatively stable and distinctive, are readily thought of as carriers of culture. Culture, an umbrella concept whose components need to be disaggregated, should be a crucial focus of contemporary socio-legal inquiry.

5

SOCIO-LEGAL STUDIES AND THE LAW SCHOOL

What promotes interest in and commitment among legal scholars and law students to socio-legal studies (SLS)? What is the importance of this enterprise of teaching and research in law school contexts? Addressing these questions, this chapter is a personal (and opinionated) account viewing, from one scholar's perspective, SLS specifically in the law school world. As such, it tries to assess conditions of work and prospects for socio-legal research today.

A View from the Law School

My outlook has been shaped in part by the having always worked in a law school environment. I came to sociology of law (which, in this chapter, is not distinguished from SLS) because I became dissatisfied with the kind of theory that legal philosophy offered in law schools. I was convinced, even as an undergraduate law student, that law, if it was to be an interesting focus of scholarship, must be a theoretically sophisticated subject. But I thought it was struggling towards that like a poor swimmer who had not learned efficient strokes and so made little headway, just treading water despite apparently making huge efforts to move forward.

Legal philosophy offered theoretical resources. But, because law exists only in *specific times and places*, the concerns of philosophers seeking apparently timeless and absolute answers to such questions as 'What is law?', 'What is the relation of law to morals?' or 'What is the foundation of legal authority?' seemed inadequate to make legal scholarship realistic and in touch with law's changing socio-political conditions.

Most important theoretical questions about law are not at all timeless but very timely – they are issues about the way law is shaped, works, and develops

DOI: 10.4324/9781003340324-7

in *specific* historical contexts. They are about what law means to those concerned with it or confronted by it, and this meaning cannot be abstracted as if it were unrelated to time and place. Indeed, the claim of legal philosophers that there are genuinely timeless, essential, or universal characteristics of law[1] might ultimately be no more than arbitrary stipulation, in the absence of a full examination of conditions of 'the legal' in all possible times and places – an impossible task. Perhaps a designation of the concept of law and its related concepts can be useful only for the purposes of empirical study of ideas in practice in *specific* social and historical settings.

So, I sought theory that could help, and looked for it in social science. I thought that philosophical legal theory merely went round and round in circles in trying to address 'timeless' questions about the nature of law – covering the same issues endlessly, never resolving them – like, to use another writer's metaphor, a continually replayed game of football (Honoré 1973, 1–2). Social theory suggested the possibility of breaking out of that circularity[2] and linking big issues about law to observation of the varied, changing social and political contexts in which legal ideas must find meaning and significance.

I am optimistic that socio-legal theory can do what legal philosophy has failed to do; that it can be profoundly relevant in the law school world in ways that perhaps some legal philosophy is not. But I am also aware of obstacles. Legal theory – theory aimed as explaining the nature of law – depends on empirical socio-legal research to keep it grounded in experience and sensitive to social variation. And most academic lawyers in Britain still have relatively limited awareness of or exposure to empirical socio-legal research, except perhaps where it relates directly to their legal specialism and where they have the sort of favourable conditions for wide-ranging scholarship that the best law schools allow.

American legal scholars have sometimes claimed that 'We are all legal realists now' (Singer 1988, 467; Schlegel 1995, 2) and it might be tempting to say, 'We are all socio-legal scholars now.' It seems true that many legal scholars in the English-speaking world are often reluctant today to call themselves 'black letter lawyers'. What once was a label of pride to denote single-minded,

1 See Raz 2009, 104, describing what he sees as 'the difference between the philosophy of law and the sociology of law. The latter is concerned with the contingent and the particular, the former with the necessary and the universal.' As used by legal philosophers, however, this way of characterising the distinction tends to imply misleadingly that sociology of law (unlike legal philosophy) is not concerned with or does not provide general legal theory. In fact, the key issue is: what is the object to be theorised? Is it law as experienced in particular kinds of society or civilization, or law as some kind of pure form detached from social context?

2 For a different – and brilliant – way to portray the strangeness of timeless speculation about time-bound law see Twining 1978, though the author rightly insists that his vivid and exotic 'dream', including its hilarious vision of the 'Legal Philosophers' Circle', is, like all dreams, open to many interpretations.

rigorous, and precise logical analysis and systematisation of legal doctrine, now is more often treated as an admission of myopia, which no one wants to make.

But socio-legal research has not invaded the law school. In the UK, unlike some continental countries, it is surely generally viewed sympathetically by academic lawyers of most persuasions. But socio-legal research has not modified the most basic patterns of legal thinking. It has not, so far, much disturbed the jurists.

Its value certainly does not depend on whether it has influence in the lawyers' world of doctrinal argument, dispute processing and practical regulatory design, but its long-term security probably does, to some considerable extent. In recent years, in Britain, posts in socio-legal research have been created in law schools, and part of the motivation for this – apart from any intellectual arguments – may have been that SLS is seen in some university environments as a promising focus for attracting external grants to support research.

Funding from sources other than the usual state higher education support (for example, from charities, industry, or foreign institutions) is increasingly valued in British universities for its own sake, quite apart from its financial value, as a mark of external recognition and esteem. In such a climate, support for socio-legal research in research-active law schools may make good practical sense. Yet this is a fragile foundation for the development of SLS in law schools because external funding opportunities can disappear and fashions in academic planning can change. SLS remains vulnerable unless it becomes more clearly associated with doctrinal law teaching and research. That means that it must engage with the idea of law as doctrine directly.

Insofar as SLS focuses on law it must compete with juristic studies of law and in some way impose itself upon them. Hans Kelsen's (1945, 175–7) famous claim to relegate sociology of law to the periphery of legal concern as a dependent study should have outlived its relevance, yet it still echoes today. As Kelsen saw, if sociology of law does not find space to address the meaning of law in *something like* a 'juristic sense' – that is, as ideas and doctrine – it may have no central concept of law except insofar as it borrows this from lawyers. No one can really believe that a concept such as – to use the sociologist Donald Black's (1976) term – 'governmental social control' captures the full meaning many people attach to the idea of law. So, the intellectual situation seems parallel to that in criminology. 'Crime' seems to be what law says it is; and 'law' seems to be what the state and the lawyers say it is.

Where then do the social scientists stand in relation to concepts of crime and law? Are they just bystanders waiting for the lawyers to clarify founding concepts of their intellectual field? The way out of this problem is surely to admit that SLS must engage seriously with theoretical ideas about the nature of law, it must take *its own stand* theoretically on the nature of law as ideas, practices, and experiences; and that theory must take careful account of (but certainly not be limited by) juristic legal theory.[3] Juristic theory provides part of the 'raw' material (indicators of legal experience and legal practice) available for empirical socio-legal theory to work with.

Part of the object of social studies of law should be to show how juristic ideas find their meaning (or fail to do so) in relation to their time and place. And it is for social science to study law's time and place and to clarify the nature of law through such study. So, legal ideas (as well as behaviour in legal contexts) must be interpreted sociologically; that is, systematically and empirically as social phenomena. By this means one can ask why legal ideas take the form they do, what social forces drive their development, and why some kinds of legal arguments typically prevail over others in hard cases. Legal ideas are part of the subject-matter of sociology of law, but to be seen always in terms of their social origins and effects. And legal analysis that lacks any sensitivity to what social science can offer is likely to be inadequate and blinkered, because it cannot gain an informed understanding of the currents of socio-political change in which legal problems arise and legal aspirations are formulated.

Socio-legal scholarship (both theory and empirical research) must *invade the law school*. But this is certainly not to turn law schools into social science departments, and not to make legal analysis into sociological jurisprudence (that is, social science on tap to help the lawyers when they feel they need it). It is to make the study of law a great *conversation* that draws on the whole range of types of knowledge necessary to make that conversation an informed one.

This approach could be illustrated in many contexts, but two illustrations will have to suffice here. Many lawyers are actively concerned with the numerous kinds of transnational extensions of law beyond the boundaries of the nation state that have occurred (Cotterrell 2018, 103–55). Old forms of juristic legal theory often seem inadequate to inform these developments, because much traditional juristic thought and legal philosophy presupposes the state as the source and guarantee of all law; belatedly this situation is beginning to change.

Many kinds of social theory are now exploring forms of 'the social', 'the political', and 'the economic' that are no longer contained within state boundaries. So too is socio-legal research. We need the mainstream intellectual communities in the law school to recognise just how profound the changes underway now are and to convince these communities that such massive changes in legal regulation and its environment cannot be understood through the 'internal' resources of traditional legal thinking.

The other matter, discussed in previous chapters, is *multiculturalism* or cultural pluralism. Lawyers have rediscovered legal pluralism (Roughan and

3 See further Chapter 13, pp. 200–3. The problem of formulating concepts of law in sociology of law was considered earlier in Chapter 2.

Halpin 2017) – the phenomenon that legal anthropologists studying faraway lands always lived with, but which has now 'come home' because of increased cultural diversity to the old established metropolitan centres of law – that is, especially to the legal systems of Western Europe. It is obvious now that legal aspirations are rooted in culture. Which cultures provide the home for which legal aspirations and ideas? How is the interplay of cultures through law to be managed? These matters were discussed in Chapters 3 and 4.

Academic and practising lawyers working on questions of law and religion and legal problems of minority groups are aware that these issues are never 'purely' legal in some positivist sense, but thoroughly socio-legal, so that they must be seen as deeply immersed in cultural understandings and concerns (Grillo et al. 2009). As these topics become more pressing interests for lawyers of all kinds, socio-legal research should gain further openings to invade the law school environment.

So, my thinking is much influenced by the intellectual problems of the law school world, and by a sense that the brightest future for SLS may depend at least to a significant extent on forging strong links with this world. In Britain it has long seemed clear that university social science departments, in general, are not very interested in law. Perhaps they are somewhat frightened of it – with its endless technicality and its confident claims to organise and govern the social. Or perhaps they still see it as of limited significance – they think that life goes on without law intruding (as litigation) into most (middle class) people's lives. And where law *does* intrude *forcefully*, especially into the lives of marginalised populations, a special field – criminology – is left to handle that.

Otherwise, perhaps law is seen by many social scientists as an intellectual no-go area, best avoided. They may think it obvious that in the intellectual division of labour of the modern university and the organisation of modern professions, law has its own disciplinary structures, its own demarcated field – perhaps beyond the social, somewhere in the humanities; so, to study law one goes to law school – a different part of the academy where people grub around with regulations rather than study social life.

These are caricatures of attitudes and of practical and intellectual divisions – but they have some residual substance. They imply a range of problems for socio-legal research which, as discussed in Chapter 2, sits uneasily on the institutional borders between the knowledge fields of social science and law. Perhaps there is a degree of insecurity among some lawyers (who sense a social world out there which they really ought to understand better) and also among some social scientists (who might even admit to a little resentment at the great accumulation of professional and political power supporting law financially and giving it prestige as a focus of study and practice).

Socio-legal scholarship can, of course, study these tensions alongside its other agendas. Its insights might help reshape aspects both of law and social science. As noted in Chapter 2, sociology of law has been called an intellectual stepchild on the edge of established disciplines. But the view from the periphery of orthodoxy is often clearer than from its centre.[4] And government support for socio-legal research has to some extent displaced issues about disciplinary boundaries or competition. Perceived practical usefulness has become the sole criterion of the worth of research in most governmental perspectives.

Legal Scholars and Social Theory

SLS, in most understandings, is founded on empirical social scientific methods. But how far is social theory – theory about the nature of society or social life in general – important for SLS? For many legal scholars, empirically oriented social theory, and the sociological heritage in which it is grounded, can seem intimidating. When, as an academic lawyer, I first became seriously interested in sociology of law I had had no formal education in sociology. I found that with sufficient curiosity and motivation it seemed possible just to begin reading and learning anyway, and not to be afraid of unfamiliar concepts and methods of inquiry. But, when I had the chance, I enrolled for formal study in sociology and was guided in depth by good teachers through key ideas and research traditions and the great classics of social theory – Marx, Weber, Durkheim, and others.

Having the opportunity to devote much time as a student to mastering key writings in social theory without any need to orient that study immediately to the needs of legal inquiry (although I continued to teach law full-time while I was a sociology student) was an important confidence-booster. It provided a theoretical and conceptual language to set alongside juristic legal theory. But many socio-legal scholars do not follow that route. They start from a particular knowledge-field – perhaps law or one of the social sciences – and then read themselves beyond it as seems necessary for their specific research projects.

Most people do not consciously straddle two or more intellectual disciplines equally. They see their roots as being primarily in one such discipline and, from that base, they explore outwards. So, how important is systematic exposure to fundamental unifying theory in law and social science? Is there is any ideal recipe for a well-grounded socio-legal awareness in research?

I am sure, at least, that it is not necessary to become a social theorist to engage in SLS. But nor is it enough to stay firmly rooted in lawyers' thought or even perhaps to adopt in practice empirical social science research methods. I do think there is a need for a *strong sensitivity* to empirically oriented social theory to gain a broad perspective on the nature of social change (and legal change within this) and to have access to frameworks for thinking *in general*

4 See Chapter 8, developing this idea in the context of Ehrlich's juristic thought and sociology of law.

terms about the nature of social relations, institutions, and structures – that is, about 'the social', the environment law inhabits.

Perhaps because of my background I have found myself returning endlessly to the sociological classics: especially to Durkheim for his efforts to build a sociology of morality and the challenges he poses to rethink what meaning might be given to social solidarity today, and how this solidarity might be fostered, and to Weber for his coldly anguished portrayal of capitalism, and of the modern state with its formidable bureaucratic apparatuses and dense layers of technical, instrumental law.

Why go back to this kind of theory? A century has passed since these scholars of genius left us their intellectual legacy. But this temporal distance does not make them irrelevant now; it reveals them as master mapmakers of the whole vast social terrain of modernity (in which all contemporary ideas of law have been formed). They wrote in the youth of social science and so had no professional constraints to inhibit their ambition to explain all the key features of social life as they understood them, seeking the widest sociological perspectives.

Classical social theory brings into sharp focus the key features of a modern Western social world that, since this theory was proposed, has undergone the most radical transformations but in relation to which legal and social change can still usefully be measured. Using this theory as a base marker is a way of gaining deep perspective on the present; a set of frameworks for analysis that (properly supplemented, adapted, and critiqued) can still inform contemporary empirical and theoretical research in productive ways.

By contrast, contemporary social theory is in some respects *too close to us* to give this deep perspective. For all its essential insights, it gives competing accounts whose enduring value often cannot be properly judged at present: it includes theoretical approaches that, perhaps dominant for a time in debate, rapidly succeed each other or gain cohorts of combative adherents to defend them against other contenders. Some are destined to be powerful maps of the unfolding future, but some are fated to be, to use a striking term, 'provincial in time'.[5]

None of this is to deny in any way the importance of many kinds of recent social theory insofar as, like the classics, these are richly informed through empirical study of social variation. It is only to suggest that the kind of theory necessary to give perspective to SLS is not necessarily always the latest

5 'What is lastingly important [in intellectual life] can easily be unfashionable in its day. . . . [I]t is possible to be provincial in time as well as in place' (Magee 1998, 30, 31). To see this 'provincialism' as a possible defect is not to contradict the claim made earlier that theory should avoid efforts to portray law in some timeless way. There is a 'middle position' – an optimal 'broad view' that good social theory can provide; one that is neither too focused on recent experience nor so generalised as to ignore variation between societies and across history.

products.[6] Just as law as a field of doctrinal scholarship can appeal to a tradition of juristic theory that stretches back through several centuries and shows a powerful continuity of concerns (and a frequent reinventing of the wheel), so SLS should appeal to a long theoretical tradition that stretches back at least to the founding classics of social theory that established some still fundamental parameters of inquiry.

It may seem strange that I have emphasised this so much. And here I offer only a very personal view: I think it is becoming necessary to retrace some steps in social theory and to link that retracing to the contemporary challenges that SLS faces, to make its directions most relevant to address current social issues about law. There are many such issues. But there are now some that are dauntingly large – somewhat comparable with the vast issues that classic social theory addressed.

These are issues about the conditions of social solidarity; the social character, effects, and future of capitalism; the possibilities of giving meaning to ideas of community in modern society; the consequences of unchecked economic inequality; the links and contrasts between legal and economic rationality; and the prospects for democracy. All of these are major themes in the writings of one or other of the classic theorists Durkheim, Weber, and Marx, and are prefigured, developed, or reinterpreted in much other social theory. But in the modern development of sociology of law these big themes have often been largely discarded.

The reasons for putting then aside have usually been sound enough. We quite properly recognise that few if any writers today can hope to embrace the full ambitions of the classic theorists and it might be foolish to try to emulate the range of their intellectual concerns. We live in an age of necessary specialisation and of precisely defined professionalism; and the age of 'grand narratives' has been said to be over (Lyotard 1984). Yet in fact, remarkably, each of the big issues I have just listed as part of the agenda of classic social theory is now rapidly and forcefully pushing itself back on to the contemporary agendas of debate.

When, as now, the word 'crisis' is regularly linked to such big themes as the future of capitalism, 'Europe' (and the UK's relation to it), financial regulation, social cohesion, the nature of democratic politics, and ecological catastrophe, it might be suggested that there is a need, if not to invent new grand narratives of social theory, at least to focus existing research methods and conceptual resources on large-scale issues again. In other words, perhaps to

6 The ongoing relevance of classical social theory is signalled by the fact that a major scholarly journal, the *Journal of Classical Sociology*, is devoted to exploring its contemporary interest and significance.

develop *middle-range* socio-legal theory[7] of limited scope (Cotterrell 2009, 494, 499–500) to shape analyses with *long-range* significance.

Undoubtedly this reorientation is happening increasingly in SLS. For example, the field of regulation and governance which has always been an important focus is becoming very much more so, with a wealth of important research activity and journals devoted specifically to this field. Surely this will continue as pressing questions are addressed, for example about the prospects for effective regulation of national and international economic, financial, and ecological systems: systems that have been brought to the edge of disaster by regulatory inadequacies, 'white-collar' and corporate criminal activity, obfuscation of transactions through complexity, and intricate forms of corruption. Exciting developments are underway to recover old ambitions for an economic sociology of law (Swedberg 2003; Edelman and Stryker 2005; Ashiagbor et al. 2013; Williams 2022) to fill a sensed void left by orthodox economists' thinking about the legal regulation of economic life. And the ongoing transformations of feminist, postcolonial and ecological thought are reshaping SLS agendas (Cotterrell 2023b, 6–10).

Accounts of the imminent 'death of the social' (cf. Rose 1996) will surely be seen as much exaggerated, as it becomes clearer that our most prominent public anxieties relate precisely to the nature of the social and the need to rebuild and strengthen many of its foundations – partly through a wise use of law. Under these conditions the responsibilities and opportunities for SLS in assessing the conditions, limits, and consequences of legal intervention can only continue to grow.

7 'Middle range theories consist of delimited sets of assumptions from which specific hypotheses could be logically derived and empirically tested, yet are sufficiently general to apply in a range of domains' (Lee 2021, 515):

PART II
Juristic Radicals as Socio-Legal Pioneers

6

JURISPRUDENCE IN CONTEXT

This chapter has two related purposes. One is to provide an intellectual bridge to the four chapters that follow. These examine specific writers' contributions to the literature of jurisprudence – distinct theories, each apparently presenting an intellectual world of its own – so they differ greatly in character from the chapters in Part I, which have surveyed aspects of social scientific approaches to law. What connections can be made between these seemingly very different kinds of inquiry?

The other purpose here is to recover an old idea of jurisprudence, which the chapters of Part II illustrate. Jurisprudence has a distinctive intellectual and moral role, but it is one that has often been forgotten in current Anglophone legal philosophy. Legal philosophy in this context is often treated as synonymous with jurisprudence, so that nothing of significance in juristic theory is thought to remain beyond the contemporary concerns of legal philosophy. But jurisprudence as a theoretical resource of jurists has a unique remit which is not that of professionalised philosophy. The chapters that follow explore that remit. How then should jurisprudence be understood? As a theoretical enterprise, what kind of theory does it produce or rely on? And how do its theoretical commitments compare with those of contemporary socio-legal inquiry?

Theory and Variation in Socio-Legal Inquiry

The term socio-legal inquiry can conveniently embrace both socio-legal studies (SLS) and sociology of law. As suggested earlier, it is not important to differentiate these when emphasis is on their common focus on empirical study of legal phenomena using social scientific methods. To that extent these terms indicate a single field of research.

DOI: 10.4324/9781003340324-9

But, as earlier chapters have suggested, when the topic for discussion is explicitly sociology of law, what can be evoked is not only a century-long research tradition, but also a sense that *theoretical* contributions to social scientific studies of legal phenomena are especially important. Often, sociology of law reflects the long heritage of modern sociology as a distinct academic discipline which has always been concerned with social theory as well as empirical social research. The literature of sociology of law often evidences an almost natural, unselfconscious concern with theory. The idea is well established that sociology of law must be a theoretically sophisticated field. Perhaps this idea originated in the fact that many pioneers and classic contributors to sociology of law had their intellectual formation in fields where theoretical inquiry was commonplace, for example in philosophy and jurisprudence.[1]

Earlier chapters have presented SLS as, generally, differently oriented. Its focus has usually been *contemporary* rather than aware of a long historical tradition; it has been synchronic not diachronic in considering the nature of the research field (although a flourishing field of socio-legal history has evolved in parallel with the contemporary concerns of SLS). Contemporary legal issues are usually a prime focus for SLS, studied with a view to some plausible relevance for lawyers and legal policymakers. Where theory is important, it is typically theory about how state law works, how it achieves (or fails to achieve) its effects in society. The typical SLS focus is on law's current practical working, rather than on general theory about the nature of law as a social phenomenon.

The place of theory – its nature and its relevance – is the key issue. Classic sociology of law in the work of, for example, Durkheim, Weber, and Gurvitch, was much concerned with theorising the nature of law.[2] It did so by treating law as an empirical social phenomenon set in time and place, not as a concept with an essential meaning applicable universally. It considered the nature of law in particular kinds of society or culture.

This concern with theory should give sociology of law an important area of common interest with jurisprudence because jurisprudence also embodies a concern for theories of law's nature as jurists experience it. But this link is very hard to pursue if jurisprudence is seen as philosophy largely uninterested in empirical observation of the variety of social life, and of the diverse kinds of law that reflect that variety.

The gulf between sociology (and social science in general) and philosophy centres on the idea of social *variation*, the variability of social phenomena across time and space (Cotterrell and Selznick 2004, 295–6). In general, philosophy

1 For example, Durkheim began his career as a teacher of philosophy and remained interested in it through his career. Weber was well grounded in legal philosophy and economic theory when developing his sociology of law. Gurvitch had studied law and was well schooled in philosophy. Ehrlich remained a juristic theorist even as he evolved his sociology of law: see Chapter 8. On the backgrounds of later legal sociologists see Chapter 2.

2 See Weber 1968, ch8; Gurvitch 1947; Cotterrell 1999.

has little interest in this variation. But sociology, and sociology of law, are centrally concerned with the empirical study of social variation. Sociology of law can recognise law only as a phenomenon varying in character with the diversity of social life in general. So, it is not possible, sociologically, to have a theory of law's essential meaning or a concept of law that makes sense for all times and places; one derived *a priori*, in advance of any systematic social observation.

A robust concept of law in sociology of law will be one that demarcates empirical phenomena that the researcher finds useful for research purposes to designate as law. That will include those phenomena widely understood in ordinary everyday linguistic usage to warrant such designation. But nothing is essential in such a concept. Its value is in its utility for the purposes of research in the researcher's environment. Law understood in this way will be an ideal or pure type (Weber 1949, 90–3). As such, it is a concept constructed by the researcher to serve specific purposes of inquiry, not one expected to have any independent philosophical value as an idea. When the ideal type ceases to serve its specific purposes, it can be discarded or altered to reflect changing experience and knowledge of the social world. So, a concept of law for sociology of law must be seen as a *working model* of law – a way of thinking about and delineating certain phenomena as 'legal' for whatever purposes seem useful.

By contrast, SLS very often presupposes that the nature and scope of law are what lawyers and state officials assume these to be. So, law is usually seen as state law – law recognised, applied, interpreted, and enforced by state agencies. I suggested earlier that the theoretical interests of SLS are most likely to be in theory that helps to explain the *working* of law, its operation, impacts, and effects in social life (and perhaps the reasons for its failures to achieve intended effects). So SLS may seem to have few obvious potential points of contact with jurisprudence. Legal theory for jurisprudence is theory about the nature of law as a body of practices and ideas experienced and applied by the jurist. By contrast, theory for SLS is most likely to be theory about how legal phenomena affect the social world or are shaped by social conditions.

Everything written here involves broad generalisations. They can be challenged when made in relation to specific contributions to socio-legal inquiry. But generalisations may be warranted if they can point, even if vaguely and controversially, to intellectual fault lines, tension points between bodies of scholarship, or difficulties in communicating across intellectual divides where researchers are accustomed to operating within the protocols and assumptions dominating their intellectual field.

A Bricolage Method

If SLS focuses primarily on the legal professional and legal policy worlds, rather than on its relation to distinct social science disciplines, its approach can be characterised as one of open interdisciplinarity or multi-disciplinarity. It could be called a *bricolage* approach, one that takes from any available source in the social sciences or beyond whatever is needed to clarify specific socio-legal issues or to guide specific studies of law. To do this it does not often need to discriminate rigorously between different disciplines of social inquiry on which it draws.

As noted, SLS in practice often – but not always – adopts an assumption that law is what lawyers or government officials assume it to be. But, perhaps more often, SLS shows limited concern with the nature of law (distinguished from other regulation with which law might be confused), or with any need to 'define' law. Seeing SLS in this way opens the perhaps surprising possibility of a direct comparison with jurisprudence despite what was just written about seemingly different attitudes to theory in these two fields. It can be tentatively suggested that the 'bricolage' view suggested here of SLS' relation to social science, *very closely parallels* the idea that I have defended elsewhere of jurisprudence as itself a kind of bricolage knowledge (Cotterrell 2018, 45–6).

What this means is that jurisprudence is not a kind of philosophy drawing its interests and methods from academic philosophy (and thus securely located within the protocols, methods, and field of interests of philosophy) but a diverse, pragmatically assembled compendium of insights about law drawn from many different intellectual sources. Its method of drawing from these sources is not indiscriminate – it is dictated by the specific purposes of jurisprudence as a resource serving the needs of jurists. But the bricolage assembly is not pursued with any strong concern to preserve the integrity or autonomy of distinct academic disciplines from which the insights are drawn.

Like a magpie collecting found objects, jurisprudence in this 'bricolage' sense collects what is needed for its purposes. But needed by whom? By jurists: that is, by theoretically minded lawyers serving the interests of preserving and optimising their own legal system and others with which they are concerned, guided by an idea of what law is and should be. Jurisprudence is the practical theoretical resource of jurists. Its purpose is to give insight into the jurist's task of promoting and preserving an idea of law, allowing that idea to flourish in the jurist's environment, interpreting and working with it to cope with the continual challenges brought about by social, political, and legal change (Cotterrell 2018, ch3).

This idea of law is not a philosophical system. It springs from the realisation that under certain conditions law is popularly expected to serve certain ultimate values – easily referred to by lawyers and lay citizens alike as *justice* and *security*. These values are understood in many ways but the task of the jurist, and of law, is to make sense of them in time and place, to realise as fully as possible what is often popularly expected (or hoped for) from law.

There is also a third ultimate value directly relevant to the jurist. It reflects what jurists often recognise as a modern *unifying* task of law – the idea of law as a regulatory system that is in some reasonable degree integrated and intelligible as a body of norms (not just a mass of them).[3] This idea of law as a unity, as system, which is at best an aspiration, might be extended into the idea of a corresponding unity of *society*. That is, into the idea that social life might be more than just a chaotic mass of individuals in chance or transient relation to each other. Social life might be integrated, interwoven and cohesive to some significant degree despite the inevitability of conflict and friction in it. Seen in this perspective, an aspiration to system and normative unity in law, however unrealisable and perhaps undesirable if carried to a stultifying extreme, may be generalised into a social value which law should serve. This is the value of *solidarity* – the normative aspiration to integration and cohesion in social life.

The promotion and protection of these three values – justice, security, and solidarity – can be seen as the key elements of a juristic idea of law.[4] Stating them is easy to do. But their realisation in changing times and places is a matter for great juristic craft and, ultimately in certain circumstances, of much wisdom. The juristic task involves balancing many kinds of popular demands for justice, many different asserted needs for security, and the complex working out in practice of the social value of solidarity, which itself depends on how far this value is recognised and prioritised politically, as well as in popular opinion.

Jurisprudence is a practical theoretical resource of insights for the jurist faced with the task of realising, as far as possible, ultimate legal values in ever-changing circumstances. As such, jurisprudence cannot be considered an academic discipline like modern philosophy or any of the distinct social sciences. It is a body of knowledge and insight unified only by the juristic tasks it must serve. It is a box of disparate ideas, an intellectual treasure trove, a magpie's hoard. It exists only to serve practical juristic purposes, providing the resources of theory that should help in pursuing those purposes. Its literature can *only* be a bricolage assemblage.

SLS might be compared with jurisprudence insofar as both are bricolage projects. SLS takes from the social sciences whatever is needed to study law as an empirical social phenomenon in time and place. SLS, focused on law as practice and experience, relates potentially to all the social sciences. It seeks insight into the empirical reality of law wherever it can gain this insight. And jurisprudence is similarly grounded in the practice and experience of law – a

3 Cf. 'When somebody takes his starting point somewhere other than in the unity of the legal system . . . he is not a legal scientist in the classic sense. The societal role of the latter is . . . to interpret the legal roles so that they comprise a single legal system': Aleksander Peczenik, quoted in Petrusson and Glavå 2008, 100.

4 For full discussion see Cotterrell 2018, where the idea of law associated with these specific values is developed from an interpretation of Gustav Radbruch's (1950) work. It is an idea tailored to the conditions of modern, complex Western societies, though it may well be appropriate in other contexts.

professional practice and a popular experience. Its relation, like that of SLS, is with any knowledge fields that can provide insights about law as practised and experienced. Viewed in this way, both SLS and jurisprudence rely on a bricolage approach to knowledge but find their secure intellectual grounding in their relevance to the practice and experience of law. Given this strong commonality of orientation, SLS and jurisprudence seem to be drawn closer together – as parallel fields of inquiry. I shall argue in Chapter 13 that they can be further envisaged as actually intersecting fields, but that SLS needs a special relationship to social theory.

However, sociology of law, in this context, must appear differently. It has its origins in consciously fostered relations with specific social science disciplines even if, as argued earlier, it should not be seen as a sub-discipline of any of them. As described in Chapter 2, sociology of law has an intellectual autonomy that derives not from any disciplinary links but from its positioning as an independent field of practice existing to address tensions at the intersection of political, juridical, and social fields.

Scope and Uses of Jurisprudential Theory

It is sometimes assumed that legal theory – theory about the nature of law – is a monopoly of legal philosophy; that it is a conceptual inquiry undertaken for its own sake as the unravelling of a puzzle posed by the question: 'What is law?' It is also sometimes assumed that addressing this puzzle requires only a kind of introspection about the uses of language. Following this assumption each philosopher seeks to think out, in substantial isolation from the findings of any of the human or social sciences, how law can be most rigorously envisaged as an idea. The rewards for this exercise may be measured in terms of elegance of formulation, the coherence and completeness of a system of thought, the personal satisfaction of intellectual effort, the correction of logical flaws in other people's thought, or the ongoing refinement of one's own.

This might be called a caricature. But my aim is to draw as sharply as possible a line between jurisprudence as a hesitant, always revisable set of provisional insights about law, a disorderly but curious bricolage, on the one hand, and a philosophical ambition towards certainties, absolutes, and finished intellectual systems of thought, on the other. Such certainties often do not last; such systems remain finished only until the next one comes along. And where philosophy purports to be far more modest – for example to concern itself only with the clarification of ordinary language to unravel puzzles in philosophical understanding, it turns out that there may be no such thing as 'ordinary' language, but only many different uses of language that linguists, anthropologists, and others have empirically studied.

Philosophy has its own projects, and this book is concerned with them only in one respect: insofar as they may hamper an understanding of the nature of jurisprudence as a resource to serve the practical tasks of the jurist. But the question remains: what is theory for? What are concepts for in jurisprudence? And where are jurisprudence's resources most productively to be found? The four chapters that follow are all concerned with these issues.

I have suggested that theory in jurisprudence should be much concerned with examining ultimate legal values. The idea of law as a combination of the three values of justice, security, and solidarity is built – but modified – from the 'idea of law' as a variable structure of values that is presented in the work of the German jurist and legal philosopher Gustav Radbruch (1950). Radbruch used philosophical methods to proclaim a profound philosophical *modesty*; indeed, he used them to deny the utility of comprehensive philosophical systems of explanation for the jurist, and to propound a cautious, revisable, contextualised approach to the specification of legal values.

Justice and security may seem relatively straightforward as values promoted in law, as they are for Radbruch. They emphasise the fair balancing of claims, fair trial, conscientious judging, the willingness to hear and assess both sides of a legal conflict. They emphasise the need for certainty and predictability in legal procedures, and for citizens to be able rely on established law, rights, and duties, and to be protected from arbitrariness and uncontrolled discretion in state processes. But it is not difficult to extend Radbruch's legal values of justice and security; to make them also social values of justice and security outside the courtroom and the trial, extending into the negotiation of relationships of everyday life.[5]

Radbruch's third and somewhat vague value, requiring law to be 'fit for purpose' – appropriate to the demands of culture and civilisation in time and place – can be given a sharper, more precise significance when adapted (Cotterrell 2018, 40–2, 224–6), into a value of solidarity. The idea of solidarity is often associated with Durkheim's sociology. Durkheim treated solidarity as a fact. Solidarity, he argued, was the natural condition of societies, even if this condition could be upset by pathological factors. But, even in his own work, doubts about this purported normality appear almost as soon as he proclaims it (1984, 291–328). Solidarity should not be seen as a natural social fact. It is a social value. As such it may or may not be recognised and promoted.

If solidarity is understood in this way and seen as an important focus for the work of the jurist, social science can aid significantly in explaining conditions under which promoting this value is a meaningful aspiration, and how this might be pursued. Sociology, as in Durkheim's own work, can show how different kinds of solidarity may be appropriate (meaningful values) in different

5 In Chapter 13, justice is considered in the context of cultural pluralism, and security is considered in the context of ecological crisis.

kinds of society, and what solidarity can mean in practice if it is translated into the quality of social relations of community.

The idea of *theory* in jurisprudence – when seen in the way proposed here – is necessarily a very different matter from theory as understood either in legal philosophy or in sociology and other social sciences. Jurisprudential theory is piecemeal and non-cumulative, tailored to the specific environment in which juristic work is done. That does not mean that this theory created in a certain society and historical time can never have application beyond the specific intellectual, social, and political environment in which it was created. But it does mean that to understand jurisprudential theory it must first be related to its original context. And this will colour and inform its meaning and significance. Context will fill gaps in the way theory is to be interpreted. And, on that basis, judgments can be made as to how far theoretical ideas can escape their 'local' contexts, how far they can be more than provincial in time[6] and place. This is a central concern of Chapter 10.

These considerations serve to introduce the profiles of individual jurists presented in the following four chapters. The profiles are self-contained and not directly related to each other. This in itself partially exemplifies the concept of jurisprudence proposed in this chapter. If jurists' concerns are rooted in their time and place there is no reason to suppose that the theories they create or adopt for their work should dovetail neatly with other jurisprudential theories created in other contexts, nor that they should cumulate into an integrated body of knowledge.

The theories presented originate from diverse countries and periods: from Tsarist Russia; from the final years of the Austro-Hungarian Empire; from unstable twentieth-century Italy moving towards fascism; and from relatively stable Sweden in the era of the founding of the welfare state. These chapters do not suggest a progression of knowledge, as in a systematically developed academic discipline, but rather an indirect response to their environment, an interpretation of juristic responsibilities coloured by it. They originate in papers written for diverse occasions, though all have been modified here.

Why profile these scholars and not others? As noted earlier, all appear today as mavericks, when judged against contemporary assumptions about the nature of jurisprudence. One attraction of considering them is that their time and place put them sufficiently far from the contemporary legal philosophical mainstream to provide a distancing perspective – a revealing displacement of current jurisprudential orthodoxy. In all cases they exemplify a rich juristic imagination, unlimited by contemporary intellectual fashion or disciplinary protocols.

A more personal answer about the choice of subjects would just be that these scholars interest me deeply: first, because of their radical outlook;

6 See Chapter 5, p. 74.

second, because of their location in an often crisis-torn Europe from whose history much can be learned, and third, because of the close interplay of ideas and context which their work exemplifies. Reconsidering them together, comparisons between their lives come to mind. So, it may be appropriate to say something of the biographies of each of these scholars, to set them context – just as the following chapters seek to set their ideas in context, while emphasising their continuing independent value.

Four Jurists and Their Times

The legal philosophy dominating contemporary Anglophone jurisprudence grew in conditions of relative peace and stability, which characterised most Western societies in much of the half century after the end of World War II. Cold war tensions were serious, and important social fractures existed. But post-war Anglophone countries did not suffer the pervasive recurring political violence, disorder, or revolution that had affected much of pre-war Europe.

Did this situation encourage legal philosophers to accept the possibility of timelessly valid, stable, context-free understandings of the nature of law, or at least to think that the search for such free-floating understandings was worthwhile? Did assumptions of underlying security, and reasonable solidarity and progress towards justice, allow main currents of jurisprudence to aim at constructing ideas about law that had scant concern with social variation and processes of social change? After all, if society seemed fundamentally stable and secure why should jurisprudence need to examine its nature?

Whatever the answers to these questions, the conditions in which Leon Petrażycki in Tsarist Russia (Chapter 7) and Eugen Ehrlich in Austria-Hungary (Chapter 8) lived were far less stable. Anyone studying the lives of these scholars in detail might experience a melancholy sense of the vagaries of history and of the abrupt, dramatic, sometimes tragic changes of circumstance that they can produce. Yet both Petrażycki and Ehrlich in their heyday were very successful, internationally renowned jurists. Their work brought them widespread fame, making them leaders in legal thought in the two decades preceding World War I.

Petrażycki (1867–1931)

Leon Petrażycki studied in Berlin and contributed to debates around the new German Civil Code of 1900, the core legal expression of the newly unified German state. Returning to Russia as a professor, he dominated the St Petersburg law faculty and devoted much energy to promoting liberal legal reform and political progress. Though respected as a dazzlingly original legal thinker, he was also officially suspect in a hostile, authoritarian political context.

After the Bolshevik revolution of October 1917, Petrażycki had no place in the new communist order. He had risen to prominence as a Pole working in the multinational Russian Empire. Now he decided to relocate to his newly independent native land, to a new chair specially created for him in the University of Warsaw. But his best work was already done. For reasons that are still not entirely clear, he could not come to terms emotionally with his new situation in Poland. He lived and worked through the chaos and turmoil of the early years of Polish independence during which dictatorship succeeded democracy. But in 1931 he took his own life.

If violent disruption changed Petrażycki's circumstances, the same is true of Ehrlich. Chapter 8 notes much about the context in which Ehrlich developed his life work. While Petrażycki worked at the heart of the Russian Empire in St Petersburg, Ehrlich, his near contemporary, was born and worked for almost all his life at the remote eastern edge of the Austrian Empire. Both scholars were state jurists of vast empires. And as reformists committed to the wellbeing of the idea of law in their environments, both had to consider the position and capacity of the state as a regulator over huge territories and the diverse cultures contained in them. This is explicit in Ehrlich's work and Chapter 8 devotes attention to it. A key concept relevant to both scholars (though used by neither of them) is that of 'moral distance' between the regulator (the state and its agencies) and the vast diversity of citizens of the state.[7]

Petrażycki had to find a modus operandi as a jurist committed to ultimate legal values (which I postulated before as justice, security, and solidarity) while working in a repressive, often vicious, and inefficient state. Perhaps, in such conditions, the jurist's focus had to shift. Petrażycki may have thought it possible to displace (even subvert) state authoritarianism juristically, while not directly attacking it. The method would be to relocate the very idea of law itself, rethinking its ontology as something ultimately located *outside* the state. Perhaps one could prise apart the assumed inseparability of state and law. If so, surely one could deny that law must be accepted, in its very nature, as the violent instrument of autocracy and coercion of the individual. As Chapter 7 explains, Petrażycki relocates law in the most radical way by seeing it as living in the mind of each thinking individual. It is a mental phenomenon. All law's attributes of authority, ethical worth, and rights and duties, live in the individual's private mental experience, not in state imperatives.

Of course, a place had to be retained in Petrażycki's thought for 'official law', the law applied by the state. It is immensely important, but only one of four kinds of law, and perhaps it exists at a tangent to what he really thinks of as law. The state has no way to repeal the legal intuitions of the citizen. Perhaps

7 Moral distance (Cotterrell 2019, 199–204; 1995, 304–5) indicates a cluster of potential failures of the regulator: (i) overgeneralised, imprecise knowledge of circumstances; (ii) too rigid or alien values imposed; (iii) inflexible regulatory techniques; (iv) impressionistic view of regulatory effects; and (v) weak democratic bases of regulation.

it is a romantic strain in Petrażycki's thinking that preserves liberty of thought and action in the individual mind, even as the state aims to control it through police power. So, he presents a vision of law that links it directly to the idea of the flourishing of human personality, the idea of perfectibility in human experience, however far from reality that might seem. He hoped, indeed, that reality would change; that official law might in a better world even become unnecessary. Education and enlightenment might create better citizens.

In the work of his follower, Pitirim Sorokin, this possibility is even introduced as a focus for sociology, expressed in terms of communal fellowship as an ideal that sociology should serve. But as the following chapter notes, the idea is also already present in Petrażycki's jurisprudence as a social aspiration, reflecting a philosophy utterly different from any that today seems a viable juristic resource. Nevertheless, a connection to the value of solidarity is easy to envisage.

Ehrlich (1862–1922)

What of Eugen Ehrlich's view of the state? Chapter 8 suggests that he did not solve the problem of how the state relates to social life. In the Austro-Hungarian Empire the problem was acute. With so many centrifugal political, cultural, and nationalistic tendencies in this empire, which was fated very soon to collapse, it is inconceivable that he was unaware of the dangers and of his obligation as a jurist to address them. His main juristic work focused on promoting judicial 'free law finding' (Ehrlich 1917a). He advocated that, in cases of gaps in the codified law or of its unclear meaning, judges should use free discretion based on understanding of the needs of socio-economic life to resolve legal uncertainties. Able and socially aware judges should not wait for legislation because, addressing cases before them, they might appreciate everyday problems far more than a legislator could. Perhaps free law finding would be a step towards reducing moral distance. Ehrlich admired English common law judges who, he thought, were more willing than continental ones to pursue this approach with skill and insight.

The idea of free law finding has been much criticised, considering its subsequent abuse by dictatorships (notoriously in Nazi Germany) to deny the values of security and justice in application of law. But, in the careful way in which Ehrlich advocated it, free law finding demanded wise, well-informed judging, and a circumspect use of social science knowledge. It gave encouragement to a sociologically aware jurisprudence (Cotterrell 2018).

Perhaps Ehrlich, like Petrażycki, was a romantic. If the latter romanticised the individual's absolute liberty of thought, Ehrlich may have wished to believe in the state as indispensable unifier of a diverse society, and this despite all his strictures against state ignorance of social life. Significantly, his given name was not 'Eugen' (or Eugene), but he chose to use it because of his admiration for the famous Austrian soldier-diplomat, Prince Eugene. The Austrian novelist Franz Werfel (1937, 37–8) writes about Eugene:

> No one had understood so clearly as he the imperial idea. . . . But . . . his intelligence forced him to realise that . . . [it] must suffer shipwreck . . . that everything which he accomplished, in the face of the embattled idiocy of regents, politicians, bureaucrats and the military, would before long be as though it had never been.

Did Ehrlich too eventually glimpse the 'idiocy' of the inefficiently bureaucratised, ill-informed state trying to rule many ethnicities, nationalities, and regions in the empire?[8]

Soon after the outbreak of World War I in 1914, Czernowitz, the location of the university where Ehrlich taught for almost all his career, was occupied by Russian troops. Thereafter the region became a battleground, and the university closed. The environment of reasonably peaceful multicultural existence which he had enjoyed, and which is the background to his sociology of law, disappeared under the onslaught of occupying powers, nationalist agitation, and ethnic discontents. Ehrlich (1936, 71) wrote that society would not disintegrate even if the state ceased to exert any coercion. One can ask what he meant by 'society', what qualities it would need to have to deserve the name; but he does not make that clear. The halcyon period of his career in the quarter century before the outbreak of the war in 1914 was not the historical normality that he perhaps thought sustainable. It was a short period before the often-murderous turmoil that, in the following half century, engulfed his region and uprooted the legal culture he had enjoyed.

Like Petrażycki, Ehrlich enjoyed much international recognition. But, displaced by war in 1914, he roamed Europe unsuccessfully seeking a place to work, think, and regain security. After the war, his city and university became Romanian.[9] Ehrlich, ultimately trying to return to teach in the Romanian language was attacked by antisemitic and Romanian nationalist activists. Ill with then untreatable diabetes he ended his wandering, dying in Vienna in 1922.

His dissatisfaction with the jurisprudence of his day led him to create a pioneer sociology from his observations of his own pre-war social environment. As Chapter 8 insists, his insights still have much juristic relevance. But neither

8 The writer Stefan Zweig (2009, 55) noted that Austria, where Zweig grew up before World War I, 'was an old state ruled by an old emperor, governed by old ministers, a state that, having no ambition, hoped only to preserve itself intact by rejecting all radical changes in Europe'. See also Fillafer 2022.

9 Ehrlich's city is now in Ukraine and called Chernivtsi. When I visited it in 2017, it showed many traces of the Austrian era in its buildings and squares, and its central street layout was hardly changed since Ehrlich's time.

his conception of the state nor of society is acceptable today. His concept of society governed by living law was criticised in Chapter 1. As regards the state, Ehrlich recognised its need for greater sensitivity to problems of moral distance but did not explore its co-ordinating role among the communal networks of society. Perhaps he romanticised a state that, whatever its faults, had seemed to preside with relative benevolence over security in the multinational empire, and this prevented a radical analysis of its nature, problems, and tasks. Certainly, as World War I drew to a close and the breakup of the imperial state was being envisaged, Ehrlich (1917b) fought hard to preserve it.

Romano (1875–1947) and Lundstedt (1882–1955)

Santi Romano's era was certainly turbulent and violent, marked by the crises and eventual collapse of parliamentary government in Italy in the early twentieth century, and the emergence of fascist rule. His key writings show no trace of fascist ideas but reflect conditions that foreshadowed fascist thinking about law and the state. A phone call from the dictator Benito Mussolini summoned Romano from his lecture room in 1928 to accept high judicial office in Rome (Sandulli 2009, 29), but by then his unique contribution to legal theory had been made.

Romano's career thrived through the turmoil of his times.[10] No desperate personal tragedy upended his scholarly work as with Ehrlich and Petrażycki – there remains just an enigma as to how far and in what ways his remarkable, entirely unique theory is really situated in 'the thick of events'. As Chapter 9 explains, it is emphatically a *lawyer*'s theory, explicitly distanced from sociology[11] yet it was authored by a scholar acutely aware of social conditions; it should provoke much reflection about democracy, populism, and authoritarianism today.

Like Ehrlich and perhaps Petrażycki, Romano is ambiguous about the role of the state (Sandulli 2009, 30–1). And it is perhaps this issue that most haunts jurisprudence today. Contemporary legal philosophy, little concerned to analyse structures of power, gives minimal guidance. But socio-legal inquiry has almost always been interested in power exercised by the state. For this reason alone, jurisprudence should take careful account of sociology of law and SLS.

10 'Shortly after fascists seized power in October 1922, Santi Romano became one of the regime's active advisers, providing counsel especially on constitutional reforms. He was one of the five scholars who joined the commission of fifteen members named by Mussolini in January 1925 to draft the Fascist constitutional reforms. In 1928 he joined the Fascist party and was named president of the Consiglio di Stato (State Council). However, scholars are cautious in labelling him a fascist' (Conte 2023, 7–8).

11 Yet the sociologist Renato Treves (1995, 117–9) saw Romano's jurisprudence as a sociological theory of law.

It needs to understand the environment in which law is formed, enforced, and aims to achieve its effects.

Of the four jurists considered in the rest of Part II it is only Vilhelm Lundstedt who has no doubt about the role of the state in relation to law. That role is assumed to be entirely central. Law, for Lundstedt, is the instrument of the state by which society is to be steered to prosperity.

Sweden avoided the disasters of involvement in the two World Wars. It stayed on the side-lines of world conflict and had different problems to solve. It had to transform a poor, agricultural society which, because of poverty and disparities of wealth, could be amenable to revolutionary ideologies of class struggle, into a securely democratic, modernising society built on a high degree of consensus and cooperation to the benefit of all citizens.

The societal environment and its challenges could hardly be more different from those in which the other three jurists profiled in Part II existed. Lundstedt's society eventually became, during his lifetime, one of carefully engineered and controlled stability and social progress. Chapter 10 tries to show how, in a very special context, juristic values of justice, security, and solidarity may be interpreted in a 'realist' light that illuminates the distinctive characteristics of the society in which the jurist works. In stable, peaceful Sweden, it was the state that – by popular consent and with the support of jurists – took responsibility for balancing and securing these juristic values. At least, this is the picture that Lundstedt's jurisprudence presents.

Radbruch is invoked again in that chapter, to be compared with Lundstedt, and it is important to be aware that Radbruch, like Romano but unlike Lundstedt, lived through desperate, violent times that led to totalitarianism in his country. As a twentieth-century German jurist he too worked in the thick of events. Radbruch's idea of a never ceasing juristic responsibility to try to balance always shifting interpretations of fundamental values reflects the sense that history never stops; security, justice, and social cohesion are never to be taken for granted. Jurisprudence cannot be a system of legal philosophy that floats free of history and context; to treat it as such is to abrogate juristic responsibility.

The context in which Lundstedt wrote is explained in detail in Chapter 10, but the most significant argument of the chapter is that, even when context has been fully considered, an important juristic theory may be able to speak outside this and do so precisely because context has informed understanding of the theory. This is true not only for Lundstedt, but for all the jurists profiled in Part II.

Perhaps most interesting about Lundstedt, and entirely neglected in previous international discussion of his work, is the way that ultimate juristic values are transmuted (but not abandoned) in a sceptical, realist vision that purports to eschew all metaphysics. So, justice and security as values are not topics to be handed over to philosophers in his thinking. They are what ordinary citizens understand them to be in the context of their lives. Most interesting is what happens to the value of solidarity – which is my reformulation of Radbruch's third ultimate legal value. For Lundstedt it becomes 'social welfare', and its content (always a work in progress) is to be provided by politics, not philosophy.

The four jurists profiled in this book show through their work how jurisprudence, properly understood, can extend knowledge beyond the lawyer's immediate professional concerns. They show jurisprudence as an affair of ultimate legal values that must be interpreted endlessly in context. As a way of looking at the world through a legal prism, jurisprudence must serve the lawyer's essential task of confronting that world with the professional resources of law. At the same time, it has to present itself in an open, intellectually curious way that should welcome insights from socio-legal inquiry. How this might be done and how jurisprudence and social inquiries about law can and do intersect will be the particular concern of Part III.

7

THE JURIST AS HUMANIST POLYMATH (PETRAŻYCKI)

The work of Leon Petrażycki holds a paradoxical position in the literature of legal scholarship. Indeed, the polarisation of indicators of its status may be the most extreme in modern legal theory. On the one hand, often lauded as a supremely valuable contribution to knowledge about the nature of law. On the other, widely neglected, and little known.

Certainly, 'generations of scholars have been drawn to his heritage' (Kojder 2006, 333) and those who have seriously studied his writings almost always hold them in high respect. He was called 'possibly the greatest scholar of law in the twentieth century' by one of his leading followers (Sorokin 1950, 322), his work 'unexcelled, even hardly rivalled, by any other theory of law and ethics' in that era (Sorokin 1956, 1150). Reading Petrażycki's writings one can be dazzled by the ambition, perceptiveness, and rigour of his thinking over a vast intellectual terrain.

He offers a systematic, intricate legal theory, utterly different from those that now dominate juristic thought, and also an original system of psychology to underpin it.[1] He outlines a new policy science to direct legislation, informed by a morally rich vision of what a truly civilised society might be. He provides subtle, psychologically informed ideas about the relations of law and morality. And he foreshadows contemporary concerns with legal pluralism, developing one of the most elaborate discussions of this phenomenon in legal literature.

1 Edoardo Fittipaldi 2012, 14, thinks that Petrażycki adopted 'a typical 19th-century psychology that is hardly compatible with the research' since his time, but that this in no way prevents productive use of his ideas about law. Walicki 1967, 236, suggests that since Petrażycki's method has 'very little in common with the methods of empirical psychology . . . it would be more proper to emphasise its closeness to phenomenology'.

DOI: 10.4324/9781003340324-10

Finally, his distinctive ideas on the nature of social science, developed mainly in unpublished manuscripts and in his teaching, have been publicised by his followers.

But this vast project has not attracted the Anglophone interest one might expect. Petrażycki's contribution has been called 'unrecognised' (Gella 1977; Podgórecki 1980). His theories are still unknown to most English-speaking jurists and socio-legal scholars.[2] He certainly belongs to the intellectual cultures of the main countries where he pursued his career – Russia (in St Petersburg between 1898 and 1918) and subsequently Poland (in Warsaw until his death in 1931). In these places he is celebrated, but not yet beyond them.[3]

Much of Petrażycki's writing is available only in Russian or Polish, so scholars not having access to these languages cannot hope to evaluate his work comprehensively. The only work by him easily available in English is a translation of about one fifth of his two primary Russian works (Petrażycki 1955; Sorokin 1956, 1150). However, Russian, Polish and other scholars have written extensively in English explaining his ideas. This chapter asks how far Petrażycki's theories might provide insight for contemporary legal studies. What aspects of his work can speak to major current issues and inform current debates? What obstacles stand in the way of this?

Petrażycki in the World of Jurists

Since the centre of Petrażycki's work is a theory of law it might be assumed that its best prospects of exerting influence would be in the juristic world. But some comments on his legal theory may show why its socio-legal rather than juristic significance may be most important to explore at present (though these should not be seen as mutually exclusive).

Petrażycki aimed to produce a *scientifically adequate* theory of law. An adequate theory, in his view, is one that holds true for all phenomena in the class of phenomena to which it is said to apply, but not to others outside the class (Kotarbiński 1975). Such a theory requires that law be rigorously conceptualised to indicate such a class. Arguing that all juristic conceptualisations of law (e.g. as the will of the state, or the law applied by courts or other official agencies) fail in this respect, Petrażycki conceptualises law in a radically different way, as something that exists only in the mind.

Law, he claims, is a particular kind of *mental experience* or impulsion, a bilateral (active-passive) experience that is distinctively *imperative-attributive*:

2 On Western reception of Petrażycki's ideas see Kojder 2006, 346–9. See also Treviño 2013, Deflem 2008, 78–89, and Banakar 2002. Fittipaldi 2012 is an elaborate study of legal ontology developed from Petrażycki's ideas.

3 For an important recent effort to rectify this see Fittipaldi and Treviño 2023.

that is, every individual experience of law combines an active (attributive) element of right or entitlement and a passive (imperative) element of obligation or duty (Petrażycki 1955, 47). Law differs from morality in that in morality only the imperative element of duty and not the attributive element of right is present.

As a purely mental experience, law has no objective observable reality; it remains the subjective experience of each individual. But by a psychological process of *projection* this experience is often 'externalised' so that it is understood by individuals as a norm somehow standing apart from them and acting on them, as if from 'outside'. Strictly speaking, then, all normative expressions of law (such as statutes, judicial decisions and other legal phenomena studied by jurists) are just mental experiences 'projected outwards and viewed as objective reality' (Rudzinski 1976, 111); they are 'phantasms'. However, where for various reasons these projections tend to become uniform (so that they are *widely shared* by many individuals) they begin to appear as a social reality, not just a subjective experience of each individual. The projections themselves are then often thought of as law, in the form of norms.

Often, but not always, the mental experience of law refers to 'some authority or reason outside that experience itself' (Northrop 1959, 87) which Petrażycki calls a *normative fact*. Such facts can include any sources of authority that the individual recognises. These give content to psychological experiences of law, fixing the sense of right and duty.

Law derived from the individual's acceptance of normative facts, Petrażycki calls *positive law*, but it is important to recognise that this is not what lawyers typically understand as positive law. For one thing, normative facts are not at all limited to juristically recognised sources of positive law (legislation, judicial decisions, etc.); they may have no 'official' character, nor be accepted by the state as legally significant. For another thing, normative facts have legal significance only as elements in the individual's mental experience of law.

So, in a claim that must have bewildered many of his lawyer readers, he notes that normative facts can be *purely imaginary*: a contract with the Devil may be a normative fact that operates to determine the ethical impulsions of someone who *believes* in its existence. Where these impulsions are imperative-attributive they are examples of law. Indeed, following Petrażycki's theory, contracts could be made between imaginary beings (Babb 1938, 518; cf. Petrażycki 1955, 83). Law is entirely a matter of normative mental experiences.

Law that is not related to normative facts, Petrażycki calls *intuitive law*. In this case the experience of right and duty arises directly in the individual's mind unmediated by any accepted authority, so intuitive law encompasses the sense of justice (which may or may not correspond with positive law). Thus, Petrażycki makes justice, as a sense of entitlement and obligation, a kind of law existing intuitively in the citizen's mind. Justice 'is nothing but intuitive law in our sense' (1955, 241).

So, law as a class encompasses *all* imperative-attributive experiences without exception. As one writer notes, this definition of law is 'arguably the widest . . . ever proposed' (Motyka 2007, 34).[4] And it would seem at this point as though Petrażycki's theory has few direct links to juristic thought.[5] The distinction between what (positive) law is and what it ought to be (justice), which is at the base of modern positivist jurisprudence, is brought *inside* the Petrażyckian concept of law. And even positive law seems to be merely a mental experience, rather than the objective datum that jurists study.

Alongside the positive-intuitive distinction, Petrażycki also introduces an entirely different one between *official and unofficial law*. Official law is the law 'to be applied and sustained by representatives of the state authority in accordance with their duty to serve society' (1955, 139). So, at least here, we are clearly addressing the law of jurists. However, there is also unofficial law 'which does not possess this significance in the state'. Petrażycki seems to identify official law as an objective social reality (the state representatives and their use of law can be generally observed) and this makes it a phenomenon that jurists can recognise as their normal province of law. However, the idea of unofficial law, which Petrażycki defines only negatively, indicates vast horizons of 'law' (such as the internal regulation of families and of organisations and associations of all kinds) which jurists would typically not recognise as such. But, still, both official and unofficial law are, in essence, mental phenomena.

With the notion of unofficial law, Petrażycki confronts state law with a radical legal pluralism; he indicates types of regulation that from some standpoints (sociological, non-juristic) can be considered as law but from others (those of state representatives) cannot. He puts at the heart of his work the idea of a plurality of effective regulatory regimes co-existing in the same place and time, with possibly diverse determinants of their relative authority.

These characteristics of Petrażycki's theory show why it has been resisted by many jurists who have studied it. As a descriptive account of law, it entirely avoids normative evaluation. So, it recognises law in each of the four categories (positive, intuitive, official, unofficial) it identifies and in their combinations. It makes no judgment about the general value or validity of any of these kinds of law, treating this as a matter for decision in particular contexts.

But such valuations are juristically fundamental. So, it seems that Petrażycki's theory inhabits a different intellectual terrain from the juristic one. Yet it

4 It has even been claimed that Petrażycki's concept of law is 'so comprehensive that it contained all human and social phenomena' (Gella 1977, 76) but this is to miss its specific analytical focus and purpose.

5 Walicki 1967, 216, notes that 'he was often accused of representing an anti-juridical approach, dissolving law in the vast variety of socio-psychological phenomena; on the other hand . . . he saw law as virtually omnipresent in human life. . . . '. Compare the criticisms of Ehrlich's 'megalomaniac jurisprudence' in Chapter 8.

contains many juristically relevant insights, especially about the law-morality distinction, the unifying tendencies of law, the various kinds of sanctioning of law and their development, the significance of intention and motive in law, the place of third-party intervention in legal disputes, and the role of law in economic life and in the emergence of structures of political authority.

Petrażycki's Influence on Legal Sociology

In the light of the way Petrażycki conceptualises law, the prospects for using's his work today might seem greatest in fields of research not tied to juristic concerns but aimed at studying the nature of law empirically in a socio-legal perspective. After all, his aim, as has been seen, was to develop a scientific legal theory and he came to recognise the importance of a sociological approach (Lande 1975; Pałecki 1984; Walicki 1967, 245–51).

But obstacles seem to have existed and can best be identified by noting how the three most prominent Western sociologists of law who have been deeply influenced by Petrażycki and who have tried to apply his ideas have felt the need to modify or supplement them. It is significant that each of these scholars (Pitirim Sorokin and Nicholas Timasheff in the United States, and Georges Gurvitch in France), as Russian speakers and former students or colleagues of Petrażycki in St Petersburg, had exceptional access to his teachings.

Sorokin

Both Gurvitch and Sorokin asked whether Petrażycki's psychological theory of law could give rise to an appropriately *sociological* perspective. Sorokin felt the need to defend Petrażycki against criticisms of the 'alleged one-sidedness' of his theory in confining the reality of law to psychological experience and 'its alleged neglect of the objective social form' of this reality by treating it as a mere projection or phantasm (Sorokin 1956, 1153).

Sorokin insisted that 'Petrażycki deals with trans-subjective, social forms of law as a reality' and he summarised how this reality arises: the projection of mental experiences as norms allows them to be 'objectified' or 'externalised'; they can then be communicated (in speech, writing, etc.); through such communication they can 'become diffused among many individuals and groups' and take on 'a sociocultural form' (1956, 1155–6).

Indeed, Petrażycki writes that the inevitable and potentially dangerous conflicts arising between individuals' different personal sense of rights and duties make harmonisation among these different senses essential. In the face of such conflict or the threat of it, they cannot remain purely subjective experiences of individuals. They have somehow to become trans-subjective, so that they are shared and take on a social character. Differences between individuals' mental experiences of law must be removed. On this basis, generally recognised positive law and official law may develop and large structures of social and political life (such as the state and its agencies) arise (Petrażycki 1955, 112–13, 129–37). What we might call a crystallisation of harmonised individual legal experiences takes place to form a sociocultural reality. Thus 'objective' socio-legal phenomena emerge from their origins as purely individual mental phenomena.

In emphasising such ideas, Sorokin notes that he draws on Petrażycki's writings, on his teaching in St Petersburg (which Sorokin experienced) and on unpublished writings. Unfortunately, much of what Petrażycki wrote on sociology was not published and, it seems, no longer survives (Pałecki 1984, 134).

Elsewhere Sorokin was more critical of Petrażycki. He claimed that the theory did not explain why people have particular law-convictions, why some such convictions prevail in certain groups but are absent in others, and why in a complex society only some law-convictions become official law while others are suppressed and persecuted. If the state's power exists only in the law-convictions of its subjects, why do people continue to accept state authority which they despise? How and why do only a few people determine what official law is? Sorokin thought that 'the law-factor appears principally as a mere channel through which numerous non-law forces find their aggregate outlet' and that the power of these forces is what determines law's power (Sorokin 1928, 704–5). In other words, there were things that the psychological theory of law and state could not explain but that sociology had to address.

Later, however, Sorokin restated the essence of Petrażycki's legal theory in his own sociological terms, emphasising the 'objective' social reality of what he called law-norms and seeing these as 'the skeleton, the heart and the soul' of every organised group calling forth 'a government-power' within it to enforce them (Sorokin 1947, 677, 679). Thus, for Sorokin, official law is seen not (as by Petrażycki) merely as the law administered by state authorities. It is the primary law of *any organised group*, backed by the coercive power of the group or its governing agents. Thus, an attempt is made to retain the idea of norms as grounded in law-convictions but to foreground the need *to analyse them sociologically as instruments of power and control.* At the same time Petrażycki's commitment to a radical legal pluralism is maintained because law is found in every organised group and pervades all social life.

Gurvitch and Timasheff

Georges Gurvitch accepted (like Sorokin) the psychological basis of law in imperative-attributive experiences but insisted that law's thoroughly social character had to be emphasised in a way that he thought Petrażycki had failed to do. Seeing legal experience as 'necessarily *collective experience*' (1947, 45, emphasis in original), Gurvitch treats it 'as the convergent recognition of values by group members', thereby overcoming Petrażycki's 'principal shortcoming . . . the treatment of law as a phenomenon of individual consciousness' (Timasheff 1955, xxxiii).

So, for Gurvitch and contrary to Petrażycki's view, *all* law must be positive (in Petrażycki's sense) and the normative facts on which it relies must 'really exist and incarnate spiritual values'; they must be an 'objective social reality'; in this way all 'subjectivism' is abolished from the theory;[6] all kinds of law are fully *social* phenomena, none exists only in *individual* mental experiences. Gurvitch (1931, 292) saw Petrażycki's 'psychological individualism' as having led him to accept too wide a range of normative facts (including many having no social significance) as legally relevant. It was the necessary positivity of law that brought together authority and regulatory effectiveness in a specific social milieu.

Thus, while Sorokin thought that the observable socio-legal phenomena that sociology of law can study arose from individual law-convictions as Petrażycki envisaged, Gurvitch considered it necessary to depart decisively from Petrażycki to insist that all law-convictions *ab initio* have an inbuilt *social* element. But he went on to build on Petrażycki's rejection of the juristic view that nothing can be law unless it is recognised as such by the state. Gurvitch (1947) enthusiastically accepted that many other kinds of law can and do exist.

The radical legal pluralism of Petrażycki, Sorokin, and especially Gurvitch (who identified sociologically a vast array of types of law) surely has the great advantage of giving socio-legal scholarship ways of thinking about law that are entirely independent of juristic concepts. Thus, sociological approaches to legal inquiry are not limited by any juristic or 'official' demarcation of law's scope. In fact, however, as noted in previous chapters, socio-legal studies have often been content to accept lawyers' or state officials' assumptions about this scope, perhaps on the basis that it is realistic to recognise the dominance of state law and the practical power of state agencies (legislatures, courts, etc.) to determine conclusively what is to count as law.

Nicholas Timasheff's sociology of law reflects this thinking (Schiff 1981, 405). He advocates 'a narrower concept of law' than Petrażycki's to 'emphasize enforcement by politically organised society' and he sees 'no cogent reason to consider [as] legal all social phenomena in which rights and duties are involved' (Timasheff 1955, xxxvii). For Timasheff (1939), the task of sociology of law is to study how behaviour is determined by legal norms, treating law as the intersection of social power and ethics, represented in complex modern societies by state law.

These various ideas of Petrażycki's admirers are of interest as attempts not only to engage directly with his theory but also to relate it explicitly to the concerns of socio-legal research. Taken together they suggest problems, or at least ambiguities or absences, in the theory.

6 Gurvitch 1931, 292; 1935, 166; Gurvitch 1947, 45–6, 75.

The Value of Conceptual Maps

The task of purely *conceptual* legal analysis (the effort to specify rigorously a coherent 'scientific' concept of law), which Sorokin, Gurvitch, and Timasheff inherited from Petrażycki, was pursued by them in different ways as a fundamental part of sociology of law. But, in general, socio-legal researchers today leave the task of formulating a concept of law to jurists and legal philosophers.

They do not typically see a need for rigorous definitions of law and finely delineated categories of law – scientifically 'adequate' concepts in Petrażycki's sense. Instead, as noted earlier, they tend to adopt juristic demarcations of 'the legal', or to use provisional, pragmatic notions of law that are sufficient for their specific projects of research. The elaborate classifications of types of law (almost entirely distinct from juristic classifications) produced by the Petrażyckian sociologists tend to appear merely *formalistic* to many contemporary socio-legal researchers. Petrażyckian conceptual analysis is not part of the main agenda of socio-legal studies (SLS) today.

This rejection of formalism has much merit. SLS should not pay excessive attention to the projects of legal philosophers who seek a *universal*, *timeless* definition of law or a concept *conclusively* marking off the legal realm from the rest of social experience, declaring the *essential* nature of the legal. Socio-legal inquiries need only flexible frameworks for analysis and provisional models of law, working conceptions that lend themselves to revision and adaptation as the task of studying changing forms of regulation and their sources and consequences proceeds.

Today, the classic Petrażyckian sociologists of law can best be seen as having provided conceptual *maps of legal experience* as they recognised it. These maps should not be taken as ends in themselves (as comprehensive theories or 'true' understandings of the nature of law) but as suggestions of where and how to look systematically and empirically for insights in studying regulation. They should be used to help to refine and extend the *methods* of sociology of law; in particular, inspiring provisional conceptual frameworks to guide research. And such frameworks are especially important where the forms and conditions of regulation are rapidly changing under the impact of technological developments and intensifying cultural interactions.

It remains to consider some prominent elements in the contemporary agenda of socio-legal inquiry, and how far aspects of Petrażycki's theories can relate to them.

Petrażycki and Current Socio-Legal Inquiry

After Petrażycki's time, sociology of law became a well-established international research field, as discussed in Chapters 1 and 2. Subsequently, a broad idea of SLS has developed, implying a willingness to seek insights about the social character of law from a range of disciplines, or to resist any specific disciplinary allegiances. Today, socio-legal research observes the forms that contemporary governmental regulation takes, and the ways in which it is experienced. Much research focuses on the law of the state, but some adopts a pluralist view, finding law, as Petrażycki did, in social settings not addressed by state law.

Three developments important to SLS concerns and noted in Part I of this book seem significant in considering Petrażycki today. They are (i) the dominance of instrumental conceptions of law, (ii) the impact of cultural pluralism, and (iii) the growth of transnational law and new forms of international law. In what follows each of these will be related to Petrażycki's work.

Legal Instrumentalism and the Ethical Worth of Law

Much modern socio-legal research has presumed – and been strongly promoted by – an instrumental view of law.[7] Law has been generally treated, not necessarily by jurists but usually by legislators and administrators, as an *instrument of government*; a means of framing and implementing policy, setting social goals, encouraging and regulating economic life, and shaping desirable behaviour by citizens. Alongside this it has often been treated as a *private resource*: an instrument available to citizens, corporations, and others to promote and secure their interests, through litigation if necessary.

Socio-legal scholarship in general has adopted this instrumental approach as its dominant, if often implicit outlook on the nature of law (Cotterrell 2009, 488–91). On this basis Western socio-legal research has flourished to support legal policy, especially in combating racial and sex discrimination, organising welfare provision, supporting family life, controlling crime, and regulating economies. Research has often identified what Roscoe Pound (1917) called 'the limits of effective legal action' and the conditions under which law can and cannot achieve the results envisaged by lawmakers. But to treat law as no more than an instrument is to ignore the question of whether law should have qualities that allow it to flourish as a valuable cultural phenomenon, rather than merely for what it may be used to achieve.

Petrażycki saw the imperative-attributive character of law as valuable in this non-instrumental way. The consciousness of rights would be a means of entrenching in individuals a sense of dignity and self-respect and the firmness, confidence, energy, and initiative 'essential for life'.[8] Thus, if the legal experience of right and duty is well organised in its social settings it can serve not

7 See the discussion in Chapter 3.
8 Petrażycki 1955, 88–9. For related ideas see Jhering 1915.

only pragmatic or short-term aims but a larger ethical purpose. The development of a general legal consciousness has, so it seems, an independent cultural value. On this Petrażycki is explicit – law can be a powerful *educative* force as well as a motivating force. In terms that few modern scholars would dream of using, Petrażycki suggests that law can, indeed, create ethically better people.

It is easy to mock such claims. Many decades of empirical research have shown the limits of law's ability to achieve intended effects and there is strong resistance in socio-legal scholarship to moral prescriptions of any kind. But one can also note in the literature urgent criticisms of the excesses of legal instrumentalism, on the basis that this can make law seem no more than a weapon available for use in socially irresponsible ways by anyone able to gain control of it (Tamanaha 2006). The image of the lawyer as 'hired gun' is very familiar.

Petrażycki was in no way opposed to the use of law as an instrument of policy – indeed he pioneered the project of a 'science of legal policy' and developed this idea extensively (Babb 1937; Gorecki 1975a). But his image of what legal policy could be is so alien to the assumptions of contemporary socio-legal research as to seem, at first, shockingly naïve or bizarre. He sees law's ultimate task as to promote 'the complete dominance of active love'.[9] What this means in essence is the promotion of a social life characterised by communal solidarity, altruism, active citizenship, public spiritedness, and social responsibility. Law, in this view, is to shape not only behaviour (through incentives and penalties) but also *character* (by inculcating experiences of duty and entitlement).

These are long-term aims for law but they set immediate challenges: for example, to make official (state) law as comprehensible and accessible to the citizen as possible, to adapt it carefully to the psyche of those subject to it, to make it vivid and clear through factual illustrations, and to enforce it firmly and consistently. The ultimate aim of legal policy is to make official law increasingly unnecessary insofar as the ethical regulation of social life becomes more effective (Babb 1937, 810, 826–8).

Petrażycki's extensive work on the science of legal policy is hardly represented in English translations of his work. But available indications of its content suggest that it points to ideas absent from, but an important supplement to, those inspiring much contemporary socio-legal research. One of its important messages for today seems to be that SLS should link its existing concerns about the effectiveness of legislation and the legal experience of citizens

9 Babb 1937, 810. The idea reflects wider currents of thought in the Russia of Petrażycki's time, and it became, in effect, the central focus of Sorokin's sociology (as 'Amitology') in the last phase of Sorokin's career in the United States. See Johnston 1998, 5, 42–9.

to a wider sense of law's potential *moral meaning*.[10] It implies the need for renewed attention to the often-neglected *expressive* functions of law – attention not restricted merely to this function in the context of criminal law. At a time when law is often seen as a mere technical calculus, divorced from the moral experience of citizens, Petrażycki's voice from a century ago insists that studies of law in action can and should be guided by a vision of what an ethical life and a well-organised society might be.

How far can the vigorous assertion of rights really be seen in contemporary conditions as a way to promote ethical life in a society? Durkheim drew an important distinction between what he called egoism (the selfish assertion of right to promote only one's private interests) and individualism (a moral position characterised by respect for and willingness to defend the rights of all individuals to their personal autonomy and dignity, no less than to defend one's own such rights) (Cotterrell 1999, 112–13; 2018, ch13). Hence, this moral individualism recognises commitment to the rights of others as a basis for defence of one's own rights. Mere assertion of one's own rights without concern for others does not promote ethical life in any sense; such conduct has no ethical value to the individual or moral worth to society. What then is to be made of Petrażycki's enthusiasm for the active assertion of rights?

A Petrażyckian concept of law treats the experience of right or entitlement and that of duty or obligation as *inseparable* (Petrażycki 1955, 46), as two sides of the psychological impulse to which the word 'law' refers. Current legal thought often puts strong emphasis on securing private rights (especially of property) as the primary purpose of law, alongside guaranteeing basic personal security. But the very structure of Petrażycki's imperative-attributive concept of law suggests that the sense of obligation is as fundamental as that of entitlement. The recognition of duty by one person, in this conceptual architecture, is not a mere consequence of the assertion of right by another. The recognition of duty can equally be seen as the psychological experience that, in law, *allows rights in others to exist*. One might also say that although the sense of right or entitlement is what gives law the special quality that distinguishes it from morality, this sense gains its truly 'legal' quality only because it also embodies a *typically moral* experience of prescribed duty. The attributive (sense of right) and imperative (subjection to duty) elements in law are inseparable – they are experienced as one.

This quality of law is, I think, what for Petrażycki can make it valuable independently of its instrumental value. It makes possible legal *relationships* as social relationships. This is not to confuse law with morality, or to imagine

10 For somewhat related ideas about the expressive, communicative, and rhetorical potential of reflexive legislation in a dialogue with societal values, see the thoughtful discussion in Witteveen 2005.

that law is always (or even often) intuitively experienced as morally good; it is merely to note that *as psychic phenomena* law and morality are closely related, especially when understood as expressions of a vibrant culture.

Cultural Pluralism, Intuitive Law, Positive Law

Some 90 years ago, praising Petrażycki's emphasis on legal pluralism, Gurvitch (1935, 164) noted the emergence of many new forms of regulation that it was becoming hard for jurists to ignore – legal institutions outside the scope of state law, but existing inside national society as well as in the international sphere. In the national sphere he mentioned the regulation of working practices produced in enterprises through processes of industrial democracy. Today we might think especially of the demands of minority cultural groups for legal recognition of their religious or traditional norms.

As noted earlier in this book, the issue of the female Muslim veil – the right to wear it, or a legal duty not to do so in certain contexts, has attracted much attention in continental Europe (Ferrari and Pastorelli 2013). More broadly, the claims of many Muslims to have some effective legal recognition of their distinctive practices – for example, of marriage, divorce, inheritance, and commerce – have led to unending debate in several countries. These claims have also often posed problems for state courts faced with the need to apply official law (in Petrażycki's sense) to situations and practices already shaped by other kinds of legal ideas such as interpretations of Islamic *Shari'a* law, or the customary norms of minority groups.

A persistent question in much discussion has been how far such ideas, which may possess great authority and be firmly applied in the groups that recognise them, should be generally accepted as 'law'. If so, what kind of law would this be? What would be its relation to official state law? How could its status as law be understood? By whom should it be accepted as law? What situation exists if some groups in the national society consider it legal, but others do not? What happens if it is inconsistent (perhaps irreconcilable) with state law? Increasingly these are matters for everyday juristic practice.

State law in Western societies may, for example, refuse to recognise polygamous marriages, but how should it deal with the position of wives married and divorced from polygamous marriages when, being dependent and perhaps destitute, they seek financial support from their former husbands? Should state law ignore their situation? More generally, how can state law purport to regulate family life in communities where couples marry (and perhaps divorce) under the authority of religious law but not state law?

Petrażycki's legal theory allows the organisation of such issues *entirely in terms of law*, cutting through the limitations of a rigid demarcation between state law and all other forms of authoritative social regulation. The claim of the deserted polygamous wife, even if not based on an appeal to religion or custom, can be interpreted in terms of intuitive law (a sense of justice). But it may well be a claim referring to the 'normative fact' of religious or customary authority. As such, it is a claim of positive law (in Petrażycki's sense), irrespective of whether the state recognises it. In Britain, as noted in Chapter 1, Muslim arbitration bodies decide family cases brought before them by applying their interpretations of religious and customary sources to try to find reasonable solutions consistent with the expectations of the communities they seek to serve. So, in practice, in these conditions, it is possible to observe, *co-existing*, all Petrażycki's types of law (various kinds of official and unofficial, positive and intuitive law, and their combinations).

And Petrażycki's idea of legal policy might suggest some specific responsibilities of official law: to encourage conditions in which all individuals can flourish, their sense of social responsibility as active citizens is promoted, and communication and solidarity between communities in the larger society as well as within them is promoted. Petrażycki's legal pluralist conceptions may not solve regulatory problems. However, they make it possible to see that a radical, irresolvable conflict between different and exclusive conceptions of 'law' can be replaced by a *single* perspective – one that accepts the *co-existence* of a variety of distinct *types of law* and the need to facilitate their stable interaction or interrelation. This implies that the relative authority of different kinds of law should be recognised and negotiated so that society can be regulated in a practical, effective, socially meaningful way.

A critic of this approach might say that it is unimportant whether the conflicts and interrelations of regulatory regimes and aspirations are thought of as problems of *legal* pluralism or simply of normative pluralism. Are the problems made any easier by choices made in applying the word 'law'? Isn't the real issue the clash of expectations as to what regulation is to be applied to specific problems? Whether or not regulation is called law by jurists or legal theorists may not alter popular convictions as to whether the regulation should be applied to cases that concern them. The activity of defining should not be confused with empirical study of conditions defined.[11] The point is well taken. As suggested earlier, a socio-legal perspective should not become entangled in efforts to define conclusively what counts as law, as contrasted with non-legal regulation.

However, Petrażycki's radical reconceptualisation of law, extending it to embrace much that jurists serving state legal systems would not accept as law, may make it possible to reconsider issues of normative (or legal) pluralism in illuminating ways. In particular, it shifts focus from the positivist position of seeking to identify particular social sources (e.g. legislative procedures, judicial decisions) that determine whether or not a norm is valid law. Such a positivist

11 As it was once memorably put (Bentley 1908, 199), 'Who likes may snip verbal definitions in his old age, when his world has gone crackly and dry.'

position often provides no useful answers in cases where popular opinion refuses to accept that the linking of norms to such identified sources is the only conclusive way of attributing operative authority to them. Equally, legal positivism provides no adequate answers where regulatory regimes are in conflict and competing social sources of validity can be identified, with no established hierarchy of importance accepted as between these sources.

A Petrażyckian approach would focus not on identifying 'pedigree tests' of what is to count as legal or non-legal by looking to see by what social sources the regulation in question has been brought into being. Instead, it would focus on the subjective experience of those who encounter the regulation. It would not need to treat as irrelevant the sense of the 'legal' held by those who experience, as law, types of regulation that the state does not recognise. It would presumably seek to understand the phenomenon 'law' at least partly in terms of *their* legal aspirations and *their* sense of what for them is authoritative regulation. It would not see the regulatory problem as demanding acceptance of the state's legal prescriptions irrespective of citizens' understandings (or, conversely, of accepting those understandings as the only legitimate basis of state law). Instead, it would aim at appreciating, influencing, and organising citizens' complex and often contradictory senses of legal authority.

Petrażycki's approach appears to downgrade state law to merely one kind of law among many – a radicalism that may seem highly dangerous. Yet we should recall that in pre-revolutionary Russia he was a jurist serving the official law of a huge multicultural empire. It may be that his approach is best seen (like that of his contemporary Eugen Ehrlich, considered in the next chapter) as directed to protecting the state from itself; that is, from its own regulatory hubris, and from isolation and alienation from the perceptions of citizens. It would do this by encouraging a view of law that is sufficiently wide to allow jurists (who are professionally committed to the idea of law) to see the realm of state law as if 'from the outside' – that is, from the imagined standpoints of citizens who recognise many kinds of intuitive, positive, official, and unofficial law.

In this kaleidoscope of many kinds of legal experience, the experience of positive law held in place by the state is just one element. This does not mean that it must be seen as in any way a minor element; rather it should be continually confronted with (and enriched in) a larger regulatory environment that is not rendered juristically redundant simply by having been denied a priori – by definitional fiat – the designation 'law'.

The Nature and Authority of Transnational Regulation

Petrażycki recognised international law as a reality, but he could hardly have envisaged the vast range of different regimes of regulation that exist today in, for example, international trade law, international criminal justice, international human rights, international financial regulation, and European Union law. International law is no longer necessarily confined to regulating the relations of states. It can also often directly address individuals (as, for example, in the prosecution of offenders in international criminal law) or indirectly shape the conditions in which they live and work, as in the case of international economic law, such as that of the World Trade Organisation. As noted in Chapter 4, much recent legal regulation can be considered not only as governing relations between states but also as operating transnationally across, or irrespective of state boundaries.

Some of it arises from treaties or conventions between states, some from national laws that have effect extraterritorially, some from the creative activity of transnational communal networks such as the business networks in which international commercial arbitration (the new *lex mercatoria*) has developed, some from international agencies (such as the World Trade Organisation or the International Criminal Court) claiming independence from specific national allegiances, and some from within transnational professions, industries or interest groups defining 'best practice' through authorities which they support to set uniform standards.

The growing importance of transnational law and, in some cases, its controversial character as 'law' raises the question of whether Petrażycki's legal pluralism can help in analysing this phenomenon. Much transnational law is not official (state) law in his sense. Yet it is sometimes applied by officially recognised institutions (international courts, regulatory agencies, standard-setting bodies). It is often created and imposed 'top-down' on those it regulates. But some of it is created 'bottom up' through the interactions of those for whom it is useful (transnational traders, financiers, internet technologists, etc.) as what is sometimes called 'transnational private law' (Calliess and Zumbansen 2010). What seems to be emerging is not a single new transnational realm of law but a multitude of legal regimes claiming different kinds of authority, arising from different sources, and regulating in different ways.

Petrażycki's legal theory teaches that many forms of positive law can exist outside state law. This makes it possible to portray the entire complex universe of transnational law as an array of different kinds of positive law. And if, as Sorokin argued, Petrażycki's theory shows adequately how law as a trans-subjective social form can arise from the harmonisation of individual psychological experiences, it is not difficult to see how legal structures can arise through interaction in social groups and networks and the common recognition of normative facts as the basis of positive law. The varieties of transnational positive law created in this way may have different kinds of relationships with state law.

By separating the idea of positive law from that of official state law Petrażycki moves us past unhelpful debates as to what kinds of transnational regulation should be recognised as law. Instead, the issues become: how do these different kinds of law relate, from where do they derive their ethical meaning as structures of rights and duties, what gives them authority over those they are supposed to regulate? Ultimately, the key juristic question is: how is their relative authority – their authority *relative to each other* – to be judged when these kinds of law clash, purporting to regulate the same people, or the same situations or transactions?

Surely this Petrażyckian perspective is helpful. It makes possible a focus on law's practical authority rather than its abstract definition. Petrażycki's open, flexible, and minimal model of law in terms of imperative-attributive experiences seems to undermine any assumptions that the challenges of normative pluralism can be dealt with simply by defining them away as outside juristic concern. Positivist legal theorists might adopt concepts of law that exclude from the 'province of jurisprudence' many regulatory forms and normative ideas now populating the socio-legal world that do not correspond with orthodox conceptions of state law. But Petrażycki shows that law can be thought of coherently in ways that do not depend on the concepts that have traditionally served to police the boundaries of the juridical world.

This was surely the scandal of his theory in his own day, and it remains so today. The socio-legal realm does not need positivist juristic theory to mark out what is to count as law within it, though it should take account of the ideas offered by that theory. The freedom to think about legal development *inside* but also *beyond* orthodox juristic categories is a main legacy of Petrażycki for scholars seeking to understand evolving forms and characteristics of transnational law.

However, it is still important to bear in mind Sorokin's claim that important questions are not satisfactorily solved by Petrażycki's psychological theory. Some of these seem to be about the authority of official (publicly organised or recognised) legal agencies. What Petrażycki calls official law (law 'to be applied and sustained by representatives of the state authority') is often remote from individual citizens. Although they may recognise the normative facts that authorise it (and so they experience it as positive law), those normative facts are not necessarily (or even typically) their own choices.

The psychological theory of law may show how some law can take social form as a development from the legal experiences of individuals interacting and communicating with each other. But it is surely important to ask sociologically how official law exerts its 'psychical effects' (Pałecki 1984, 137, quoting Petrażycki), how it gains coercive power over individuals who have had little influence on its creation, and how the authority of the state comes into being, is sustained, and in various conditions is challenged or overthrown. Official law, wrote the legal realist Karl Olivecrona bluntly (1948, 178), 'cannot be reduced to psychical experiences, to "law-convictions"'. However, it might be more accurate to say that it cannot usually be reduced to those of *citizens at large* (Pałecki 1984, 150).[12] Its nature requires sociological explanation.

If these issues are pertinent to state law, they may be even more so for the kinds of transnational law that are created by agreement between states (treaties, conventions) – processes in which most citizens are even less involved. The central problem is that of the 'moral distance' (Cotterrell 2019, 199–204) between official lawmakers and law enforcers and those whom they seek to regulate.

The available materials by and about Petrażycki do not resolve these issues. It seems that the following conclusion can be reached. His theory points towards the important idea that a great deal of transnational law might be understood as created in transnational communication between individuals in groups, organisations, and networks. This communication gives rise to various kinds of positive law as sociocultural phenomena. So, transnational law as a social form can be produced 'bottom up' in such a way. Thus, it is easy to see where the source of its authority lies. We might say it lies in the culture of those who interact to create it; that is, it has *cultural* legitimacy. But the problem of where 'top-down' law (such as much international law created by conventions) gets adequate authority to achieve widespread recognition and wide-ranging effects as social regulation seems to remain (Cotterrell 2018, ch9).

Where does the regulatory authority, for example, of the World Trade Organization, lie? Why, by whom, under what conditions, and with what limitations, is such international regulation experienced as positive law in Petrażycki's sense? Must it be seen as having only a relatively weak *political* legitimacy so that it is experienced as law only by the relatively few officials directly involved with it, but has little or no resonance in the legal consciousness of most of those who live within the jurisdictions it addresses?

Does, then, top-down, cross-border law-making depend entirely on the support of the governments of nation states that authorise international law-making institutions or international judicial processes? If so, the authority supporting it is not culturally based but technical-political. But the stability of contemporary transnational regulation might need cultural as well as political sources of authority. A sense of the acute current inadequacy of cultural sources its authority is surely one reason for popular antagonism to this regulation.

12 For example, it might represent only the law-convictions of its creators. Claims have been made that Petrażycki's (social) category of official law cannot be derived from his (individualistic) psychological definition of law: see Motyka 2007, 37; Motyka 2006; Peczenik 1975, 94.

Petrażycki's Hidden Legacy

Because much of Petrażycki's work remains untranslated and so inaccessible to most international scholars it is impossible for them to draw firm conclusions with any confidence about the overall significance of his theories. At best, his available writings are suggestive: a store of imaginative ideas about law that imply fruitful avenues for contemporary theoretical development, such as on the topics discussed in this chapter. There is no doubt that, if more of his extensive scholarship could be made available to international scholars, more productive debate around his ideas would be possible. To achieve this, it would be very desirable to have more of his writings translated into English.

Petrażycki suffered both during his lifetime and posthumously because of the accidents of history. Uprooted from pre-revolutionary Russia where he had been a dominant intellectual force and one of the most celebrated jurists of his day, he found his career almost entirely driven off-course after the Bolshevik revolution and his subsequent relocation to Poland. Thereafter the political and cultural crises and divisions of twentieth-century Europe and the dislocations of war further hampered the development and long-term reception of his thought.

However, such of his work as is internationally available, together with the many informative and accessible commentaries on his ideas,[13] makes it possible to recognise something of the scale of his achievement. This chapter has examined intellectual obstacles that have limited his international influence. However, its main purpose has been to suggest that Petrażycki's thought can still inform debate around pressing contemporary socio-legal issues.

13 For a sample of valuable commentary, see Gorecki 1975b; Motyka 2007; Motyka 2006; Rudzinski 1976; Kojder 2006; Walicki 1967; Fittipaldi 2012; Fittipaldi and Treviño 2023.

8

THE JURIST AS LEGAL SOCIOLOGIST (EHRLICH)

'I had found Ehrlich, and been somewhat crushed in spirit, because he had seen so much.' So wrote the American jurist Karl Llewellyn about his discovery of Eugen Ehrlich's 1913 book on sociology of law (quoted in Hull 1997, 291). What seems most remarkable now about Ehrlich, more than a century after he wrote his *magnum opus*, is that it was *as a jurist* that 'he had seen so much'.

Ehrlich created his sociology of law – which many scholars today recognise as the first major manifesto for a new social scientific field – as a by-product of juristic inquiries. And it is serious sociology, even if homespun. It is ambitious social analysis, not the kind of rhetoric of social awareness adopted by many progressive lawyers in the early twentieth century. Ehrlich aimed to save juristic scholarship from itself – from its intellectual narrowness and delusions of self-sufficiency as a science of law – by explaining sociologically the place of that scholarship in society.

In a sense, he aimed to promote a new juristic modesty, relating the jurists' world to citizens' social experience. He argued (1936, 390), indeed, that the 'centre of gravity' of legal development lies outside the usual work environments of lawyers and state officials. For Ehrlich, more than most other pioneers of legal sociology, the question of whether lawyers are to be central or peripheral to social life is of the utmost urgency.

These features of his work make it especially interesting to study in terms of a dynamics of marginality and centrality. His writing is very relevant to any discussion of distinctions between 'internal' (normative) and 'external' (behavioural) viewpoints on law, or assumptions about the existence of a centre and a periphery of legal experience – lawyers usually being assumed to be at the centre. Indeed, Ehrlich raises the whole question of what being a legal insider or outsider means and who has authority to decide such statuses. The

DOI: 10.4324/9781003340324-11

issues readily broaden out to more general ones about intellectual and cultural centrality and marginality.

It is tempting (but, this chapter argues, ultimately not sufficient) to try to explain how Ehrlich 'had seen so much' by emphasising his own marginality or 'frontier' situation which gave him a special viewpoint (cf. Likhovski 2003). He taught Roman law for almost the whole of his career (from 1896 until the disruptions of World War I closed his university) in a city (Czernowitz) on the remote, easternmost edge of the Austro-Hungarian Empire of which he was a life-long committed subject.

Culturally too, he might be seen as located at the periphery of his own (Germanic) cultural universe, living in a region (the Bukowina, today part of Ukraine) populated by at least nine different national and ethnic groups (Rehbinder 1986, 17). Temporally too, he was at a margin, the end of an era, living through the Austro-Hungarian Empire's final years and its dissolution at the close of the World War.

In some of his last writings (Ehrlich 1917b), he argued passionately but fruitlessly, like many other Austrian intellectuals, to save the old Austria after 1919 as a unified multicultural entity. He wanted to preserve a centre that, in fact, would not hold. His life and work related strongly to this centre, and any professional or cultural marginality from it could not have been enough to allow him to achieve what he did.

This chapter attempts, then, to look at Ehrlich's sociology of law – the creation of a jurist – not as a product of marginality, but in terms of a *dialectic or interplay of marginality and centrality*, which reflects both Ehrlich's own personal and professional situation and the consistent strategy of his work. My argument is that this dialectic accounts not only for the most valuable contribution of his sociology of law – its full-frontal challenge to juristic certainties about what legal inquiries encompass and how they are to be pursued – but also for its most frequently criticised weakness – the vagueness of its concept of law. To develop this argument, it will be necessary to consider aspects of Ehrlich's biography and the scholarly reception of his work, as well as the bearing of centre/periphery distinctions on his legal outlook.

The Relativity of Centres and Peripheries

Margins and centres are never absolute locations but are endlessly re-definable. A situation marginal in some respects, or from a certain point of view, may be central in other ways, or when seen from a different viewpoint. Indeed, a different perspective might show the marginal and the central as reversed. But legal thought and legal studies are particularly susceptible to the idea that there really is a fixed centre (and a clearly identifiable, permanent periphery) of law, legal experience, legal studies or legal theory, and lawyers inevitably occupy the centre of the legal world.

A main reason why Ehrlich's work is still important is that it demonstrates the falsity of any reification or hypostatisation of centre/periphery or inside/outside dichotomies in legal studies. What Ehrlich called 'living law' (*lebendes Recht*) – the law that lives in citizens' experience – may not even be law at all from a lawyer's perspective, but merely non-legal social norms. Yet, for him, it is fundamental. By contrast, 'legal propositions' – the rules that lawyers invoke and to which they most readily attach the status of law – are, for Ehrlich, when viewing matters sociologically, no more than *derivative* law. They are abstract normative generalisations from decisions aimed at resolving conflicts arising in social relationships. Otherwise, they are rules created by the state that may or may not operate to regulate social relations – their social significance is not to be assumed.

So, central and peripheral forms of law, as lawyers understand them, are turned on their head in Ehrlich's legal sociology. More accurately, their exact status – how central or peripheral particular kinds of regulation are – is deliberately left open. This destabilising of the idea of centre/periphery in law is important. For some jurists, sociological views about law are 'external' views, outside the scope of juristic scholarship (cf. Dworkin 1986, 13–4), and some legal sociologists accept this characterisation (Black 1976). Lawyers typically see themselves as at the heart of law and legal experience, treating non-lawyers' legal experience or awareness as, at best, a pale derivative of lawyers' understandings, or otherwise as external to any reliable (professional) legal understanding.

But the only reason these views of what is central and what marginal can be securely maintained is because of an equally secure sense of *what counts as law*, and so of what is central and peripheral to it. Ehrlich's work, especially subversive because it is the work of a jurist, fundamentally challenges the lawyer's confidence as to what counts and does not count as law. More accurately than any non-lawyer could, Ehrlich aims at the very core of the lawyer's professional sensitivity and security.

It is this last point – that Ehrlich's theories are the weapon of a *radical jurist* – that best illustrates why any claim that his originality reflects professional marginality is unconvincing. His sociology of law gets its power and its enduring interest from the fact that he is a juristic 'insider' no less than a sociological observer and his book on sociology of law continually moves between these positions, mingling and merging them, playing juristic argument alongside social analysis.

Ehrlich's book, *Fundamental Principles of the Sociology of Law* (1936), is poorly structured, repetitive, ambiguous, and sometimes seemingly self-contradictory – but it is a virtuoso performance, nonetheless. In it, he not only intimately intertwines juristic and sociological analysis, but he makes the jurist become a sociological observer of legal processes and legal expectations while he makes the sociologist dig deeply into legal doctrine and juristic thought to see how these directly or indirectly structure and inform social relations and understandings. Ehrlich's whole strategy is to disrupt lawyers' certainties as to what is central and peripheral to law, or internal and external to juristic understanding.

Another general point needs to be made about intellectual marginality. In intellectual life, marginality is of interest only if it is linked to a process by which marginal ideas can be seen as integral to a system of thought *outside intellectual orthodoxy*. It is often said that those on the margins (of mainstream ways of thought, experiences, or cultural reference points) can see more, or see more objectively.[1] But that depends on having recognisable reference points to which they can firmly relate their perspectives. Otherwise, marginal thought becomes mere eccentricity. Marginal thinking is most productive when it *understands* orthodoxy but can also *transcend* it, reinterpreting and criticising it in broader perspective, from the intellectual periphery.

This broader perspective might embrace a cosmopolitanism, an understanding of more than one culture through personal experience, or the accumulated critical and contextual knowledge of a reference group different from that of the intellectually orthodox. So, the existence of important reference points for marginal ideas allows them to become (at least potentially) *central* ideas, but in a different intellectual universe – a universe of *critique* that establishes paradigms of thought in opposition to orthodoxy and does so by assuming a new parallel orthodoxy of its own.

The development of socio-legal studies (SLS) illustrates this process at work. In Britain, at one time, SLS was regarded not as legal research at all, and certainly separate from orthodox legal research. Orthodoxy in the juristic world relied on ideas of 'black letter law' – officially promulgated legal rules – as almost the sole focus of legal studies. As regards my own experience (surely also that of many other socio-legal scholars of my generation), much of my early writing on sociology of law in the 1970s was done in conscious opposition to this orthodox legal research paradigm.

I rarely attacked the orthodoxy directly or polemically, but I produced work that clearly did not fit it and therefore could have been seen as asserting a place in the law school for scholarly research at the margins. I did not see matters that way but merely followed my own research inclinations. But I soon realised the existence of a substantial group of like-minded researchers, and of long-standing intellectual traditions to which 'marginal' socio-legal writings could be related. Within these traditions, and with appropriate reference groups, this marginal research could seem central. Indeed, one could begin to marginalise the orthodoxy!

1 Simmel 1971 is one of the classic sociological sources of this idea.

Now, much later, it is relatively easy to see socio-legal research of many kinds as the centre of contemporary legal scholarship, at least in leading research-focused law schools. The old narrow idea of legal scholarship seems so pushed to the margins that the term 'black letter legal research' is often treated as one of disparagement. It seems that few academic legal scholars now admit to conducting it.[2]

Yet everything is a matter of perspective. What is central or peripheral in various kinds of legal research remains controversial, judged differently by different intellectual communities. And what counts as valuable legal *theory* is typically assessed differently by socio-legal scholars (in their various constituencies) as compared, for example, with the way it is judged by many legal philosophers today.

Ehrlich in Empire and Culture

Generalisations about Ehrlich's personal and professional situation can only be suggestive. There is insufficient information for firm conclusions. But the tantalising evidence available, alongside the silences in the historical record, makes the question of Ehrlich's own marginality or centrality very fascinating. Enough is known, however, to make it possible to suggest that it is an interplay of his marginality and centrality, intellectual and cultural, that explains most about him.

Even his geographical marginality suggests interesting ambiguities. The train journey from Czernowitz (now called Chernivtsi) to Vienna is stated as 1,123 km and now said to take some 21 hours.[3] In Ehrlich's time, travel to the imperial capital from the city where he worked must have been long, slow, and arduous. Does an empire need a precise centre? Or does empire entail an idea (or ideal?) of a regime of regulation that can be carried *equally* into all its diverse regions? Is the heart of empire found in its local manifestations? Surely that depends on how its essence is understood.

In the last phase of existence of the Austro-Hungarian Empire some intellectuals saw the empire as a unity created out of cultural diversity, while others saw only vast diversity given a mere semblance of unity. Optimistic views portrayed 'a bright colourful garden of nationalities. . . . Each flower . . . was . . . praised for its own beauty. But the garden as a whole was imagined as being even more stunning because of the harmonious assortment of its diverse elements' (Weiler 2002, 3). Austrian banknotes of the time denoted their currency on one side in German and Hungarian and, on the other, in all the other official languages of the empire.

2 See the discussion of SLS in the law school environment in Chapter 5.
3 According to online travel resources.

Ehrlich's (1917b) writings vigorously defended the empire against charges that it had treated its subject nationalities unfairly. He surely subscribed to the 'garden theory'. On such a view, the remote Bukowina, the locus of his living law researches, was as integral as Vienna or Budapest to the empire. In his book on sociology of law he writes about the under-appreciated significance of state law in forming 'the people of a state' (*Staatsvolk*), even a state with different national groups, as a 'unique, unified entity' with a common constitution, capital, army, juristic science, official language, administrative system, and economic territory (Ehrlich 1936, 378).

The idea is of projection, through the law of the state, of a constitutionally defined unity that does not deny cultural or national diversity. Notions of a European constitutional patriotism distinct from nationalism (Müller 2008; Rosenfeld 2007) might be seen as reflecting a kind of recent thinking not unconnected with what Ehrlich had in mind.

Complications multiply when we consider Ehrlich's personal cultural situation. Born into a Jewish family he became a Roman Catholic and wholeheartedly subscribed to an ideal of Jewish assimilation to the dominant Germanic imperial culture.

> I myself belong to a race for which there is no other resolution of the Jewish problem than the complete assimilation of the Jews into the German culture. This applies not only to Jews living under the Germans but also to Jews here in the East who have their home among the Slavic peoples.

He worried whether anti-Semitism meant that 'this entire plan must now be given up'.[4]

He was a member of a frequently marginalised cultural minority, yet it was one that had a strong presence in his own locality and among the student body of his university. And he clearly received much recognition for his work. He took his turn as Rector of the University of Czernowitz (in 1906–7)[5] and was well respected for his writings and his gifts as a lecturer. He had begun his career as a *Privatdozent* at the University of Vienna in 1894 after publication of his first book. But this was eight years after completion of his doctorate. Probably he was in legal practice before that. Karl Renner thought that the fact that Ehrlich was Jewish had, in later life, stopped him getting beyond

4 Ehrlich quoted in Rehbinder (1986, 27). I am grateful to Derek Daniels for assistance with translation from this work.

5 It was normal practice (abrogated only during the 1914–18 war) for the office of Rector to be held by each incumbent for a single academic year. Wagner (1975, 130) lists all Rectors who held office between the university's founding in 1875 and its restructuring as a Romanian institution in 1919.

Czernowitz 'despite his research, which would have warranted his appointment at a top-ranking university' (quoted in Rehbinder 1978, 405).

Bernd Weiler (2002, 3) describes culturally marginal intellectuals in the Austro-Hungarian Empire as learning to understand the 'language, values and modes of thinking' of the dominant culture but often living 'in different cultural milieux, constantly moving across linguistic, ethnic and religious boundaries. Their own marginality combined with a high level of mobility' led them 'to view social life from different perspectives. In their works these intellectuals pointed to the importance of roots and differences. In their practical lives they often felt culturally homeless.' One way to escape the sense of rootlessness, Weiler (2002, 7) suggests, was to 'adopt' the supranational identity of the empire, becoming supranational people of the multinational state.

It is easy to understand Ehrlich in these terms. In place of (or alongside) cultural marginality is an important idea of *intellectual centrality* within a larger multicultural entity – an entity dependent for its identity on an overarching state structure with its juristic, official law. This alone suggests that Ehrlich's intellectual outlook must not be seen as setting social norms *against* state law (periphery challenging juristic and political centre). His project is rather to demand of the state a new, deeper self-awareness to ensure its essential survival faced with powerful disintegrating tendencies produced in its periphery.

Everything, indeed, points to the importance of broad, *transnational* points of reference in Ehrlich's life and work. The ultimate intellectual reference point for him was not Czernowitz, the Bukowina, or even perhaps Vienna or Austria-Hungary. He was widely known internationally as a jurist, and he knew an amazing range of languages. It seems that Ehrlich aimed to be a juristic citizen of the world. His mother tongue was probably Polish, his working language was German, he spoke perfect English and he knew French, Spanish, Italian, Danish, Norwegian, Serbian, Croatian, and Hungarian (Rehbinder 1986, 19, 23). At the end of his life, at the close of World War I, he planned to return to Czernowitz to teach in Romanian. 'To get just a mere overview of the subject matter', he explained about his legal sociology, 'I had to learn almost all European languages and undertake much travelling' (quoted in Rehbinder 1986, 19).

A vital key to Ehrlich's scholarly project lies in his commitment to a transnational identity of juristic science: a science with a scope of application as wide as the empire and Germanic legal culture but extending further – as evidenced, for example, by his deep admiration for English law and his frequent advocacy of some of its methods. A science of law 'freed from national limitations' and a 'restoration of international activity in the field of law' promise 'abundant returns', he writes. 'No science has ever grown great in national seclusion' (1936, 482).

This near-global scientific commitment runs alongside a more obvious focus in his work on legal *localism* expressed through his sociological idea of living law – the infinitely varied, effective normative regulation of everyday life. But the localised study of living law is a necessary correlate of juristic universalism – the corrective needed to prevent juristic science becoming socially out of touch as it is forced to relate to an ever-widening range of social and cultural conditions.

So, it seems reasonable to see Ehrlich's self-image as that of someone *central* to a new universal legal science as well as a celebrator of many varieties of cultural *marginality* expressed through the local customary practices of living law. As a leading jurist he could see himself as a representative of the imperial centre, teaching its law and relating, in all aspects of his juristic formation and primary cultural interests, to its Austro-Germanic dominant culture. As an inhabitant of the Empire's '"Far and Wild East", once called "Semi-Asia"' (Weiler 2002, 1) he could observe a cultural periphery in productive ways (even if resisting any thoughts of his own marginality) in order to provide resources for reshaping juristic culture from the inside – creating his legal sociology in the process.

Responses to Radicalism

I suggested earlier that centre and periphery in law, as the lawyer understands these, are turned on their head by Ehrlich's legal sociology. His most important lasting influence might have been a large-scale and permanent disruption of juristic certainties – a genuinely subversive move to shake lawyers' understandings of law to the core. But his work did not achieve this effect. It suffered the two most common (if opposite) fates of radical ideas: (i) to be co-opted and tamed into forms that allow an appropriation into the mainstream, the centre of orthodoxy, or (ii) to be condemned as so bizarre as to be unworthy of consideration, to be irredeemably marginalised.

Co-Optation

The jurist Roscoe Pound's active promotion of Ehrlich's legal sociology in the United States was not necessarily intended to condemn it to the first of these fates but may have helped to do so. David Nelken (1984) and Marc Hertogh (2004) have rightly criticised interpretations of Ehrlich's work that have largely equated his contrast between living law and legal propositions with Pound's influential distinction between 'law in action' and 'law in books'.[6]

6 Timasheff (1939, 366), for example, sees a stress on 'the discrepancies between written law and actuality' as 'the essence of the book of Ehrlich who, I believe, exaggerates it'. And see Ziegert 1979, 233–4. For more general comments on appropriations of Ehrlich's work see Nelken 2009.

Ehrlich's concern was not primarily with a contrast between the letter of the law (law in books), on the one hand, and the practice or experience of law (law in action), on the other. It was mainly a concern with the variety of types of law and their interactions, and with the fact that lawyers typically only recognise some of these types (legal propositions, state law and official norms for deciding disputes) and so fail to appreciate the great social significance of other types (the many varieties of living law). Ehrlich's radicalism is to displace state law and juristically developed legal propositions from their preeminent position in legal analysis as a whole and to demand the recognition of other kinds of (ultimately more socially fundamental) law that are usually unrecognised by lawyers.

Therefore, like Petrażycki's legal theory, but based on sociological observation rather than psychological speculation, Ehrlich's work points towards legal pluralism, the co-existence of different legal regimes in the same society. He asserts that legal pluralism flourishes even in complex, modern, politically unified societies. Indeed, any society, whatever its nature, will have a diversity of legal regimes co-existing and sometimes conflicting in the same social space. Some (indeed, especially the socially most fundamental) will not be controlled or supervised by the state or by lawyers.

By contrast, Pound's juristic thought lacks almost all this radicalism. It sees only state law as law (Pound 1943, 3–4, 20): there is no challenge in his jurisprudence to the idea that the state and lawyers monopolise the whole of law. He distances himself from sociological claims that a different view of the nature and scope of law could be taken in contrast to lawyers' typical views. The contrast between law in books and law in action is a contrast between state law as officially written and state law as experienced in practice. But the only law considered is the law of the state. For Pound the central question is: *how* is law experienced? For Ehrlich it is: *what* do people experience as law? Certainly, Ehrlich is also concerned with the effects of state law in action; with 'what is going on in the administration of justice and what the causes thereof may be' (1917a, 79). But his fundamental claim is that different kinds of law – recognisable sociologically as such, but juristically significant – come from different sources.

For Ehrlich, the state makes law, usually in legislative form, but the social associations in which people live their lives also produce law directly as the 'inner order' of those associations. Law is also produced, from both social and state sources, as norms for deciding disputes (*Entscheidungsnormen*). Other law is created as relatively abstract legal propositions, developed juristically from these 'norms for decision' or generalised from state enactments.

Finally, Ehrlich (1936, ch7) analyses the nature of the state itself. He treats it, for most purposes, as one kind of social association and as an organ of society; in this way he tries to complete the link in his theory between state law and the law of social associations. State law is the law of what Ehrlich saw as the largest social association – that of political society as a whole. If there are many uncertainties and loose ends in the theoretical picture that Ehrlich's legal sociology offers (not least about the role of the state and the legal status of social norms), its vast ambition is not in doubt.

But, if reinterpreted as a Poundian theory of law in action, it is turned merely into a functional or realist critique of the effectiveness of the official law that lawyers professionally serve. If 'we are all legal realists now' (cf. Schlegel 1995, 2), one reason is that this critique of effectiveness has become an accepted part of the legal mainstream in many advanced legal systems. When Ehrlich is treated not as a legal pluralist but as a theorist of the effectiveness of official law, co-optation is complete.[7]

Marginalisation

The alternative fate of Ehrlich's work has frequently been intellectual marginalisation, his ideas being dismissed as too lacking in theoretical rigour or sophistication to be taken seriously. This strategy of denying Ehrlich's work serious consideration on its own terms began early with Hans Kelsen's critique, noted earlier,[8] that sociology of law could not itself conceptualise law; it would be conceptually dependent on, yet unable to contribute to juristic science. The entire legal sociological project could thus not address its purported subject-matter 'law'; the conclusion might be simply that it is a non-science, certainly not a science of law.

The historical jurist Paul Vinogradoff, writing in 1920, two years before Ehrlich's death, marvelled that Ehrlich treated ethnological and anthropological issues 'in such a superficial manner'. An 'important limitation of our author's range of view and of reasoning', Vinogradoff thought, was that he found social phenomena so interesting (even if he studied them in unscholarly fashion) that he neglected juristic logic, central to understanding law.[9] In any case, sociology 'is yet too indefinite and too incomplete to serve as a scientific basis of law' (1920, 222, 223–4). In other words, even if grave defects of

7 A different kind of (cultural) co-optation is found in Max Rheinstein's (1979, 151) striking characterisation of Ehrlich: 'This man, who was born and who spent all his life in the old Austrian Empire, was an American at heart, an individualist and pragmatist, a believer in freedom and the free forces of society. He saw the task of his life in combating government by bureaucracy, which was so characteristic of the old Habsburg monarchy.' Ehrlich's intellectual prestige was certainly much greater in the United States than in continental Europe (Husserl 1938, 340). On one view, although he started no 'school of thought', '[t]he number of [American] jurists who followed him in the sociological or the realist or the relativist approach to legal problems is almost legion' (Littlefield 1967, 26).

8 Introduction, p. 6; Chapter 5, p. 70.

9 In fact, another major product of Ehrlich's theoretical work, alongside his 1913 book on sociology of law, was his treatise on juristic logic which remains untranslated into English. On this see Vogl 2009.

method could have been corrected, the project would probably still have been a waste of time.

Even some critics who might have been expected to be friendly were not. Nicholas Timasheff, sympathetic to sociology of law, objected to any attempt, such as Ehrlich's, to study social phenomena as 'law' beyond positive law (cf. Ehrlich 1936, 478). He noted that 'Ehrlich's theories are so contestable and so contradictory' that the book in its original German edition had provided no basis for new legal studies (Timasheff 1937, 122; 1939, 25–7).[10]

In England, C. K. Allen (1964, 30) noted that 'Ehrlich found the greatest difficulty in setting any boundaries to his subject and ended up by setting none whatever.' He concluded (Ibid, 32): 'I mean no disrespect to the labours of a very learned, sincere and original jurist if I call this kind of project Megalomaniac Jurisprudence . . . knowledge of everything usually ends in wisdom of nothing.' Behind even measured language in jurists' reviews, a relentless pincer movement is usually at work. Ehrlich is often caught between claims (i) that his social observation is too ambitious or intellectually unsound (sociology being seen as lacking adequate scientific credentials) and (ii) that his juristic analyses are too generalised, limited, or unappreciative of lawyers' doctrinal expertise and reasoning.

The State and Social Associations

Ehrlich should be judged on his own terms. His enduring contribution lies in his advocacy of a perspective that refuses to be confined by the scope of what lawyers and state officials recognise as law, but (contrary to some critical perceptions) certainly does take account of juristic understandings of law, and of the state's production of law. Indeed, he devotes much of his book on legal sociology to considering the role of lawyers and the state in creating and administering law. Also, as noted earlier, he insists that state law may make a very important – but insufficiently recognised – contribution to uniting a nationally diverse people constitutionally as a *Staatsvolk* under a unified legal, economic, political, and administrative regime. His discussions of the interplay of official (state and juristic) law with living law growing up spontaneously in the social associations of everyday life are more subtle and nuanced than is often suggested.

In Ehrlich's view, all social associations, of whatever kind – formal or informal, enduring, or transient – are organised by social norms that reflect the nature of the association and define the position and relations of members in it. Social associations usually also produce norms for deciding conflicts or

10 Yet he also saw Ehrlich as 'the outstanding German sociologist of law' and a brilliant critic of historical jurisprudence: Timasheff 1939, 315, 324.

disputes in the association. But such norms for decision cannot always retain the form given by their spontaneous evolution in associational life. They may need greater guarantees of permanence and clarity. And such norms are needed to resolve problems *between* social associations. In fact, as Ehrlich recognises, the practice of deciding disputes predates historically the creation of formal norms for decision. So, adjudicative practice looks first to the expectations of the associations whose disputes are to be addressed and (later, as courts develop historically) also to the state which guarantees a general judicial authority to impose norms. From norms for decision more abstract legal propositions are derived by juristic reflection, and legal propositions are also created directly by the state (usually as norms addressed to courts and state administrative officials).

Ehrlich's sociology of law presents a complex tapestry of types of regulation and sources of law, with no sharp line between state and society, or between official law and living law. His effort to balance these elements in his legal sociology reflects a combination of juristic and sociological sensibilities, and an effort to integrate them.

From a *juristic* point of view, law and legal experience exist in many forms spanning the juristic centre and the social periphery (of normative order beyond lawyers' practice). From a *sociological* viewpoint, however, law's centre seems initially located in the social associations of life that provide its normative meaning and essential authority, and law's periphery (that is, its derivative or less fundamental forms) is found in state and juristic legal activities.

The real subtlety of Ehrlich's legal pluralism, however, is that because it insists on a vast range of sources of law it implies that there is no 'objective' means of saying where legal centre and periphery are located. Centre and periphery depend on *standpoint*. The same complex legal realm might be viewed by lay citizens, by state officials, by juristic scholars or by legal practitioners as, in each case, *their* law, in relation to which they stand in a central place.[11] This dialectic of centre and periphery, which surely derives from Ehrlich's own complex professional and cultural situation, shapes his legal pluralist approach, the most original aspect of his legal theory.

It also provides the only possible meaning for his otherwise entirely opaque claim that the centre of gravity of legal development lies in 'society' (Ehrlich 1936, 390).[12] What is 'society'? It obviously includes lawyers and even,

11 See also the discussion in Chapter 2 of contrasting conceptions of law that can be assumed in political, juridical, and social fields.

12 Cf Husserl (1938, 334) criticising Ehrlich's idea of society as 'an abstract construction to which no sociological entity corresponds. His book is entirely wanting in any analysis of such basic social phenomena as a political community, a people, a nation, a community of law, and their interrelation.' Husserl's review is one of the most perceptive early critiques of Ehrlich's legal sociology.

according to Ehrlich, the state as the 'widest', 'most inclusive' of all the social associations (1936, 68, 69). To see law's developmental centre as 'society' is effectively to *decentre* law – to see it as the framework, guarantee, product, or expression of innumerable associations or communities, the relative significance of these being judged differently from different standpoints, in terms of different (social, cultural, political, etc.) experiences and commitments.

Yet this centre/periphery dialectic also accounts for his theory's most problematic aspect – the ambiguity of what is to count in it as 'law'. Virtually all the most severe criticisms of Ehrlich's legal sociology focus on this problem, including those mentioned earlier as tending to marginalise his work. They must be taken seriously – but in a context of appreciating what he tried to do and of the difficulties entailed.

Ehrlich's Concept of Law

Ehrlich's starting point in explaining the nature of law is the 'inner order' (the structure) of social associations. A social association is 'a plurality of human beings who, in their relations with one another, recognise certain rules of conduct as binding, and, generally at least, actually regulate their conduct according to them' (1936, 39). Social associations include all kinds of relatively stable patterns or networks of social relations, from contractual relationships, families, religious or political organisations, corporations, social classes, and professions to nations and states.

The lack of discrimination in Ehrlich's concept of associations does not augur well for it as a basis of rigorous theory. Nevertheless, he sees all social associations as having similar organisational problems, which necessitate rules assigning members their relative positions and roles in the association (1936, 40, 85).

It might be assumed at this point that Ehrlich will treat as law – in a sociological sense – the most important of these associational rules. Although juristic scholars might complain at such a broad redefinition of law that no longer ties it to state or official sources, the germ of a coherent concept could emerge from such an approach – the problem would be to ask what degree of formalisation or institutionalisation of social rules would be needed for such rules to be recognised in theory as law. But he does not take this course. Early in the third chapter of his book he suddenly stops the reader short with this statement: 'Not all human associations are being regulated by legal norms, but manifestly only those associations are parts of the legal order whose order is based upon *legal norms*' (1936, 40, emphasis added).

The concept of law is ultimately not tied, therefore, to the concept of social association. Some social associations do *not* produce law. Which do? Why these associations and not others? Ehrlich gives no entirely convincing answers to these questions, enabling many critics to say that no clear specification of the concept of law, differentiating it from social norms in general, can be found in his work (Kelsen 1945, 26–8). Thus, Franz Neumann (1937, 353), reviewing Ehrlich's book, complained of its 'entire lack of a genuine legal theory'.

Identifying the Legal

Nevertheless, Ehrlich presents two different strategies for identifying the legal in the social – a sociological strategy and a psychological one. The sociological strategy is related to his idea of 'facts of the law' (*Tatsachen des Rechts*). These are foundational social facts that 'the human mind associates' with the organisational rules of social associations (Ehrlich 1936, 85). There are, he claims, just four facts of this kind: (i) usage (that is, custom treated as an applicable norm), (ii) relationships of domination and subjection, (iii) the fact of possession (that is, the possibility of actual control over something), and (iv) 'declarations of will'.

While usage was an important basis of primitive law (customary law being the central form of this law), it is now, Ehrlich suggests, a merely residual fact of the law. Domination/subjection relationships and possession are legally significant in so far as they relate to matters of general economic importance in society. Law expresses economic conditions in this way. Only two forms of declarations of will – the contract and the testamentary disposition – have been legally fundamental (articles of association linking people in companies or other organisations are basically an expression of usage or agreement) (1936, 104).

Ehrlich's view seems to be that all law that arises as the inner ordering of social associations directly reflects these 'facts of the law'– which are clearly a mix of types of social action and types of social relations. The point at which law emerges from social norms cannot be specified precisely. But law concerns aspects of social organisation that relate to the *Tatsachen des Rechts* and that are recognised as of general (primarily economic) significance in society. As well as law that arises directly in social associations in this way, there is also law in the form of relatively abstract legal propositions enacted by the state or formulated juristically, and also law established as norms for decisions by courts and tribunals or various state agencies.

So, law has a range of sources and forms, but is rooted in the *Tatsachen des Rechts*, and is regarded (at least by those who formulate or enforce it) as of great social importance. Ultimately the bases of Ehrlich's sociological view of law seem to be (i) that law consists of those social norms that regulate matters seen as of general social significance and (ii) that law is rooted in certain types of action and relationships that tend to assume fundamental economic importance and attract state supervision.

If this seems a weak basis for specifying the distinctiveness of law, Ehrlich's psychological strategy is weaker.[13] He admits that it is very difficult to indicate the precise difference between legal and non-legal norms. Yet it is 'impossible to deny the existence of this difference' which is 'unmistakable' (1936, 164) and revealed in *feelings* about norms. The violation of a law produces a 'feeling of revolt' that is different from and stronger than reactions to breaches of non-legal norms. Law also gives rise to a reaction of *opinio necessitatis* (1936, 165). He does not explain this term, which others have explained as the feeling or instinct of obeying a social necessity (Cassese 1999, 797, quoting Georges Scelle).

A theory that avoids defining law in absolute opposition to non-legal norms should not be dismissed out of hand because of that avoidance. On the contrary, to offer a definition sharply dividing law from other social norms would be to subscribe to the kind of rigid centre/periphery dichotomy that Ehrlich's legal sociology aims to challenge. Sociology of law does not need a conclusive definition of law of the kind that jurists, for understandable practical reasons, have often sought. As has been argued earlier,[14] it needs rather a working concept or 'model' of law to organise empirical research; a concept that avoids dogmatism and leaves open the possibility of rethinking the scope and character of the research field to take account of the results of research. Such a provisional working concept also needs to have sufficient coherence and flexibility to allow for productive theoretical inquiries.

If sociology of law is to have theoretical integrity as an enterprise of *legal* studies, it must identify fields of social experience that can be convincingly characterised as 'legal' – at least provisionally. It needs this if it is to build coherent socio-legal theory. What is required is a set of sociological criteria to indicate how far social practices should be treated as legal practices, and social ideas treated as legal doctrine, for specific research purposes. But Ehrlich's characterisation of law's distinctiveness – even if treated as merely sketching a working concept of law – is so weak that it encourages those seeking to drive his work to the intellectual margins. Why does he get himself into such difficulties? And how might socio-legal theory avoid them?

The Jurist as Sociologist

The cause of the problem lies in the dialectic of centre and periphery discussed earlier in relation to the juristic and sociological aspects of Ehrlich's work. Despite his sociological imagination, he cannot escape his *juristic formation*,

13 Timasheff (1939, 140) calls Ehrlich's approach 'a remarkable assemblage of completely vague statements'.

14 See Chapter 2, pp. 34–5; Chapter 6, p. 81.

which puts the juristic view of law and legal experience in centre place and arranges other social experience around this as (legally) peripheral.

A thoroughgoing modern sociological approach to legal pluralism might see law as potentially arising in *all* social associations in some form. Some specific criteria of institutionalisation could then be treated as distinguishing law in these associations from other kinds of social norms (Cotterrell 2018, 86–8, 100–1). But Ehrlich does not proceed in this way. He clearly has in mind, as legal problems, the kinds of regulatory problems that jurists and state law address. So, when he introduces the idea of 'facts of the law', virtually all his discussion of these facts relates to juristic doctrine and to problems of regulation that are familiar to lawyers. It is as though he superimposes, over a (sociological) view of the norms that structure social associations, a different (juristic) perception of what is important in lawyers' experience. His discussion of facts of the law is a very uneasy attempt to reconcile these two perspectives.

The difficulties of Ehrlich's concept of law also show the underdeveloped nature of his social science, which recognises cultural diversity but does not provide an adequate means of analysing social forces and structures. So, when he suggests that laws are those social norms that are considered especially important, he does not explain the contexts in which judgments of social importance are made or the conditions that determine whose judgments ultimately count.

It is possible that he envisages a radical pluralism in which *each group or even each person* judges the degree of social importance of a norm that, for that group or that individual, makes the norm 'law'.[15] But this is to read a degree of radicalism into Ehrlich's thinking which is not at all explicit in his work. It seems more likely that he often assumes that the state, and the socio-economic elites having access to its power, will decide in practice what is to count as law. Ultimately, he seems not sufficiently interested in sociological inquiry to ask under what could happen where social sources of legal development are so antagonistic to the state's conceptions of law that controversy arises over what should count as 'valid law'. These issues seem beyond the scope of Ehrlich's sociology of law – perhaps too far from a jurist's outlook.[16]

Again, if his criterion of law in terms of the perceived social importance of norms is left aside and his alternative 'psychological' criterion is considered, the limits of his social insight are no less apparent. If law is distinguished from other norms by feelings evoked by its breach, Ehrlich does not seem to see that these feelings might vary within and between different social groups, and

15 He may consider, equally, that the feelings of revolt of each group, or each individual, in relation to a particular norm is what makes that norm 'law' for the group or the individual.

16 But, as will appear in the following chapter, the jurist Santi Romano offers an important exception.

there is no substantial analysis of how feelings about law might link with different kinds of social experience.

For all his many insights, Ehrlich does not *transcend* a dichotomy between juristic and sociological perspectives. He seems trapped in that dichotomy. He leaves his sociological insights into the nature of law undeveloped because, at crucial points, he retreats to juristic assumptions, or he lacks the incentive or resources to pursue sociological conceptualisations adequately. Ehrlich's dialectic of centre and periphery reflects the location from which law is to be conceptualised. Ultimately, he understands law in terms of a *juristic centre*. Beyond that centre, law as a social phenomenon remains vague and undefined in a sociological periphery.

Yet, in principle, it should have been possible to shift location: to see law from a sociological centre; in other words, to adopt a distancing from (but not a rejection of) the juristic world. Ehrlich could have achieved this if he had adopted an approach that treated the kinds of doctrine and practices that lawyers recognise as law as special instances (even perhaps especially important, clear, or well-developed ones) within a wider sociological conception of law.[17]

For example, consistently with his general sociological outlook Ehrlich could have seen law as one kind of normative regulation of social associations – I should prefer to say, of communal networks[18] – distinguished from other kinds of social regulation by its distinctive *institutionalisation*; that is, by the existence of specific agencies for creating, interpreting or enforcing normative regulation as doctrine (but not necessarily providing for all three of these activities) (Cotterrell 2018, 86–8, 100–1). This is only one of many strategies for conceptualising law sociologically. But it offers a working concept that embraces juristic law but can also extend beyond this to cover other normative orders based on institutionalised doctrine.

An Assessment

Ehrlich saw 'so much' because he could occupy different standpoints, trying to see as far as he could from each of them. As a jurist in a huge empire, he could stand in the centre of a sophisticated legal professional world, which he could envisage as transcending all cultural differences and local social conditions. But as a participant observer of provinciality and multiculturalism, he

17 Hans Kelsen's (1945, 175) claim that any sociological concept of law must be derivative from juristic understandings of law is unwarranted. Legal sociologists may recognise and make use of juristic understandings of law. But that does not entail that they must derive their working concepts of law from such understandings or tie these concepts in some way to them. Reasons for this lack of dependence of the sociological on the juridical in conceptualising law were given in Chapter 2.

18 See Chapter 1, pp. 21–2.

could create a different perspective in the social laboratory that he found on his doorstep in Czernowitz. From that vantage point, the imperial centre, with its state bureaucracy and official legal order, stood at the periphery of a rich if unstable concentration of local cultures with diverse regulatory expectations and traditions.

Ehrlich lacked the sociological insight of some other pioneers of sociology of law – certainly Weber or Durkheim. As was emphasised in Chapter 1, his concept of living law is a portmanteau idea that needs disaggregating. It cannot reflect the diversity and complexity of socio-legal reality. An approach in terms of relations of community promises much more for middle-range socio-legal theory.

What makes him special and still important is the continual movement of his thought between juristic and wider sociological perspectives, which allowed him to go beyond typical lawyers' thinking about law. Ehrlich's presents sociology of law as intimately bound up with juristic perspectives yet also potentially powerfully subversive of them; aiming to respect these perspectives yet also to relativise and decentre them in a far wider sociological vision.

9

RADICAL LEGAL PLURALISM IN THE SHADOW OF FASCISM (ROMANO)

Legal pluralism, the idea that haunts several previous chapters, indicates 'a situation in which two or more legal systems coexist in the same social field' (Merry 1988, 870). The term is used descriptively but also often to indicate a normative problem: how to manage juristically a plurality of competing legal orders, systems, or bodies of law co-existing in time and place but in unclear relation to each other.

For lawyers such an idea can be disturbing. It can suggest laws in unresolvable conflict or endless competition so that the question of what law should apply, and when, might no longer be answerable by using orthodox legal reasoning. It can suggest legal insecurity, even chaos. As in the theories of Petrażycki and Ehrlich, it can put in question the modern idea that it is *the state* and no other institution that creates and controls law. Can there be sources of law not dependent on state authorisation, asserting their own jurisdiction? If so, a plurality of legal systems can indeed exist within the political society of a state. They may present conflicting claims to regulate – potentially challenging each other's authority or jurisdiction.

Many social scientists agree with lawyers in adopting a firm state-focus in thinking about law and legal systems. More interesting, however, is the fact that others accept the ubiquity of legal pluralism so completely that it is no longer seen as a matter for debate. This is especially so among legal anthropologists in a tradition stretching back almost to the beginnings of their research field. In this tradition, law is often given a specific *social* location without reference to the state. So, for Leopold Pospisil (1971, 107), 'every functioning subgroup in a society has its own legal system . . . necessarily different in some respects from those of the other subgroups'.

DOI: 10.4324/9781003340324-12

This tradition (social scientific legal pluralism) finds law rooted in social relations and group life and may then project out from this location to find a place for state law. All of which might even make state law look *peripheral* to, set apart or derivative from, law's real social sources. As seen in Chapter 8, Ehrlich's view of law also points in such a direction.

Jurists, however, have rarely recognised legal pluralism as pervasive in modern states. The idea is too disturbing to the idea of a stable, unified, centrally co-ordinated, securely authoritative legal system. But the Italian jurist Santi Romano's *The Legal Order* (2017) presents just this idea in completely uncompromising form.

An Enigmatic Classic

Romano's work, first published in book form in Italy as *L'ordinamento giuridico* in 1918,[1] is the product of an otherwise conservative jurist who reached very high judicial office. Yet his book seems drastically to de-emphasise the place of the state in jurisprudence. It denies that the state monopolises all law in its territory; and it claims that non-state sources of law have their own autonomous existence. Indeed, these may sometimes be hostile to the state and its law and can exist although the state condemns them. Romano argued that a pervasive legal pluralism is an entirely general feature of modern societies whatever their constitutional structure or state law system. Yet such radical claims did not stop Romano's rise to official prominence in Italy from the late 1920s. Some reasons will be suggested later in this chapter.

In Italy the book's ideas were much discussed from its first appearance (Zanetti 2011; Barberis 2013, 31) and there have been translations into several European languages. In continental Europe, *The Legal Order* has become an enduring juristic reference, a classic source of ideas.[2] But in the Anglophone world it long remained little known. Only in 2017 did an English translation appear. What explains this difference in reception – widespread in the European civil law world, minimal in the Anglophone common law world?

Like the works of Petrażycki and Ehrlich, Romano's book signalled, early in the twentieth century, a crisis of uncertainty about the relations of state and law. The book's Anglophone neglect may well reflect a deep-rooted assumption in the common law world that law is a matter of integrated, stable, national legal systems guaranteed by strong states. Yet, when Romano

1 The text, originally two journal articles, was republished in book form and in a second edition in 1946.

2 Translations into Spanish (1963), French (1975), German (1975), and Portuguese (2008) exist. A summary in English of some of the book's ideas appeared in Stone 1966, ch11.

wrote, Italy was a relatively new nation with a weak state. More generally, continental Europe's twentieth-century history was one of frequent political instability and widespread occupation of national territory in war; conditions in which sometimes uncontrolled legal plurality (conflicting legal claims across the same socio-political spaces) and unstable legal orders with unstable relations between them, were far from uncommon.

It may be that thinking about such conditions now has much relevance in major common law countries. Do debates around legal pluralism often implicitly reflect more general issues about political conditions – especially about possible political instability? This question underpins discussion later in this chapter of the historical context in which Romano's book appeared – a context that in some respects is still contemporary, or at least is very relevant to a contemporary politics of legal pluralism.

From this viewpoint, part of the book's significance lies in its enigmatic relation to Romano's other writings which can be linked to political debates that preceded the emergence of fascism in twentieth-century Italy. It is important to draw out that political linkage, even though it is indirect as regards *The Legal Order*. In doing so I try to highlight a dimension of legal pluralism not often explicit in the literature: how it links to contemporary issues about political stability in Western societies, and the conditions of existence of Western states.

Legal Pluralism for Lawyers

Up to a point, lawyers routinely live with legal pluralism. Legal pluralism in *some* sense is often recognised as existing in nation state legal systems (Woodman 1998).[3] Federalism is an obvious case with its frequently variable legal accommodation between federal law on the one hand, and provincial or regional law on the other, and with all this legal variety sheltering under the umbrella of the constitutional order of the nation state. Colonial legal structures provide another familiar example. Here the imposed law of the colonist is often juxtaposed with and presupposes the indigenous customary law of the colonised (Merry 1988, 876). Indigenous law itself is frequently reshaped by colonial power and limited in its reach by 'repugnancy' rules which invalidate custom-based claims seen as incompatible with colonial law. In these cases of what is sometimes called official or state legal pluralism, the different legal orders can be associated or integrated with each other in the state legal structure.

To take a different case, international law, over the past century, has greatly increased its scope and formal significance, forcing itself on lawyers'

3 Legal pluralism may also arise from differences in legal practices between state agencies see Dalberg-Larsen 2000, 103–14.

consciousness. This suggests, if not legal pluralism, legal *dualism* – national state jurisdiction co-existing with international legal jurisdiction. And international law itself is becoming pluralistic, partly fragmenting into a plurality of distinct fields, sources, and competing or indeterminately related institutional locations (Varella 2013). As always, the juristic instinct is to affirm the absolute primacy of state law faced with the spectre of pluralist uncertainty. So, the fiction is often maintained that international law is merely the consensual legal outreach of states, embodied in treaties that could in practice be terminated without adverse legal consequences for the states involved – so, all law remains tied to the state. But many lawyers engage in transnational legal practice in which the interplay of laws across nation state borders, the negotiation of relations between legal systems, and the complexity of conflicts of legal authorities are commonplace. In these conditions, the field of conflict of laws may be increasingly important as a bridging mechanism between legal orders (Berman 2002; Joerges 2011).

So, even lawyers, their gaze fixed on their own state as the centre of their legal universe, try to accommodate a plurality of legal sources not easily reduced to those of state law. Yet juristic thought falters when legal pluralism is not confined inside the boundaries of a state legal system, or when the legal systems to be considered are not just a plurality of state legal systems.

Contemporary juristic scholars adopt one or more of four distinct strategies to banish the pluralist spectre (Cotterrell 2018, 78–81). First, using *conflict of laws* rules, conflicts between legal systems are addressed as they arise in specific cases without theorising any overall relationship between these systems. A second approach seeks an overall, *unifying legal structure* to organise plurality within this unity (as with federalism); this may or may not entail asserting a hierarchy of authority, but it aims at least to fix a demarcation of jurisdictions. A third approach tries to establish a *hierarchy of authority* for practical purposes so that conflicts of authority can be easily resolved. A final approach treats some normative systems other than state law as juristically significant but judges that significance by how far these systems *operate like state law*.

For lawyers the ongoing issue is whether these devices can keep at bay the potentially disruptive forces of legal pluralism. Can they handle plurality when plural law cannot all be subsumed in the state law model? How is law to be identified and validated?

Legal Pluralism for Social Scientists

Things can seem very different from a social scientific perspective. For many socio-legal scholars, lawyers' conceptual questions no longer impede empirical research. Legal anthropologists, for example, have dropped 'semantic questions and focus . . . on how social needs are met'; defining law is 'too complex to be worth arguing about' (Conley and O'Barr 2002, 871). Specifying a social scientific meaning of 'the legal' is just a practical device to set the scope of empirical inquiry for a particular project about certain kinds of social regulation and the conditions of social order.

Much valuable empirical research can be and has been done on this basis. But, as argued earlier, if *legal* anthropology or *legal* sociology takes 'law' as its field of research, some sense of the scope of this field is needed and concepts of law help to provide this.[4] Socio-legal researchers often recognise this and devise such concepts for research purposes; it is not necessary to rely on lawyers' concepts of law. But it is hard realistically to separate the idea of law entirely from its juristic associations. To conduct socio-legal research on contemporary Western law – especially where issues of legal plurality arise – it may be counterproductive to reject entirely juristic understandings, not to accept that the law reflected in juristic thought will be *at least part* of the legal pluralism that social science aims to study.

Ultimately a question for social scientific study of law is how to treat jurisprudence itself – the systematic thought and knowledge of jurists – as a social phenomenon. Debates in jurisprudence can have sociological significance when they contribute to and even help to shape wider ideological and political climates of thought about law. Such debates might then be properly recognised as part of the socio-political reality of law itself. I shall argue later, putting Romano's ideas in political context, that some legal pluralism controversies in his time and ours are very much part of this socio-political reality.

Socio-legal research does not need always to tie the idea of 'law' to state law. And lawyers' reluctance to analyse non-state regulation can be bypassed by social science. But the coherence of the socio-legal research field may require some conceptual link to the juridical. A shared enigma exists for lawyers and socio-legal scholars. That enigma, as Romano explores it in his book, is *how to combine juristic understanding and social observation, without distorting either.* At least this is what I shall suggest in interpreting the key messages of *The Legal Order*.

If jurists and socio-legal scholars tend to see legal pluralism differently, solving their problems with this concept might require bridging the juristic-scientific divide without denying its existence; presenting legal pluralism in a way that makes this idea equally meaningful to both constituencies. On the one hand, jurists need to appreciate the variety of communal networks that produce law, and the many kinds of law-like regulation (codes, orders, standards, etc.) that lawyers increasingly need to consider. On the other hand, social scientists need to ask: if juristic understandings are completely marginalised is something lost? One criticism of social scientific legal pluralism has been that, in recognising many non-state legal phenomena, it does not ask how

4 See further Chapter 2, pp. 33–6.

far non-state law can serve ultimate *values* that state law is typically expected to serve, for example the value of equality before the law (Woodman 1997, 159–62). In general, is the concept of the rule of law relevant to non-state law? If so, what meaning is to be given to it?

Romano's Juristic Radicalism

Romano recognises in his book a vast plurality of regulatory systems in modern society. He emphasises phenomena that contemporary legal pluralists often focus on, such as the independent legal identity of religious law or of the regulatory systems of corporate entities (such as business enterprises, factories, hospitals, schools, and trade unions). But he goes far beyond this. For him, families can also be thought of, under certain conditions, as independent legal orders, as political parties can. Even *organised revolutionary groups* and *criminal organisations* can be properly seen, from their own subjective standpoint, as legal entities, with their own legal identity (Romano 2017, 58–60). When states seem to act unjustly some such entities gain popular approval even if the state condemns them. 'After all, everyone knows how arbitrary, contingent and variable the criteria are that the state adopts for considering certain entities as lawful or unlawful' (Ibid, 59). This extreme legal positivism allows no moral judgment to be made in recognising law's existence. That the state condemns criminal groups or revolutionary cells does not mean they cannot exist as legal entities.

Romano's view of international law may seem less scandalous. The international legal order is, he claims, an autonomous entity; international law is not derived from state law, although its recognition (or not) by nation states is important, and it presupposes the existence of state law (Ibid, 75). In fact, he claims, the independent identity of nation states derives from international law. The state itself, as an autonomous legal entity, produces the rules through which it acts, as well as those that structure it. However, an international community of states must exist before the system of mutual recognition of states and their sovereignty is legally possible. The system of legally interacting states *presupposes* an international community that allows the recognition of states as independent legal actors. But *within* the states, the international legal order exerts minimal legal control.

Originally Romano saw international law as having no legal significance for the internal legal affairs of states (Ibid, 73, 75). But he later recognised that international law was beginning to assert claims over internal state activity (Ibid, 77). The key point, however, is that the legal order of the state is far from being the only legal order that can independently exist.

It might appear, then, that Romano fully embraces a social science view of legal pluralism. Law resides in the organisation of social life, not solely in the state's prescriptions. But the book is explicitly a contribution to *jurisprudence*, not social science. His aim is 'to include in the legal world a fact of social order [the vast plurality of self-regulating social entities] that was generally believed to be anterior to law'; he insists that he seeks 'a jurisprudential definition of law', *not a sociological one* (Ibid, 20). The concept of 'institution' is the key to (indeed a synonym for) the concept of legal order; jurists must 'draw this concept into their own realm, *which is not that of sociology*' (Ibid, 20, my emphasis).

An Institutional Theory

The concept of institution has a special meaning for Romano. An institution is 'any entity or social body' that has 'borders', 'organisation', 'a firm and permanent unity' (2017, 17, 18, 19) and a 'yearning towards the realisation of a shared purpose' (Fontanelli 2011, 104).[5] Law is nothing but 'an arrangement, an organisation' of such an entity (Romano 2017, 25). Although the institution may be a social group, it is not reducible to the members of such a group or to social relationships between individuals. It has *its own existence*, irrespective of the individuals associated with it. It can continue although these individuals are all replaced by others. And it facilitates collective projects that transcend individual lives.

An institution need not be made up of individuals at all (it could be an enduring trust, capital fund or organisational idea), but it always needs individuals to manage it (Ibid, 18). This could suggest the legal personality of a corporation, distinct from those of its officers or employees. But personality is, for Romano, a different concept from institution. An institution only 'takes on the character of personality when it is considered as an entity with a will of its own' (Ibid, 38). Asserting its personality (so that individuals can act for it in fulfilling its 'will') or having its personality recognised by others allows it to interact legally with these others.

It could be easy to see this as indicating the kind of law-producing social units that social scientific legal pluralism presupposes, a way of conceptualising numerous law-creating groups or associations, as in Ehrlich's theory. If so, the next step would surely be to study institutions empirically to see how, and in what sense, they have law, and what kind of law. But this approach is not Romano's. If the institution is a social entity, a feature of observable social life, 'institution' is nevertheless a *legal* concept. It is not that institutions *create* law (or that social groups *have* legal systems). For Romano (2017, 16)

5 He also writes (2017, 36) that 'it will have a leader, a legislator, subjects, laws of its own, an ensemble of authorities and administrative gears', but what form any of these elements can take seems entirely open, and it is not clear whether they can all be found in some form in every entity that, for Romano, counts as an institution.

institutions *are themselves* legal orders; 'legal order' and 'institution' are synonyms. So, juristic theory must recognise the vast plurality of law, which is the vast plurality of organised social life regulating itself.[6] The entire second part of Romano's book considers the numerous ways in which legal orders in this plurality can interact legally or, more broadly, may be 'relevant' to (that is, have some effect, influence, or bearing on) others.

Legal orders appear fully formed as integrated, unified entities; in Romano's view, they cannot be recognised as legal orders unless they have this unity. So, French law, Italian law or the law of the Roman Catholic Church are legal orders to the extent that they can be seen as totalities to which all legal issues relating to them can be referred. This juristic perspective does not deny the complexity of social regulation, or sociological questions as to how it comes to exist. But it *leaves aside* these questions (Romano 2017, 46–7). It presumes that legal thought can only work when related to what appears as a unified legal order.

Social entities are legal orders when they are institutions in Romano's sense. So, contrary to the assumptions of much jurisprudence, legal *rules* are not the fundamental phenomena of law. Behind the legal rules stands the legal order (institution) to which they relate. A legal order operates by means of, and is structured by, its rules but is much more than them. The institution is 'the body, the frame, the limbs of law' and, equally, law is 'as inseparable from the institution . . . as life from the human body' (Ibid, 22). Romano notes, as an analogy, the idea of the relation of soul and body: 'we are spiritual and corporal entities at the same time' (Ibid, 23). The implication is that, at base, law is the *spirit* of organised social life. This spirit must be embodied in social form; but social existence would be lifeless without it.

Although these ideas are very abstract, they suggest something important: that law, understood realistically, is something even beyond social scientific observation, a kind of *animating spirit*, although it presupposes and cannot exist without the social entities that social science observes. Law is a juristic idea that arises directly out of social life and motivates and organises social life. So, Romano's theory is a rare bridging, from a juristic point of view, of pluralist social observation and jurisprudence, and has been influential as such (Fontanelli 2011, 70–1; Francescakis 1975, xiv–vi). It is not a sociological theory of law. Instead, it is a jurisprudence that incorporates as *legal* ideas – the juristic thought of a lawyer – everything that sociology can teach about the life of groups.

6 Cf Marilyn Strathern's (1985, 111) comparable formulation from an anthropological (not juristic) point of view: 'the sense of social order enshrined in legal/governmental [i.e. state] institutions is simply a more complex, rigid and systematic version of what people do everywhere to sustain ordered life'.

The book addresses practical legal issues of Romano's time that are not irrelevant to ours – notably the legal position of collective bargaining in industrial relations (2017, 61, 96–8). He notes that the state legal order typically sees in the workplace only legal relations between individuals and the enterprise, governed by the individual employment contract; and this is part of a wider legal marginalisation of social groups. But the *institution* of collective bargaining, he insists, is its *own* legal order, distinct from that of the state, and recognised subjectively as important by those involved in collective bargaining processes. The theory of the institution gives no inevitable primacy to either the state legal order or the collective bargaining legal order. So, it forces jurists to consider each of these and their relations – not to assume that only the state legal order deserves juristic attention.[7]

Essentially the question is posed: when two legal orders confront each other how are they to be co-ordinated if each is subjectively valid in the eyes of those who represent it and operate through it? What social scientific legal pluralism identifies empirically is, in Romano's work, rethought as a jurist's *normative* problem: what is to be done when the state's law confronts the regulatory understandings of many different social groups?

Crucially, in Romano's theory all legal orders are viewed 'from the inside', from the perspective of a legal participant, someone inside the institution: the approach is 'perspectival' (Croce 2017, 127). The focus is on (i) what is involved in *experiencing* a regulatory order as an enveloping environment, and then (ii) how to look beyond this 'inside' experience to try to appreciate how the reality of other such orders is experienced. Any idea of the inevitable centrality of state law is rejected as a matter of legal theory, while the internal viewpoint of the jurist (which is the experience of *anyone* trying to make normative sense of law as an insider in a legal order) is retained and extended.

So, social life is *brought inside jurisprudence.* But equally, in Romano's understanding the concerns of jurisprudence are part of organised social life. In other words, the social experience of living inside regulatory systems can be studied using long-established juristic methods of interpretation and management of regulatory conflicts. And, insofar as legal orders are recognised subjectively, the issue of conclusively defining law is peripheral. One just inhabits law (and recognises others doing the same), rather than looking at law as an *object* to be delineated.

As regards the state, once in being, it is undoubtedly a legal order and *from a certain point of view* is all-embracing and dominant. But its legal significance is not necessarily obvious to those who do not subjectively experience it

7 Compare the discussion in Chapter 7, pp. 105–7, of ways in which Petrażycki's ideas might reconceptualise juristically the relation of state law to other normative orders in conditions of cultural pluralism.

strongly as a legal order (as, for example, its officials typically do). Citizens may be utterly alienated from it, and have a legal consciousness set up in opposition to it, or indifferent to it. State law must co-exist with other legal orders subjectively recognised as real by those associated with them.

The Rise of Fascism and the Context of *The Legal Order*

Romano's book, with its laconic, lawyerly style, leaves it entirely to the reader to draw conclusions about where his theory might lead. We can ask what really motivated him to present the most radical conception of legal pluralism ever proposed by a jurist – and to do so in the face of lawyers' clear general hostility to strong pluralist perspectives on law. He makes scarcely any reference to political context and offers no systematic survey of social issues of his time. Yet many of these issues must have been in his mind when he wrote his book, and they are strongly in evidence in some of his other writings. In fact, these can suggest the hidden politics of *The Legal Order* and, as I shall argue, provoke reflection on the politics of legal pluralism today.

In 1909, a few years before *The Legal Order* first appeared, Romano published an essay on 'The Modern State and Its Crisis'.[8] It came at roughly the mid-point of a glittering academic career, which was then subordinated to a no less spectacular judicial career. From 1929 to 1944 Romano was President of the Council of State, Italy's highest administrative court.[9] So he was hardly a legal outsider, and the apparent iconoclasm of his radical legal pluralism seemed to do him no harm in terms of his career in the state establishment. Why not? Perhaps because of aspects of Romano's thinking that are not revealed in *The Legal Order*.

He was a political conservative with 'no penchant for the limelight of politics' (Croce 2017, 112); a technically-minded lawyer through and through.[10] He held high judicial office during the fascist period in Italy, but it is claimed that his appointment to the Council of State 'did not imply at all a "fascistization" of the Court' over which he presided 'with a great dignity' (Sandulli 2009, 30). The context of fascism, however, is an important matter to return to later.

Some themes of *The Legal Order* are present in the essay on 'The Modern State and Its Crisis'. For example, he writes that the state is an autonomous

8 Originally published as *Lo Stato moderno e la sua crisi*. I used the French translation (Romano 2015) as a basis for the following discussion. See also Sandulli 2009, 17–21.

9 He also held part-time academic posts during his judicial career and continued his academic writing until his death in 1947. On his very prominent career in academia and public life see Sandulli 2009, 5–7.

10 Sandulli (2009, 32), discussing his later writings, refers to 'his typical reasoning, a strict legal logic, just as if it were mathematics'.

entity, transcending the ephemeral existence of individuals with their specific interests (Romano 2015, 3). However, the state must present itself as a synthesis of diverse social forces. And many new social associations characterise modern society – trade unions, agricultural, merchant, industrial, and public officials' organisations, co-operative societies, mutual institutions. The formation of organised economic groups is 'the major fact of the present era' and 'a more solid and organic social cohesion is needed' (2015, 6). In his essay this theme takes on much clearer political significance than in *The Legal Order*.

The state prefers to recognise legally individuals not social groups, he notes, and *cannot control these groups* (Ibid, 7). It confronts a social movement that 'organises itself according to its own laws' (Ibid, 8).[11] And some powerful social forces are implacably hostile to the state, aiming to replace it with syndicalist social organisations. Corporatist developments (self-regulating groups) are not entirely unwelcome and can challenge excessive individualism (Ibid, 11); they might cure some deficiencies of the state. But inadequate current electoral systems undermine faith in the state; electoral colleges representing diverse social groups would be useful and need not challenge the state's unity (Ibid, 13–14).

Despite all its problems, the state is essential because there must be 'a higher organization to unify, moderate and harmonise the minor organisations. This higher organisation can for a long time continue to be the state' (2015, 14). So, it seems that when he wrote this essay Romano in no way wished to displace state law from the centre of the universe of legal plurality, as *The Legal Order* (2017, 50–3) a few years later seemed to suggest. Instead, the essay advocates a form of *state corporatism*; that is, state supervision of self-regulating social groups.

The ideology of Italian fascism also promoted state corporatism from the 1920s, but it is unlikely that Romano would have welcomed fascism's total idolisation of the state – 'everything in the state, nothing against the state, nothing outside the state' (Mussolini 2000a, 66). The fascist state under fascism regulated society in part by creating and supervising social corporations – syndicates representing occupational groups. But it envisaged the state pervading all aspects of social life (Mussolini 2000b, 164), whereas *The Legal Order* proclaimed the autonomous legal existence of entities distinct from that of the state (Romano 2017, 53–4). Occupational syndicates approved by the fascist state were legal entities (Welk 1938, 54–5) but had no significant autonomy from the fascist regime and the state legal order.

Why are these comparisons of fascism with Romano's writings important? They might suggest a progression from a certain attitude to legal pluralism

11 Cf Romano 2017, 54 noting the 'tendency of an enormous number of social groups to constitute independent legal circles of their own'.

towards an ***authoritarianism*** addressing this pluralism and aimed at controlling it. There seem to be significant differences between Romano's ideas and the politico-legal environment that arose a few years later in fascist Italy. However, even if *The Legal Order* treats the state as just one legal entity in a vast plurality of such entities, Romano was without doubt a loyal state jurist (Soldini 2015, 16). He has been called 'theoretically a pluralist but ideologically a monist', propounding 'pluralism in the service of the state' (quoted in Soldini 2015, 11).[12] This is why his apparent juristic radicalism in no way damaged his official career.

The real aims of *The Legal Order* are never revealed in it.[13] Perhaps he wanted no more than to represent the fundamentally pluralist socio-legal reality he saw around him (on which see Zanetti 2011). But the book may have been intended to alert jurists to the seriousness of threats to the state from social fragmentation. It highlights phenomena that Romano, no doubt, thought must be brought to the attention of the state but had been neglected.

So, it highlights a need to regulate collective bargaining properly by presenting this need in the dramatic form of legal pluralism – a confrontation of state and non-state legal orders. And when the suggestion is made that some organised crime groups and revolutionary political groups can be seen as having their own law even if the state utterly rejects this perspective, that could be a way to emphasise the threat of weakening or collapsing state authority in the face of organised social groups that might usurp or destroy that authority. Finally, Romano's insistence on the total legal autonomy of international law, independent of national interests, might be a reaction to the disastrous fracturing of the international community in World War I, which was still being waged when he wrote. *The Legal Order* strongly suggests that international law must not be subordinated to the play of state interests.

Legal Pluralism in Contemporary Politics

Two linked ideas inspired by Romano's book are, I suggest, critical for contemporary juristic thought. They are (i) the idea of ***self-determination*** of legal orders and (ii) the idea of ***legal identity*** as a vehicle for asserting claims to self-determination by social groups within the jurisdiction claimed by a state. For Romano, any legal order has, for those associated with it and often for outsiders, a unique identity and this may be legally 'relevant' to other legal orders

12 Caranta (2009, 102–4) suggests that Romano's authoritarian views shown in his minor writings would have made him sympathetic to fascism. But Fioravanti (2016, 442) claims he was never 'completely a jurist of the regime' but aimed 'to be a man of the State and never gave up this intention even during the fascist regime'.

13 Most commentators agree that the book's firm positivism admits no normative commitments. Cf. Vinx 2018.

in different ways (2017, 69ff). Can we go further and say that the appeal to group legal identity is an appeal experienced as *collectively empowering*, and a similar empowerment may arise from rejecting group subordination to what is seen as an *alien* legal identity?

This question has great significance in the context of contemporary cultural pluralism, discussed earlier in this book, or the context of societies experiencing various kinds of social fragmentation. Often it is against the state and state law that assertions of separate legal identity, or claims to legal self-determination of social groups, are directed. Independence movements sometimes begin to make their claims by invoking the idea of autonomous legal orders, or freedom from 'alien' legal orders. The effort to assert legal self-determination has, for example, been important in the politics of Native American identity and efforts towards greater cultural autonomy (Goldberg 2000, 264–5).

The claim to legal self-determination was strongly present in the movement to 'take back control' that led to the British vote to leave the European Union in 2016. The integration of Member States' law and the structures of European Union law can be seen as a kind of legal pluralism (Barber 2006; Arnaud 1995, La Torre 1999), or even as a component in a larger legal pluralism that includes varieties of international law. Brexit can be viewed, in one perspective, as an effort to take back control of national law as an *entirely autonomous* legal order and to redefine afresh the points of 'relevance', to use Romano's term, of national law to other legal orders, including European Union law. So, 'take back control' is said to mean 'control our own borders', 'make our own laws', 'have only British judges to enforce them', 'set our own trade rules', 'be masters of our own budget'.[14]

General resistance to international legal entanglements created by treaties establishing transnational trade rules intended to be relatively permanent can be seen in a similar light. Legal monism (here meaning the exclusive, autonomous jurisdiction of the law of the independent national political society) is asserted against legal pluralism (here meaning the uneasy co-existence of state law and various regimes of international law as distinct, but interacting or competing, legal orders applicable in the same territory). This resistance may also be driven by the belief that transnational law based partly on treaties made by participating states is building a global legal order to which state law may be subordinated.

In other words, the concept of *state* legal pluralism, in which various legal orders are all organised and co-ordinated under the umbrella of the state, might appear to be a template for a comparably structured *transnational* legal pluralism – that is, a global regime within which all national legal orders can be organised and co-ordinated. This vision is far from reality. There is

14 Aspects of Brexit summarised in Taylor 2017.

no such overarching legal umbrella. But the imagined spectre of something like this may be a factor in resistance to the legal pluralism created by intersections of the law of nation states with transnational and international legal structures.

Also important, perhaps especially in continental Europe, are fears about legal pluralism inside the political society of the state. These arise in parts of public opinion from the legal aspirations and claims of some minority groups in multicultural societies. As discussed in previous chapters, these aspirations and claims often centre on religious law, and especially on the place of Islamic law in Western societies. Many commentators frame debates around this specifically in the terminology of legal pluralism. To assert elements of Islamic law, or some kinds of customary law, as resources for individuals or groups wishing to use these, is treated as a claim for recognition of legal pluralism within the state (Fourneret 2006; Bader 2009; Tas 2014).

The terminology of legal pluralism is easy to adopt in this context, both by those who welcome regulatory diversity and those who want to resist it, when the regulatory orders involved can be seen as 'law' in some sense. Islamic law is readily recognised (not only by those subject to it) as a legal order, but not as a state legal order in Western societies. So, the issue of legal pluralism here is, from one perspective, much like that presented by Romano. *When can non-state regulatory orders be accepted juristically as law*, on the basis that they are subjectively experienced as law by those associated with them and are distinct organised social entities – that is, when they are what Romano would call institutions?

Certainly, an organised Muslim community is an institution in Romano's sense and so, to use his terms, it is 'the body, the frame, the limbs of law' and law here is 'as inseparable from the institution . . . as life from the human body' (2017, 22). The politics of legal pluralism thus centres, in this kind of case, on cultural assertions of legal self-determination, which is just another way to refer to relatively autonomous communal social organisation and regulation. Today, these issues of legal pluralism are never seen as purely juristic but always as inseparable from social scientific perspectives. Romano's statement in *The Legal Order* that he adopts the concept of institution to make it possible for jurists to conceptualise organised social life in 'their own realm, which is not that of sociology' (2017, 20) might reflect an unease at the popularity of sociological perspectives on law early in the twentieth century.

Sociological jurisprudence at that time, in the United States and several European countries, was a critical response to the failure of state legal systems, and juristic thought, to adapt to changed social and political conditions (Cotterrell 2018). Today, as when *The Legal Order* was written, jurists are challenged to understand empirical social conditions. Correspondingly, a socio-legal challenge is to assess how social scientific study of law relates to the juristic responsibility to make legal sense of social complexity.

An Uncertain Role for the State

Sociology in the early twentieth century emphasised a need to understand the social bases of *political* processes. Romano's Italy was a relatively new nation state with limited experience of stable democratic structures and parliamentary government. Both in *The Legal Order* and in his 1909 essay he stressed that the state must be *juristically* seen as a unity, a single legal entity, independent of elite groups, factions and interests associated with it. But a very different account of the state was developed at around the same time by Romano's more famous compatriot, the political scientist Gaetano Mosca. Mosca's book *The Ruling Class* (1939), a foundation text of modern elite theory in political sociology, argued that elite groups will always dominate *in any state*, democratic or not, whatever the legal structures.

Mosca suggested that the separation of powers doctrine should be radically reinterpreted and developed – not just as a formal separation of legislature, executive and judiciary, but as the conditions for a plurality of social groups to influence events, competing with and checking each other through state institutions and beyond them. By this means, dominating elites might at least be refreshed and renewed. Romano fiercely rejected Mosca's *sociological* treatment of the state, insisting that it must be seen as an entity distinct from interest groups. But Mosca saw how, without these checks (essentially social rather than legal) the state might be monopolised by a despotic faction with entrenched monopolistic power. Thus, as fascism developed in Italy Mosca became its firm opponent (Benewick 1992; Meisel 1962, 224–7).

Compared with Mosca's thought, Romano's is politically ambiguous. What kind of pluralism, in practice – as a matter of socio-legal reality – would follow from his juristic legal pluralism? He does not tell us, but three possible scenarios can be suggested.

- In the first scenario a stable state asserts exclusive dominance over all legal regulation by co-opting other legal orders within it. A preliminary step towards this might be the recognition of non-state legal orders so as to work out their relations with the state juristically (a task which *The Legal Order* undertakes). But these relations would ultimately be those of *subordination*, with one legal order (that of the state) dominating all others (which might themselves be arranged hierarchically). This would be a state corporatist order. Towards the extreme (as the state becomes more powerful and more ambitious) this order moves towards fascist corporatism – that is, a corporatism that confines individual liberty in a legally framed, hierarchical structure of collective organisations. The possible endpoint is totalitarianism – state-controlled direction of all social and individual life and destruction of all opposition. But there is no reason to suppose state corporatism must move to this extreme.

- A second scenario is a more 'even-handed' pluralism, entailing a 'respectful conversation' between legal orders to produce social-political equilibrium. The same preliminary step (of juristic recognition of legal orders) as for the first scenario would be required. But, as it moves towards an extreme, this second scenario becomes what might be called full or genuine legal pluralism, a pluralism in which the jurisdictions of legal orders as well as the nature and extent of their authority are *negotiated* between these orders and, depending on contingencies, revised. The underlying assumption is the value of or need for maximum *legal self-determination*. In political terms the objective is pragmatically ordered liberty and justice.

This genuine legal pluralism, if it is not to disintegrate into a third possible case outlined next, needs co-ordination. This is likely to be by the state but could be by some other superior legal order. And superiority is not exercised, as in the first case, to subordinate inferior legal orders but to supervise legal plurality to maximise legal self-determination, doing this under a structure of minimal common values necessary to guarantee overall social solidarity across this plurality and membership and participation rights within it. Some such value structure may be indispensable to realise pluralism with any degree of stability (Cotterrell 2018, 164–7, 190–3). But it should 'have nothing sacred and immutable about it. When power rests on a system of ideas and beliefs outside of which it is felt that there can be neither truth nor justice, it is almost impossible that its acts should be debated and moderated in practice' (Mosca 1939, 139). The superior legal order itself must be responsive to pluralist negotiation.

- A third scenario is one of *irreconcilable conflict* between legal allegiances, with no centripetal force such as a strong, controlling state (as in the first scenario) or ordered, negotiated, principled compromises between legal orders (as in the second) to give legal stability. If this third scenario arises in the political society of a nation state, each faction often tries to capture state institutions to make them instruments of its purposes. This becomes a crisis when not enough forces prioritise maintaining the integrity of state institutions over politically partisan purposes, and not enough social forces accept an overriding value of solidarity as essential to the whole political society. This situation moves, at the extreme, towards anarchy (lack of any effective regulation), perhaps resolved by the triumph of one political force over all others.

Romano's juristic pluralism does not set out any scenario such as those outlined, but it should inspire an inquiry as to how legal pluralist concepts translate into political consequences. In other words, where can the politics of legal pluralism lead when pluralism appears in an extremely radical light as in *The Legal Order*, and the state must come to terms with it?

The Limits of a Lawyer's Focus

Is legal pluralism to be welcomed or regretted? Where it amounts to significant legal self-determination it may often be welcome. It may reduce remoteness of the regulators from the regulated, make meaningful democratic control of law more of a possibility, recognise and express the complexity of preferred legal allegiances and of social complexity generally, and give people more of a sense of ownership of the law that governs them.

Taken to extremes, however, it may lead to legal unpredictability. Settled meanings of justice and security might be overwhelmed by jurisdictional chaos. Law still exists, but too much competing law, too uncertain in its scope of authority and normative status. In fact, legal pluralism rarely moves to such extremes. It typically finds overarching, controlling or co-ordinating legal frameworks that, if strong enough, limit its potential for disorder. These frameworks attract supervening allegiances that temper pluralism's centrifugal tendencies.

All of these contrasting possibilities for the destiny of legal pluralism are left open, not only by the silences of Romano's text but by his lawyer's method of analysis. He has been seen as wanting to frame issues of social change *in legal terms* without addressing social change itself (Croce 2017). In Filippo Fontanelli's view (2011, 76), his book proposed 'a framework that could account for the developments of the times'. For Aldo Sandulli (2009, 7), Romano's 'use of [legal] dogmatics was . . . a means for understanding the surrounding reality'.[15]

The narrowness of a lawyer's purely doctrinal focus can make strong alliances with social scientific projects difficult. But *The Legal Order* forces the reader in its indirect, enigmatic way – especially if put into its wider political context – to ponder questions about the nature, significance, and challenges of legal pluralism that go far beyond those encountered in many contemporary juristic and social scientific debates around this concept.

15 Fontanelli's comment (2011, 101) that Romano's pluralism 'is on the verge of turning into sociology, but never does' is accurate.

10

A FUNCTIONAL JURISPRUDENCE FOR THE WELFARE STATE (LUNDSTEDT)

In part, juristic theories can be seen as responses to political conditions and to conditions of legal professional practice, in the time and place in which they emerged (Cotterrell 2003, vii). But this does not mean that the ideas are to be *reduced* to their socio-political context, explained away as having no significance outside it. The point is rather that understanding a theory's historical and socio-political context may give *essential* insight into its aims, meaning, and scope. It can change understandings of the theory, sometimes in very fundamental ways. This chapter applies that approach to the work of one strikingly original but unfairly neglected jurist, to present his work in a revealing new light.

A Method of Reading Juristic Theories

The historian of political thought, Quentin Skinner (1969), originally argued, on the one hand, that theoretical texts should not be seen as autonomous 'self-sufficient object[s] of inquiry and understanding' but also, on the other, they must not be reduced to a 'context of other happenings' that might be thought to 'explain' them. Neither the 'autonomy' approach nor the 'contextual' approach is adequate. The 'contextual' approach cannot explain a text's meaning (but only the conditions of its production), yet it also denies that the text itself can explain this meaning. By contrast, the 'autonomy' approach implies timeless, universal meanings of the text, but it cannot solve the problem of how 'timelessness' and 'universality' are to be recognised and established.

In practice, 'we' readers in 'our' cultural context may decide what is timeless for 'us' – but an author's questions and the context that inspires them may be very different from ours. Skinner (1969, 52) writes that classic texts

DOI: 10.4324/9781003340324-13

'help to reveal . . . not the essential sameness, but rather the essential variety of viable moral assumptions and political commitments'. They address not timeless, universal problems but historically and culturally specific ones. A study of context cannot explain an author's meaning, but it can show the range of possible meaning available to an author in time and place. It adds to the resources available to interpret the text.

Most contemporary scholars of jurisprudence are surely mainly interested in how they can use theoretical literature to address current issues. Given such aims, a familiar temptation is to *ignore* the historical, socio-political context of that literature and to assume an aspiration to timelessness and universality in its arguments and conclusions. Another temptation is to assume that literature from another time or place addresses essentially the *same* context of problems and assumptions as that which the reader inhabits. So, one could simply read the literature as if it had *no significant context* other than that familiar to the reader, or one could deliberately take the literature out of context and impose on it a meaning intelligible to the reader in terms of *the reader's own context*. In each of these cases, the text is read as if it is 'autonomous', outside history; yet at least part of the author's meaning is likely to be lost in such approaches.

This chapter argues that it is not illegitimate to seek, in a text from an earlier historical time or written in a different culture, meanings that transcend that time or culture. But those meanings may be missed unless context is taken seriously into account in interpreting the text. By identifying how much of a work of juristic theory can be best understood by locating it in the socio-political conditions of its time and place, it becomes possible to understand what can legitimately be seen as *transcending* the contexts of the text's production: what can speak across time and distance to have meaning in the reader's own world of experience.

It could be said that all juristic theory reflects and expresses a certain socio-political and legal context, so that nothing can be truly timeless. Whether or not this is so, the most imaginative theoretical literature can sometimes have a range of reference broad enough to address the experience (the cultural contexts) of readers distant in place or time from the author. But it is important to reject any assumption that theoretical ideas can *routinely* do this or should be expected to.

How can these ideas about interpreting theory be explored more concretely? This chapter uses the very distinctive theory of the Swedish jurist Vilhelm Lundstedt to illustrate such an interpretive approach and show how it can help in understanding a particular body of thought.

Lundstedt's theory is chosen here to resolve a puzzle in intellectual history. His theory has been very widely seen (at least by non-Scandinavian interpreters) as 'extreme', intemperate, and deeply puzzling – even 'impenetrable' (Wacks 2012, 154) with the result that it is almost entirely neglected internationally. Yet, his key arguments had very considerable, wide-ranging theoretical and practical influence in jurisprudence and politics in his own country. They had major juristic impact. How is this discrepancy in evaluation to be explained?

I argue that Lundstedt's key arguments are *readily intelligible* in the Swedish socio-political context in which they were developed. From a certain viewpoint, they appear as an entirely reasonable response to that context. Seen outside that context they can seem unintelligible. Yet a contextual study of juristic ideas such as Lundstedt's can help to show what in them can travel *beyond immediate context*: in other words, what enduring insights about the nature of the jurist's task can legitimately be taken for more general application from ideas developed in a local context. This chapter argues that, contrary to prevailing views, Lundstedt's work has much of value to offer here.

By identifying aspects of ideas that are embedded in context one can see what other aspects of them might transcend context. The very process of contextualisation may clarify what has more general significance. Thus, the chapter argues that Lundstedt's theory has far wider relevance for international debates than has previously been recognised. By contrast, ahistorical interpretation offers only a partial, perhaps impoverished understanding.

The View from Afar: Lundstedt Abroad

Scholars having access to the extensive literature by and about Lundstedt in Swedish have written extensively on his theory and the context in which it was developed. But his ideas were presented in detail to the English-speaking world mainly through just two books: *Superstition or Rationality in Action for Peace?* published in 1925, and *Legal Thinking Revised* published posthumously in 1956. Lundstedt gained notice in the world outside his own country almost entirely through his two English books (Lundstedt 1925, 1956),[1] both written as general treatises on jurisprudence for an international audience and not presented as tied in any way to Scandinavian legal experience.

The earlier book sets out a lengthy summary of his ideas on the nature of law (focusing on criminal law and tort) together with a fierce denunciation of international law as then existing. Reactions to the book ranged from modest interest in his fresh ideas[2] to curt rejection, especially focused on his notoriously combative approach.[3] Criticism was mostly of the book's

1 However, Orfield 1956, 603–11, summarising his work, draws on his English articles as well as his books.

2 Lindsey 1926, 521: 'There is much that is timely in Lundstedt's criticism of jurisprudential theories.'

3 Randall 1926, 420: 'a shriek is not an argument . . . cogency of reasoning is not enhanced by loudness of voice'.

intemperate language rather than its arguments, with which few reviewers engaged in depth.

Reaction to *Legal Thinking Revised* three decades later was more uniformly hostile, both as to the book's content (with its apparently complete rejection of almost all orthodox legal concepts and almost all theories except the author's) and its style, seen as strikingly aggressive and opaque. For most foreign readers, it has been impossible to see behind the disconcerting and often alienating facade that Lundstedt's English texts seemed to present.

A Scorched Earth Jurisprudence

His ideas, like those of other Scandinavian realist jurists, were mainly judged internationally as an engagement with legal philosophy's perennial conceptual debates. Insofar as these debates addressed such seemingly timeless matters as the nature of rights, duties, responsibility, liability, and justice, Lundstedt's contribution, like that of Scandinavian realism generally, appeared largely *negative* and *destructive*. This is because he devoted so much effort to denying the 'reality' of all such established juridical ideas, suggesting not only their lack of practical relevance, but also the danger of basing legal practice and legal theory on such 'fantastic', 'irrational' and 'superstitious' thinking.

In relation to the concept of justice, and its invocation as a basis for legal decisions, it is not hard to understand Lundstedt's main arguments, especially as set out in *Superstition or Rationality* (1925, 23–7, 48–9). If justice requires fair or equal treatment, he claims that any law truly aimed at doing justice would need to examine an infinite range of personal circumstances of offenders or litigants to assess their relative position justly, as regards guilt, blame, or liability. It would need to inquire into moral perceptions and commitments, states of mind and life conditions, pressures controlling practical choices, inequalities between rich and poor, personal histories and experiences, the differential effects of legal sanctions on individuals, and a host of other matters.

To do all this would make law unworkable; so the appeal to justice as a basis for law is a *chimera* – a mystification and misrepresentation of a working legal system that in practice usually aims not at 'doing justice' or pursuing other 'metaphysical' ideals of traditional jurisprudence but at promoting general security and the welfare of society. Insofar as ideas of justice are important, they are not the basis and shaping force of legal decisions and policies. In fact, the relationship of cause and effect is reversed: ideas of justice are largely shaped by law's own operations and classifications; they are given substance by judgments imposed by the legal system on citizens' actions and relationships, judgments that decide their legal (and, gradually over time, moral) meaning. Insofar as law succeeds in providing long-term general security, perceptions of justice will follow it.

As regards criminal law and punishment, for Lundstedt all orthodox justifications for legal action against offenders fail insofar as they focus on deterring, reforming, or exacting retribution. This is because these justifications operate by attaching ideas of guilt, blame, responsibility, or liability to the offender, but all such ideas are subject to the same criticisms as those levelled at the concept of justice itself: law has no way to make these concepts refer to objective social conditions but only to a subjective set of considerations. They refer only to value judgments about offenders and their acts that cannot ultimately be defended because they cannot and do not try to consider all variables (possibly an infinite number) that could be relevant to the offender's situation.

So, the real function of criminal law is not to establish and address offenders' guilt but to identify acts harmful to general welfare. It designates such acts as offences and connects the offences with 'the general moral instincts' of the public. In so doing it helps to support and organise these instincts. And the sole function of punishment is to affirm, through its consistent and predictable use, the existence of criminal law as in force and effective (Lundstedt 1925, 49–53; 1956, 166, 218).

This summary may be enough to indicate both the negative and positive sides of Lundstedt's theory. The negative side involves sweeping aside all traditional juristic thought as he understands it – what in *Legal Thinking Revised* he calls the method of justice, but which encompasses most orthodox conceptual thinking about law. The positive side involves replacing this with a focus on what is called, in *Superstition or Rationality*, public welfare or the welfare of the community and, in *Legal Thinking Revised*, the method of social welfare. In Anglophone commentary the reaction to each of these sides of his thought has usually been equally dismissive. But it is the *negative* side that has most often been called 'extreme'.

To label theoretical ideas in that way is to imply that they are outside the acceptable parameters of debate (cf. Munro 1981, 76). This judgment has been specially attached to Lundstedt as 'the most extreme' of Scandinavian legal realists (Paton 1972, 39; Campbell 1958, 566). Yet it is not obvious that he takes a more extreme view of the unreality of legal concepts than does, for example, his compatriot, the usually more respectfully considered Karl Olivecrona.[4] Both writers, following Axel Hägerström's anti-metaphysical philosophy, see these concepts (including ideas of rights and duties) as mainly significant only for the psychological feelings that can attach to them, and not

4 For a brief comparison of the ideas of the two writers see Spaak 2014, 268–71. For a discussion of aspects of Olivecrona's legal theory in historical and socio-legal context see Cotterrell 2013. Arvind 2012 suggests that inadequate access in the Anglophone world to Hägerström's ideas may have prejudiced reception of Lundstedt's jurisprudence. But this does not seem to have undermined Anglophone appreciation of Olivecrona's thought, similarly much indebted to Hägerström.

as representing any 'reality' in themselves (Lundstedt 1925, 38, 126–7; Olivecrona 1939, ch3; 1971, 184).

However, Lundstedt (1925, 117–8) seems content for many basic legal concepts to be used in practice as long as it is recognised that juristic foundations for them linked to the method of justice are chimeral – mere mystification (Ljungman 1955, 356–7; Olivecrona 1971, 176–7; Bjarup 2005, 11–12). So, it is said that his 'own works on contract and tort law do not differ much from the works on these topics by other legal scholars' (Spaak 2017, 97).

The reason for treating Lundstedt as (unacceptably) extreme may be as much to do with the style of argument of his English books – especially *Legal Thinking Revised* – as with his rejection of established juristic ideas.[5] Critics note his 'polemical tirade', 'tortuous style', 'rambling . . . badly organised' work, 'arrogance of statement', 'obscurity and incoherence', 'impenetrable thoughts', 'breathtaking conceit and self-importance', and 'naïve and professorial' approach.[6] In Anglophone academic cultures not accustomed to Lundstedt's kind of blunt, intemperate assessments in which scant respect is paid to the integrity of any views opposed to his own, critics have rarely tried to grasp what lies behind the ferocity of his attacks on established juristic ideas.[7]

In international context Lundstedt might seem to be debating abstract philosophical positions about legal ideas; purely academic issues that should not justify his intense heat and passion. But, seen in a different, specifically Swedish context, his 'scorched earth' approach to jurisprudence may reflect something entirely different: an impatient sense of an urgent need to reshape national legal outlooks radically to fit them for new socio-political conditions and uses of law. I shall argue later that this is a fruitful way to see this side of his legal theory.

The Opacity of Social Welfare

As regards Lundstedt's *positive* proposals about social welfare, these have been described internationally as abstract, empty of content, wholly unclear, or no less metaphysical than the ideas he rejects.[8] The most incisive sympathetic discussion of them by an Anglophone writer (Munro 1981) distinguishes Lundstedt's two uses of the idea of social welfare: first, to explain realistically the basis of law, avoiding all metaphysics, and, second, to advocate a 'constructive jurisprudence' to guide all juristic activity towards developing law solely on the basis of what is 'useful to the community' (Lundstedt 1956, 131–6, 193). Yet

5 One review suggested that, faced with Lundstedt's 'remorseless analysis', specialists in private law 'may find themselves hard put to find the exact words for a fully effective defence of their most cherished working concepts': Jones 1958, 757.

6 Friedmann 1967, 307, 309; Allen 1964, 50; Wacks 2012, 154; Hart 1983, 161.

7 For thoughtful exceptions see Jones 1958; and (much more critical) Campbell 1958.

8 Freeman 2014, 884; Wacks 2012, 155; Paton 1972, 40; Campbell 1958, 567; but cf. Arvind 2013.

Lundstedt's claims for the method of social welfare are 'significantly limited' (Munro 1981, 76). So, why did he attach so much importance to this idea?

Lundstedt says of the method of social welfare: 'I mean in the first place the encouragement in the best possible way of that – according to what everybody standing above a certain minimum degree of culture is able to understand – which *people in general actually strive to attain*' (1956, 140; emphasis in original). He stresses the words 'in the first place' because lawmakers (legislators, judges) might not be able to make these actual strivings the sole guide. They might justifiably see some of them as based on 'false conceptions', or as unidentifiable or still in process of formation in the population. Ultimately lawmakers must, as their role requires, make valuations of social welfare to benefit society (1956, 145).

Lundstedt admits that lawmakers' judgment could be distorted by the 'method of justice' but he makes no allowance for any influence on them of prejudice or special interests. Instead, remarkably, he claims that it is difficult in practice for lawmakers to make laws favouring particular interests or classes: 'the pressure exerted on the law-maker by the community interest must always be very great' and, in a modern democracy of educated citizens vigilant to watch the law-maker's actions, '*it is generally impossible to make any other laws than those which in purpose appear to benefit, broadly speaking, everyone in the community*' (1925, 133; emphasis in original). Social welfare is a matter of valuations, but these do not express any overall moral or political philosophy. They will concern the maintenance of social peace and general security, including the security of transactions and the promotion of society's economic wellbeing through 'the common production of wealth and common exchange of commodities' (Schmidt 1978, 161).

Most critics see the method of social welfare as giving little guidance[9] or as simply making ex cathedra judgments about the communal good. Because Lundstedt offers no governing principles but only suggestions of specific goods that social welfare is likely to require, the tendency has been to conclude that the method must ultimately rely on metaphysical commitments (to abstract systems of moral or political principle). Lundstedt cannot admit this, given his claim to reject all metaphysics.[10] So, critics have often assumed that what is involved is, despite Lundstedt's explicit denials, a Benthamite utilitarian justification of law-making, or a theory of the balancing of interests like Roscoe Pound's.[11]

9 Hellner 1958, 163 notes the lack of clarity and limited scope of Lundstedt's method but offers a careful assessment of its relevance in specifically private law contexts. See also the valuable discussion of Lundstedt's ideas on the law of obligations in Arvind 2012.

10 Cf. Zamboni 2002, 57, citing criticisms to this effect.

11 Rawls 1958, 170; Munro 1981, 74; Friedmann 1967, 309; Randall 1926, 421; cf. Hellner 1958, 164; Jones 1958, 757.

Based on what is said in Lundstedt's English books, and without reference to the socio-political context in which the method of social welfare is developed, these reductions of it to philosophies of law's purpose that are familiar in international juristic debate are understandable. It seems that he offers nothing new. Correspondingly, his refusal to recognise any fellowship between these approaches and his own becomes incomprehensible. But his position is clarified when put in its socio-political context. Then it appears as no longer a restatement of commonplaces. It can be seen as based on wholly different assumptions from those informing Poundian or utilitarian jurisprudence and its seeming complacency about the influence of special interests and its lack of any detailed content become readily explicable.

Lundstedt in Swedish Context

Outside Sweden, what has seemed most distinctive about Lundstedt's theory, most clearly marking him out from the other internationally best-known Scandinavian realists, has been his 'method of social welfare'. Olivecrona's most prominent writings (1971, 45, 84) say little about it; the Danish realist Alf Ross (1974, 295–6) explicitly rejects it.[12] Can this seemingly empty notion – presented by Lundstedt as distinct from all others in the international juristic literature – be given more content and meaning by an appeal to context?

The Politics of a Jurist

In Sweden, Lundstedt 'is widely known as the most "politicised" legal scholar', writes Mauro Zamboni (2002, 39), 'not only because he was for many years an active member of the [Swedish] Social Democratic Party and the Swedish Parliament. His "political" character is also derived from his legal philosophy.' It has been said that Lundstedt 'very often based his political points of view in his views on law' (Sundell 2005, 466), but it might equally be suggested that his immersion in the political currents of his time influenced the direction of his legal thought.[13] In the small, closely integrated, Swedish elite of lawmakers, opinion-formers, politicians, and academic leaders, he was well connected, and was himself an active legislator, a powerful influence in academic life, a prominent legal and political campaigner, and an eloquent contributor to the press on matters of legal reform and policy.

12 On Ross' persistent negative criticism of Lundstedt, see Evald 2014, 226–8.

13 Lundstedt is said to have called his legal realism 'a Social Democrat legal theory': see Evald 2014, 227. He joined the Social Democratic Party in the mid-1910s, and his conversion to a realist jurisprudential outlook, under the influence of Hägerström, occurred around the same time: Molin 1982–4, 376; Sundell 2005, 465–6.

My own copy of *Superstition or Rationality* offers a simple illustration of such connections. Inscribed in fountain pen ink on its first blank page are the words: 'to Rickard Lindström with the author's kindest regards'. Lindström was a journalist and a leading 'modernising' politician in the Swedish Social Democratic Party in the 1920s and 1930s (Zetterberg 1980–1; Trägårdh 2002, 81) when the party was shaping its policies to become the dominant unifying voice of Swedish politics, a position it would seek to maintain through 40 years of uninterrupted government beginning in 1932.

This process involved transformation from a socialist class-based party to a national one emphasising solidarity and unity throughout Sweden society, encapsulated in the idea, strongly promoted from 1928, of Sweden as a 'people's home' (*folkhem*) – a kind of homogeneous national family in which class conflict and 'privilege or backwardness' (Schall 2012, 456–7) would be dissolved away in an overall national interest, a common social welfare. On such foundations 'a new society marked by good sense, rationality and planning' would be built (Sejersted 2011, 47).

In fact, an idea of *folkhem* had circulated from early in the twentieth century (Trägårdh 2002, 84). And Lundstedt's concept of social welfare (*samshällsnyttan*) was present in his writings from 1920 (Schmidt 1978, 161). In 1925, while treating it as more or less self-evident, he emphasises that it requires both capitalist 'haves' and proletarian 'have-nots' to renounce irreconcilable demands; each side must give way for the benefit of the social and economic wellbeing of the whole national community (1925, 136–7). At just this time the Social Democratic party was in the process of adopting an ideal of class-free national solidarity, and convictions about the necessary policy supports, that came to seem as self-evident for the party as Lundstedt's method of social welfare was claimed by him to be.

There is no need here to postulate directions of influence between Lundstedt's thinking on social welfare and the political currents in which he operated. It is enough to recognise their very close compatibility and the ease with which, in such a climate, the largely empty juristic shell of the method of social welfare could be filled by a political programme seen, in its general shape, as self-evidently appropriate to its promoters and supporters. In other words, socio-political context remedies the 'abstract', 'empty', and 'unclear' character of the method.

Lundstedt strongly rejected the claim of some Swedish critics that his legal theory was a cover for his 'social democratic prejudices',[14] and he did not

14 In fact, this claim misses the point, which is not that one should read off the legal theory from its author's politics or vice versa, or that one 'caused' the other, but that a direct correlation exists between Lundstedt's approaches to legal theory and to politics. Common presumptions underlie the conceptualisation of each field. I think that the same is true of Karl Olivecrona's legal theory (insofar as it can be seen as a speculative sociology of law) and his published wartime political views: see Cotterrell 2013; cf. Spaak 2014, 175–6.

see the requirements of social welfare in exactly the same way as his own political party did (Arvind 2012, 178). The compatibility between his legal theory and its social democratic political context lies not in an identity of social welfare valuations in each but in the pervasive assumption that the meaning of social welfare could be rationally and objectively determined and consensually legitimated in *normal political processes.* For Lundstedt it is the everyday refinements of policy derived from the political process that guide social welfare; and what unifies these policy developments is an overriding political valuation that social solidarity and the economic wellbeing of the whole society are supremely important.

Lundstedt's denial of any metaphysical underpinning of social welfare is based on his conviction that conscientious lawmakers will follow this taken-for-granted overriding political valuation in solving problems as they arise. And because the valuation focuses on the welfare of the national community *as a whole* this is not a matter of a utilitarian counting of how many individuals will benefit, and by how much, from any particular legal policy; nor is it a matter of a Poundian balancing of interests which presupposes individual claims opposing each other and confronting social interests. Lundstedt's 1925 book argues that individual and community *cannot be set against each other*: the community exists for the benefit of all individuals and cannot be treated as distinct from them; to raise claims against the communal interest would be to undermine the very conditions that provide the individual's guarantee of security and welfare (1925, 34–5).

My aim here is not particularly to defend Lundstedt's views, which in Sweden and elsewhere (Campbell 1958) have been criticised for their potential for authoritarianism.[15] But it is to suggest that they are readily understandable in terms of a specific relation to the political ideologies and cultural experiences that complete them and which they seem strongly to support and confirm. Lundstedt's social welfare presupposes and perhaps idealises very specific socio-political conditions:

- the possibility of building consensus in a small essentially homogeneous population,
- a tightly integrated and public-spirited governing elite,
- a paternalistic political tradition in which it could be seen as natural for the lawmakers to fix valuations for society, and

15 During World War II Lundstedt defended governmental controls on the distribution of some newspapers and other publications, seeing such limitations on the free circulation of ideas as necessary to protect the country in a time of emergency from communists and others who, he thought, sought to destroy it; laws aimed at saving the nation from destruction could not be regarded as unconstitutional. He also advocated control of anti-democratic political parties: see Molin 1982–4; cf. more generally, Mindus 2009, 171ff.

- an assumption of the deep rootedness of democratic and liberal instincts, 'in the blood' (Trägårdh 2002, 77; Strang 2009a, 39), tempering any theoretical possibility of governmental authoritarianism.

Criticisms in Sweden of Lundstedt's ideas, or of Scandinavian realism in general, often focus on the attenuation of some of these crucial conditions or assumptions.[16]

A Functional Reinterpretation of Legal Values

Do these considerations 'explain away' Lundstedt's thought by reference to its historical context – which I suggested earlier a contextual approach should not do? Zamboni (2008, ch.4) has suggested that legal realist approaches present the relationship between law and politics as an 'intersecting' one, rather than as reducing the former to the latter; on this view, law has a 'partial rigidity' (an identity) not reducible to political context. Something important remains about the idea of law after it has been viewed in its specific socio-political contexts. In Lundstedt's jurisprudence, that *enduring identity of law* must be brought to light from the interstices of the theory; from the concepts that still remain important in his thinking even after its relentless attack on metaphysics, and from certain assumptions that enable him to continue to speak of law when so much of the focus of his theory is on policy.

Following this line of approach, Lundstedt's method can be seen, I shall suggest, as a way of talking about law that may help to show, *in general terms*, what could be an appropriate juristic involvement with issues of legal policy or governmental purpose. But, as a prelude to addressing such matters, the 'negative' side of his theory, his attack on the method of justice, needs also to be linked to its socio-political context.

Realist attacks on metaphysics were heavily criticised in Sweden as 'value nihilism' (*värdennihilismen*) – a reckless sweeping away of all moral foundations for law, setting it adrift without a moral rudder (Strang 2009a; Mindus 2009, 104–6). The best way to interpret Lundstedt's polemic against the 'method of justice' is as a deliberate cultural ground-clearing exercise: a relentless effort to destroy old ways of thought to make way for fresh ideas of law as an instrument to steer a rapidly changing, secularising, modernising society.

When his work is examined carefully it is clear that the *idea of justice* does not disappear from it. Instead, it is reinterpreted sociologically and pressed into service to serve social welfare. For Lundstedt, popular ideas of justice cannot guide law but are nevertheless needed to support the machinery of the legal system and cannot be ignored by it. A 'common sense of justice'

16 See Zamboni 2002, 52, on change in relation to lawmakers; and Sundberg 1986, 315, on change in relation to liberal traditions.

is present in society – a broad consensus on right, wrong, and fairness. This sense of justice originates in primitive social instincts refined and shaped by the operation of the legal system as a mechanism of coercion and persuasion over centuries. And although the sense of justice is very largely a consequence of the stable, regular, long-term application of law, the legal system must take this consciousness of justice (as a value) into account, if its operations are to be effective (Lundstedt 1925, 132, 189–91; 1933, 335; 1956, 169–70).

Thus, seen in socio-political context, Lundstedt's attack on metaphysics in law involves reinterpreting orthodox, 'irrational' juristic ideas in *functional* terms. Recognising the community's sense of rights and justice is necessary to connect the attitudes of the citizenry securely to the tasks of the legal system. Lundstedt's frequent campaigning to correct miscarriages of justice can be seen in this light. So can his efforts to promote the decriminalisation of homosexual acts between consenting adults and for repeal of alcohol prohibition legislation. In these campaigns he challenged what he saw as pointless legal victimisation of, or interference with, otherwise law-abiding citizens (Sundell 2005; Rydström 2003, 161–9). Citizens protected and defended through such campaigns could readily see them as promoting private rights or civil liberties. Yet his support for the state's power to expropriate landed property affirmed that, in his thinking, social welfare must trump incompatible public attitudes to private rights (Lundstedt 1925, 89; Strang 2009b, 66; Sundberg 1986, 316). So, justice, rights, and other legal concepts must always be understood only in terms of their utility for social welfare.

Lundstedt's idea of a common sense of justice assumes a special context: first, a history of relative peace and stability allowing the consistent maintenance of fundamental legal rules 'over centuries' to shape this sense (1925, 132, 191; 1956, 169); and second, that a consensus on ideas about law and morality does, indeed, exist within the regulated population. The assumption of such a consensus seems broadly consistent with the Swedish social democratic outlook on national homogeneity in the period when Lundstedt wrote (1920s–1950s); the movement for modernisation and social development presupposed a moral substratum to ensure stability in this process of change. An early Swedish empirical study in sociology of law, carried out in 1947–1948, was designed to examine how uniform and wide-reaching the common sense of justice was. It found differences between social groups, but within a broader picture of significant uniformity (Segerstedt 1949).

So, for Lundstedt, justice ideas must be considered in the operations of the legal system. But the 'negative' side of his theory emphasises that they can never be allowed to direct it. This is far from being a position in any philosophical debates about the epistemology of legal concepts. Justice has no essential philosophical meaning. An effectively functioning legal system *controls* justice ideas as it makes use of them; it harnesses them to social welfare and prevents the emotional claims associated with them from getting out of hand.

It is in his arguments about international law in *Superstition or Rationality* (1925, 161ff.) that Lundstedt shows most clearly why he sees the method of justice and its associated juristic concepts as not merely irrational but potentially dangerous. In a functioning municipal legal system claims of right are successfully managed, limited, and directed by the operation of law. But on the international stage, 'legal' claims of right made by states are subject to no such constraints and there are no adequately effective means to manage them. Without an international judicial system backed by immense coercive power to enforce its judgments against mighty states, claims of right made by states become excuses for war or for the subjection of weak states to stronger ones. Juridically empty rights-talk by states is significant only for the feelings of entitlement it encourages, fuelling demands against other states.

Lundstedt's views were criticised for ignoring positive achievements of international law and its potential for development (Dunn 1926); otherwise, being so completely negative, they were simply ignored. Politically, he supported Sweden's policy of neutrality in the first half of the twentieth century in a situation where, as he saw it, opting out of defensive international ties offered better prospects than relying on the hopelessly weak structures of the League of Nations to police them (Lundstedt 1933, 337; Sundell 2005, 467).[17]

A Wider Context: The Jurist's Role

So far, this chapter has developed two main arguments. First, Lundstedt's idea of social welfare must be understood in relation to a specific socio-political context at a particular time; attention to this context completes the meaning of his otherwise puzzling idea by reference to a political programme and a set of cultural factors treated as its objective foundation. The judge or legislator 'resolves his policy doubts' (Jones 1958, 757) by awareness of these factual conditions (the desires and understandings of citizens filtered through the political process) which make appeals to metaphysics redundant (Lundstedt 1925, 145). Second, attention to context also shows that ideas of justice, and, more generally, most of the apparatus of familiar juristic thought which Lundstedt criticises so heavily, are not actually abolished in his thinking but reappear as significant in it when reinterpreted in functional terms and treated as important characteristics of the social environment in which law must operate.

These contextual interpretations do not, however, 'explain away' his juristic theory. They make it possible to see what in it may properly be transported

17 Later, unusually among Swedish social democrats, he argued in favour of Sweden joining NATO: Sundell 2005, 468; Arvind 2012, 179. Seemingly he was again refusing to put his faith in law and now placed it in the effectiveness of an international pragmatic alliance of political and military power against what he saw as the threat of communism.

to a wider international arena of debate. Indeed, they can show it as far more relevant to that arena than it has usually been thought to be. A starting point for such an argument is Olivecrona's (1959, 137) seemingly casual comment that 'Lundstedt used to say that he was not a philosopher but a jurist', his practical aim being 'a complete reorientation of legal science' – that is, of the jurist's specific field of concern. This raises the question of what this field is and what idea of law must inform it. It also raises the question of how far the role of the jurist can be envisaged in international perspective, beyond the context of any legal culture.

Lundstedt's approach assumes that such a juristic role is, indeed, not that of a professional philosopher, insofar as the latter prioritises abstract philosophical problems rather than issues about relating an operational concept of law to its contexts of application. For this practical application jurists need not a fully developed philosophical system but a more provisional or adaptable idea of law serviceable to address legal issues in their time and place and perhaps to preserve, protect and promote values with which law is generally associated.

The Legal Machinery and Legal Values

The international significance of Lundstedt's thought is in pointing towards such a flexible, juristically useful idea of law. He often refers to law in descriptive, sociological terms as a governmental 'machinery' of control (1956, 8, 18),[18] an idea that offers no general *juristic* view of it in terms of normative concepts or values. But his theory surrounds this skeletal, behavioural conception of law with substantive ideas intended to guide the operation of the legal machinery and give it normative content.

Thus, the idea of law's necessary *purpose* (its governing policy) of serving citizens' common needs and wants expressed as social welfare clearly dominates his theory. Beyond this, one of his most constant references in discussing social welfare is to *security* as a pervasive value. He stresses the importance of the security that citizens seek through the predictable, consistent operation of the legal machinery (1925, 26–27, 135–6). But he also refers to the security of the social order: the reliability of transactions and trading arrangements, and the security for social life provided by a successfully functioning economy (Ibid, 131; Schmidt 1978, 161). The method of social welfare seems directed to (i) legally framing a stable socio-economic order and (ii) protecting law's own order and reliability as regulatory machinery.

Alongside these closely related concerns with law's purpose and with security, a focus on *justice* remains central to Lundstedt's thought, as has been seen, even after he rejects the method of justice. He recognises that, in the

18 Cf. Black 1976, conceptualising law simply as 'governmental social control'.

democratic legal systems that his theory assumes, ideas of justice cannot be discarded. They are a major part of the historical, social, and psychological bedrock on which modern law's effectiveness depends. So, despite his radical critiques, the 'irrational', 'superstitious' ideal of justice remains important in his jurisprudence.

It follows that ideas about law's purpose, about security as a value, and about demands for justice must be seen as the central organising elements of Lundstedt's juristic thought. Alongside the minimal conception of law as 'machinery', these elements – related but distinguishable pointers to law's essential value concerns – together encompass the entirety of the general idea of law expressed in his juristic theory. Law is 'the very life of mankind in organised groups and the conditions which make possible . . . peaceful co-existence . . . and . . . cooperation' (1956, 8). So, it expresses – through its focus on purpose, security, and justice – all the values that enable it to have this character. But Lundstedt insists that none of these values has any metaphysical foundation. Justice is no more than a popular sense, rooted in instinct and shaped by law; security is merely what people everywhere demand; law's guiding purpose is simply what makes sense in cultural and political context. There are no ultimate philosophical justifications to underpin these valuations. Their content can only be what the jurist, in support of the law-maker, identifies as relevant for the time and place.

In this light it is possible to see why Lundstedt distinguished the jurist's role from that of the philosopher. The jurist works with valuations rooted in and validated by specific historical conditions of legal practice. Law, it might be said, is an affair of distinct values – justice, security, and efficiency for purpose. Yet the content of these is not developed in or from abstract philosophical systems, but out of the exigencies of juristic work. It is the need to interpret and reconcile these values constantly in practice that gives the jurist a distinctive role.

It seems appropriate to draw a comparison here with Gustav Radbruch's (1950) view of the jurist's role, despite fundamental differences between his and Lundstedt's theories. Like Lundstedt, Radbruch recognises the need for a general but flexible idea of law to guide practical juristic activity but sees no need for (or perhaps the impossibility of) a comprehensive philosophical system adaptable for juristic purposes.[19] He similarly emphasises a triangle of values informing the idea of law: security, justice, and 'fitness for purpose' (*Zweckmassigkeit*) – that is, law's adaptability to goals set for it culturally or politically. These values are to be interpreted in relation to time and place, the triangular relationship between them shifting with a kind of variable geometry. Like Lundstedt, Radbruch sees the jurist's role as one of working flexibly with

19 See Chapter 6, p. 85.

shifting conceptions of security and justice as values sought as *social* goods, but also as values sought in law's own operations (Cotterrell 2018, ch3).

But Lundstedt, unlike Radbruch, does not see justice as ultimately the fundamental element in the idea of law; his purely functional view of it subordinates it to claims for (economic and legal) security and order. Nevertheless, his writings leave open many questions as to how the common sense of justice and the popular demand for security may interact; it seems that this could vary with time and place. And it can be assumed that part of the jurist's task, in Lundstedt's view, is to observe and assess these values, and manage the expression of their practical interaction in legal doctrine.

A Working Juristic Model of Law

Lundstedt's approach entails that law's purpose cannot be elaborated theoretically in some timeless manner: it is a theoretical (and political) datum that this purpose must be social welfare, but the detailed content of social welfare in any particular context is to be set by *political* strategies interpreted in the light of *cultural* understandings. Within this purposive framework, concerns for security and for (the popular sense of) justice can be assumed to be prominent. Juristic work involves reconciling these elements successfully in the form of law.

From this perspective, law retains its juristic identity (what Zamboni terms its 'partial rigidity') because it faces both ways – on the one hand, towards the political authority that it serves instrumentally and that guarantees its effectiveness and, on the other, towards the cultural authority that it depends on for its roots in popular acceptance and understanding. Putting this in different terms, law is partly a mere machinery of control to secure governmental aims, and partly the repository of values, aspirations, needs, and interests rooted in the character and culture of the society it must regulate.

In a particular context (such as the Sweden of Lundstedt's time) the dialectic of politics and culture plays out in its own distinctive way through law. But the dialectic itself and tasks of balancing the values of security and justice, as understood in their varied historical and social contexts, might be seen as fundamentals of a modern juristic idea of law. Seen in this perspective, the pursuit of certain intertwined and sometimes competing values of justice and security, understood in different ways in different times and places and coloured by cultural presuppositions and expectations, provides an essential dynamic of juristic practice.

However, legal forms and processes, as contrasted with legal values, may be less fundamental juristically, especially in a world in which juristic practice is faced with new challenges in conceptualising law in new forms for practical purposes. While the positive forms that law takes and the specific institutions and agencies that serve it in each environment will be of central concern to jurists in pursuing their practice in that environment, they may not need general or comprehensive theories to explain the forms, institutions, and agencies of law in some universal or timeless way.

Lundstedt was, it seems, content merely to label them collectively as the 'legal machinery' without theorisation. And other pragmatic, provisional working conceptions of law are possible. Thus, positive law in a simple, minimal sense might be seen merely as normative doctrine (of some sort) with specific agencies (of some sort) existing to manage it (Cotterrell 1995, 37–40; 2018, 86–8). In practice, of course, the jurist must understand law in any particular jurisdiction in far more sophisticated terms. But the combination of a minimal conception of legal 'machinery' and a tenacious commitment to the pursuit of basic legal values might be a realistic starting point to allow jurists to begin to address theoretically many new, unfamiliar regulatory phenomena, for example in the diverse, burgeoning fields of transnational regulation.

Lundstedt's theory must be understood as very strongly coloured by the experience of a particular society at a particular time. That puts many limitations on its relevance as general legal theory applicable beyond the context in which it was developed. Nevertheless, sympathetically interpreted, it can suggest some fundamental, irreducible elements in a juristically useful idea of law that can significantly transcend local context. It may also help to reveal general parameters of the modern jurist's role as that of balancing, through the *time-bound* forms, precepts, and processes of law, *enduring* aspirations for justice and security as legal and social values.

PART III

Mapping Intersecting Fields

11

PARALLEL HISTORIES

Jurisprudence and Social Science

How have juristic theory and social science – especially sociology – viewed each other? Can an inquiry about relations between these fields through their modern history clarify obstacles that have existed to productive intellectual collaboration between them? Can a comparison show interactions that have occurred and how these might be built on in future? This chapter addresses these questions.

It makes no attempt to present a comprehensive comparative history. It offers vignettes of intellectual attitudes and dispositions, focused on the ideas and projects of particular contributors to the modern history of jurisprudence and sociology. But these can reveal a complex picture. In part it is one of suspicion and misunderstandings reflecting the necessarily different orientations of these fields. In part, the picture is also one of cautious recognition of potential and the idea that, if obstacles can be overcome, jurists and sociologists can learn from each other, enriching their work through mutual interaction.

In social science, anthropologists have long recognised the significance of law as a part of culture (Malinowski 1926) and legal anthropology is a well-developed research field. Contemporary economists and political scientists, too, usually have no doubt of law's social and political significance. But in academic sociology, law remains a largely marginal focus of interest in the discipline as a whole, rarely recognised as a major specialism.[1] This, despite the fact that socio-legal studies often draw importantly on the disciplinary heritage of sociology. Insofar as jurisprudence, in recent decades, has been seen as synonymous with legal philosophy, and sought its intellectual validation in

1 For possible reasons, see Chapter 5, p. 72.

DOI: 10.4324/9781003340324-15

the academic protocols of philosophy, it has tended to declare empirical social research uninteresting for its purposes (Coleman 2002, 350) or too time-consuming to produce promised results (cf. Dworkin 2006, 166–7). How far do these contemporary views from jurisprudence and sociology about each other's orientations match earlier positions identifiable in the modern history of each of these fields?

Law in the Evolution of Sociology

Suspicion of juristic thought was present at the birth of sociology. Nicholas Timasheff (1939, 45) declared that sociology 'was born in a state of hostility to law'. He had in mind especially the pioneer ideas of Auguste Comte in the mid-nineteenth century, as well as earlier French social theorists such as Claude-Henri Saint-Simon. Comte's 'lack of interest in law was inherited by sociology for many decades' (Timasheff 1939, 46). Comte saw the development of human thought as reaching a final, modern stage in which positivist thought – focusing only on observable facts and discarding all metaphysical speculation – would triumph in all fields of inquiry. Science in this sense would provide an objective basis for rationally governing and administering social life. All positivist sciences would 'converge on sociology [a term Comte coined for a new comprehensive social science], because the whole hierarchy of being culminates in the human species' (Aron 1965, 101–2). Sociology would study and rationally guide the collective life of humanity.

Law, however, would have no role in this future world. Comte saw law as scientifically ignorant, losing itself in 'the vague and turbulent discussion of rights' (quoted in Timasheff 1939, 45) asserted with no wide understanding of the social conditions surrounding them. Law is 'a metaphysical vestige . . . absurd as well as immoral', and positivism 'causes the idea of law to disappear irretrievably' (Comte quoted in Gurvitch 1947, 12). This idea of an ideal rationally ordered world of societal administration, contrasted with socially irrational law, echoes through nineteenth- and much twentieth-century thought, perhaps most famously in Marx's idea of an eventual withering away of law with the attainment of scientific administration in communism.

Such an outlook could readily make juristic thought seem unhelpful and to be avoided. But in the writings of Comte and other early social thinkers, 'sociology' remained mainly just a slogan for an aspiration to study social life scientifically. Their work was generally unconcerned with systematic empirical study. Sociology was not yet distinguishable from purely speculative social philosophy. It was necessary for certain topics to be brought to the centre of attention before sociology could establish itself. These included – a merely indicative list – 'social order' (its conditions of existence), 'social change' (its causes and directions), 'social structure' (the institutions, ideas and practices framing social existence), 'social system' (the related elements that integrate social life), and 'social control' (mechanisms for stabilising society). These topics had to be studied not as unchanging essentials, but comparatively in terms of how they varied between societies and at different historical times. So, social *variation*, and the need to study it empirically and theoretically, became (and remain) essential to the sociological imagination.

Even such a schematic list of topics gives some indication of where an interest in law might or might not fit into sociological thought. In early American sociology, Edward Ross (1901, 106) developed a theory of social control and gave law a place in it as its 'most specialised and highly finished engine'. The idea was taken up by Roscoe Pound (1942, 16–26) who exerted great influence in American jurisprudence in the twentieth century, and it became important in positivist sociology of law (Black 1976) but it has otherwise had little impact in juristic thought. Law was seen as important in influential theories of social structure and social system, especially those of the twentieth-century sociologists Talcott Parsons (Treviño 2008) and Niklas Luhmann (2004), but while they wrote about law as a key topic for social theory, neither engaged significantly with jurisprudential thought.

At an early stage in sociology's evolution, sociologists tried to distance themselves from the normative, value-oriented concerns of juristic thought. Durkheim insisted that sociology had its own unique scientific field and must study social facts without evaluating them. Weber, trained as a lawyer, saw sociological inquiry and juristic analysis as having entirely different aims. In the formative years of American sociology, early in the twentieth century, sociologists seeking scientific credentials sharply distinguished their work from the policy-oriented research of social reformers who necessarily had a more explicit interest in how law might serve their purposes (Deegan 1988). And some, influenced by evolutionary theories of social change, doubted that law, especially in the form of legislation, could or should attempt to direct change deliberately in society, since social life obeyed its own dynamics (Sumner 1906).

In France, at the end of the nineteenth and the dawn of the twentieth century, several of Durkheim's followers actively pursued sociological study of legal phenomena, and Durkheim himself encouraged jurists into his intellectual orbit. Two of them, Paul Huvelin and Emmanuel Lévy, were part of his close circle of sociological researchers, and adopted key ideas from his sociological thought in their juristic work (Cotterrell 2008, ch6, ch7). Léon Duguit, whose work is discussed later in this chapter, was a colleague of Durkheim for some years in the same university and was much influenced by him in writing about public law. But Durkheim saw legal resources essentially as raw material to be transformed by sociological analysis. Despite his warm welcome to jurists as converts, the ambitions of his sociology owed nothing to jurisprudence in any fundamental way.

In earlier chapters the emergence of sociology of law, 'law and society', and socio-legal studies has been discussed along with reasons for these developments. Here, what is important is to assess how these fields related to jurisprudence; that is, to juristic theory of the nature of law as a value-oriented idea. Early continental European sociology of law was, for a time, seen as 'a discipline strictly aligned with, if not directly dependent on philosophy and theory of law' (Treves 1985, 16). Ehrlich was even accused of wanting to replace jurisprudence with sociology of law or to merge the two (Timasheff 1939, 25, 26) and fears were expressed that sociology's popularity at the start of the twentieth century would eclipse legal philosophy (Lasson 1914, 320–1).

Later, as 'law and society' studies arose in the United States from the mid-1960s, two polarised views emerged of the relation of socio-legal inquiry to jurisprudence. Donald Black's (1976) positivist sociology of law firmly distanced itself from juristic thought, defining law not in any juristic way but simply as 'governmental social control'. Law would thus be identified as a kind of behaviour, not by any normative element. On this view, what law does, and how it 'behaves', could be explained in scientific propositions about observable social facts. And at the end of the 1980s, after having taught sociology of law at Harvard Law School for some years, Black went on the offensive publicly against jurisprudence.

His new 'sociological justice' (Black 1989) could, he argued, show lawyers' efforts to predict the results of cases through juristic analysis of legal doctrine as amateurish, even sometimes redundant. What he called the sociology of the case would study sociologically the factors that actually determine outcomes in court: for example, the nature and relative socio-economic position of the parties, the behaviour and personal characteristics of judges and advocates, and the likely effects of personal and group prejudices and discrimination. This kind of empirical research was hardly new, but Black's purported aim was to help lawyers, especially in court, to work with better resources, and to give law students necessary insights to make them more effective lawyers. But could an echo be sensed here of Comte's impatience a century before, invoking sociology, as positivist science, against 'the vague and turbulent discussion' of rights?

A very different view of the relation of sociology to jurisprudence is found in the work of another American sociologist, Philip Selznick. Selznick (1961) claimed that sociology cannot avoid engagement with values, and if it studies law it must recognise that law itself is an affair of values. Hence sociology of law should engage with jurisprudence which theorises law as a value-oriented idea. The central animating value of law is 'legality', to be understood in much the way that the jurist Lon Fuller (1969) analysed the ideal of the rule of law. Selznick thought that sociology could best contribute to law by 'tending its own garden' (1959, 117), through empirical social research and social theory. But sociology of law, he argued, must accept not only that juristic values are part of the object of sociological study, but also that sociology of law loses meaning if it does not make those values central in its own studies.

Gradually, Selznick seemed to elide the distinction, which most sociologists affirm, between observing social facts and promoting values. He always affirmed his identity as a sociologist and contributed importantly to the empirical and theoretical study of the place of law in social life (especially in the context of industrial organisation) (Selznick 1969). But he came to see his approach, informed by pragmatism and communitarian values, as a 'humanist science', a perhaps uneasy fusion of a social scientist's search for social knowledge based on observation, a philosopher's exploration of ideals, and a jurist's commitment to understanding and furthering legality as a virtue (Selznick 1992, 2008).

I suggested earlier that probably most contemporary socio-legal researchers limit their theoretical ambitions within the scope of particular projects.[2] It is usually only in the most wide-ranging sociology of law that attempts are made to theorise the nature of law in entirely general terms. In that context social scientific study of law as a kind of social theory may begin to confront ideas of jurisprudence or legal philosophy directly and extensively. So, when, in its early modern development, sociology of law was a mainly speculative enterprise, not yet strongly centred on empirical social scientific research, the interaction, overlap, or confrontations with juristic and philosophical views of law was not uncommon.

For example, the French sociologist Georges Gurvitch, referred to in earlier chapters, wrote in the first half of the twentieth century with exceptional insight about the nature and tasks of sociology of law, but also about jurisprudence and philosophy, in which he was well-versed (Gurvitch 1931, 1932, 1935, 1947). Durkheim and many of his closest collaborators were philosophically trained and drawn to ambitious theoretical sociological inquiries about law. The early work of Gaston Richard (1892) on the evolution of the idea of law, Georges Davy and Marcel Mauss on the social origins of contract as a legal concept, and Paul Fauconnet on changing ideas of responsibility in history, can be mentioned (Cotterrell 1999, 107–8, 125–30). Generally, however, in all this work, sociological views of law remained distinct from jurisprudence, following Durkheim's conception of sociology as the scientifically objective study of social facts.

Sociology in the Perspective of Jurists

What about views from the other side; that is, the views of jurists observing sociology? In considering attitudes to sociology among juristic thinkers before the mid-twentieth century it is relatively unimportant to distinguish juristic theory from legal philosophy, because this latter term was readily applied to

2 See Chapter 5, pp. 73–5.

any theoretical speculations about the nature of law. Legal philosophy had not yet become a self-consciously professionalised theoretical enterprise. It could still usually be related in some way to the practical interests of lawyers committed to promoting law's wellbeing in their time and place.

In continental Europe, at least, juristic theory could encompass very abstract formal inquiries, such as the neo-Kantian theory of 'just law' expounded by Rudolf Stammler (1925) in Germany in the first years of the twentieth century. The French jurist François Gény, who thought Stammler's work 'the most considerable monument of the philosophy of law' produced by German jurists of the time, also noted 'the purely logical form' of its 'presentation . . . which scarcely lays hold of reality and keeps the mind continually in the higher regions' (Gény 1925, 493, 494). The tendency of some juristic thought to drift into philosophical abstraction – even if with concrete aims of law in view – almost necessarily pointed it away from emergent sociology's efforts to study social life systematically in terms of its empirical variation.

But jurists who did not see themselves as philosophers, or were not usually seen as such, for example Rudolf von Jhering, an older compatriot of Stammler, could appear less distanced from the practical world of law and from sociological perspectives, even if they did not explicitly appeal to sociology. Jhering (1913) saw the regulation of human interests as central to law. A critic noted that, for Jhering, 'the end in view determines law, . . . all legislation serves social interests, and . . . the welfare of society is the chief and final purpose of law. The philosophy of law is thus resolved into the correct understanding of social welfare and becomes one with the politics of law' (Berolzheimer 1912, 14). This orientation, somewhat reminiscent of Lundstedt's,[3] helped to inspire Roscoe Pound's sociological jurisprudence. Pound similarly saw the balancing of interests as law's key function. And, as he wrote, 'the doctrine that law exists to secure interests . . . requires the jurist to keep in touch with life' (Pound 1911, 146–7). He openly embraced sociology, a discipline in its infancy in America when he first set out his ideas.

However abstract juristic theorists' ideas of the nature of law might be, especially in continental Europe, their work, up to the mid-twentieth century, was often strongly linked to the political and social concerns of their time and the practical challenges faced by law in their own societies. This is apparent in the case of the four jurists who were profiled in detail in Part II of this book. Even Stammler could not stay in a philosophical ivory tower: he wrote books about various fields of positive law, and his ideas led him to analyse and criticise the anarchist and socialist doctrines influential in his time, including Marxist historical materialism.

3 See Chapter 10.

For Jhering, Stammler, and others, sociology was part of a sensed intellectual background, not an intellectual field with which they wished explicitly to engage or even, usually, to discuss. But other jurists and philosophers did express views. The Italian Giorgio Del Vecchio (1953, 11) thought that 'a comprehensive science which studies and collects all the data of social life already exists', and so a new science was not needed. Sociology was 'a study of facts which are already within the patrimony of the other sciences' (1953, 12); it was an 'often chaotic' jumble of data, 'a mass of facts of experience', and conjectures (quoted in Pound 1912, 490). Sociology's growing popularity, reflecting popular and governmental awareness of urgent social problems, could be disturbing for legal philosophers. One wrote in 1909 that 'sociology is now the subject that engages attention', but jurists might prefer to escape from 'the crumpled metaphysic which the sociological method of speculation seeks to construct' into 'the free air of clear thought' (Lasson 1914, 320, 321).

The line between juristic theory and sociology was, then as now, not always clearly drawn. So, Fritz Berolzheimer (1912), in a very wide-ranging survey of continental European legal philosophy, published at the start of the twentieth century, included a chapter of more than 150 pages on 'The Sociological Reconstruction of Legal Philosophy', a project about which he was generally unenthusiastic. He characterised Otto von Gierke's historical jurisprudence as 'primarily a contribution to sociology from the point of view of the professional jurist' (1912, 369–70). But Berolzheimer, with other contemporaries (Lasson 1914, 327), saw *economic* thought as relevant for his field, because 'legal progress is not limited to the formulation of laws, but embraces the economics and social institutions and movements which vitalize them. . . . Philosophies become effective through their practical issues' (Berolzheimer 1912, xlv). His book is still interesting after more than a century because of its careful, open-minded, generally non-dogmatic approach to social currents of his time surrounding juristic thought.

Reasons for early juristic suspicion of sociology include its tendency to stress the autonomy of *social* phenomena, while most legal thought was individualistic, assuming the centrality of individual rights and duties. Sometimes sociology was associated with socialism, an object of suspicion or hostility for many conservative jurists. Some saw sociology as seeking to offer a standard for evaluation and critique of law and thus as competing with legal philosophy (Berolzheimer 1912, 13). Even today, some commentary defensively repeats old, early attacks. Thus, a 'good deal of philosophical spadework' would be needed before social science could intrude in matters of legal philosophy; it would be unlikely 'to seek to explain the phenomena of special interest to [analytical] jurisprudence', and even more unlikely to succeed if it tried. After all: 'What social science has succeeded in delivering the [explanatory] goods . . . in the way natural science has?' (Coleman 2002, 347, 350). Thus, the same effort to marginalise, used against Ehrlich a century ago,[4] is still made, although the methods, aims, and theoretical resources of social science are very different from those of Ehrlich's time.

The idea that the conceptual problems of social science are ultimately philosophical is familiar, and often used to imply the dependence of sociological studies on prior philosophical analysis. The philosopher Peter Winch (1958, 43) claimed that 'the central problem of sociology, that of giving an account of the nature of social phenomena in general, itself belongs to philosophy'. The key words here are 'in general'. Insofar as philosophy seeks the essential ('in general') nature of anything, beyond context, beyond time and place, it is, indeed, distinct from the orientation of sociological inquiry. As noted earlier, sociology is concerned with social variation across time, and across different societies or cultures. It should have no ambition to produce *timeless* understanding, *essential* meanings of concepts, or anything else that suggests unchanging knowledge, philosophical certainties, or puzzles conclusively solved.

In sharp contrast to broadly negative approaches to sociology's relationship with jurisprudence, as sketched before, it is important to notice a long tradition of active engagement of jurists with sociology, calling upon resources of social science to aid in building theory to provide insight and guidance about legal processes. As noted earlier, Ehrlich, in his work as a jurist concerned with the operation of state law, saw a need for judges sometimes to use social knowledge beyond positivist legal doctrine in deciding cases. Indeed, leading figures in Germany, Austria, France, and elsewhere well recognised such a need in the decade or so before World War I (Wigmore1917).[5] When legal rules failed to give clear guidance for correct disposition of a case, and the scope, meaning, or intention of relevant legislation or code provisions was ambiguous or undecipherable, a court should use 'free law finding' to fill gaps left by the inadequate words of law. The judge might sometimes properly draw on wider knowledge, including sociological insight.

In a parallel simultaneous development in the United States, Pound's sociological jurisprudence advocated opening up the legal system as a whole, and especially the judicial process, to knowledge of social conditions and social change that was being accumulated (or at least promised) by the social sciences. It might be thought that there would be less need, in common law Anglo-American systems, for 'free law finding' as proposed by the continental European jurists, because the central idea of common law was arguably the organic development of law through inductive case-by-case judicial decision. Common law was assumed to be enriched by its continual reference to the culture out of which judges 'found' the law. But Pound thought that the

4 Chapter 8, pp. 121–2.
5 See Chapter 6, p. 89.

juices of life in American common law were drying up and its procedures were becoming sclerotic. Many progressive American jurists were sympathetic to his claim that sociological jurisprudence would be a necessary antidote, and that jurists could be given the tools through social science to put common law development back on track.[6]

The story of sociological jurisprudence, and its progeny, legal realism, in the United States is a complex one that has often been told. But, as a general matter, it seems that social science has been more readily welcomed into juristic practice in the Anglophone common law world than in the continental European civil law world. Legal realism, focused centrally on understanding and predicting factors that might promote certainty (or its absence) in judicial decision-making, led to pioneer empirical, social science-inspired, studies of legal phenomena (Schlegel 1995). The juristic interest in studying judges' behaviour, at least as a supplement to studying legal doctrine, eventually became so pervasive in American legal consciousness that it could be claimed that 'we are all realists now' (cf. Schlegel 1995, 2).

Pound proposed his sociological jurisprudence before World War I and continued to advocate it throughout the first half of the twentieth century. American legal realism became prominent especially from the 1930s. The relevance of both of these movements for this chapter lies in the contributions they could make to bridging juristic theory and sociology. If jurisprudence is seen, as in this book, as a theoretical resource of jurists to aid them in their practice of promoting the wellbeing of a value-oriented idea of law, legal realism certainly offered resources for understanding judicial processes in new ways. But whether it served a value-oriented idea of law is more controversial. Realist legal scholars in America were fiercely criticised for neglecting legal values and attempting to see legal processes only through the cold, sceptical eyes of dispassionate science. Realism was even condemned as unconcerned with democratic values, especially at a time when these values were challenged by the rise of authoritarian regimes abroad (Purcell 1973).[7]

Did it offer a convincing theory to aid jurists in serving the idea of law as an embodiment of values? This line of questioning might even cast doubt on the idea of legal realism as *jurisprudence* at all, in the sense of a value-oriented project.[8] And another quite different line of criticism might raise doubts about

6 Benjamin Cardozo, later a Justice of the US Supreme Court, advocated a 'method of sociology' to aid judicial practice. His widely influential lectures (Cardozo 1921) on the judicial process frequently cite with approval the ideas of European 'free law finding' theorists.

7 Similar criticisms were made of Scandinavian legal realism but countered by its defenders. See Strang 2009a.

8 Karl Llewellyn, discussed later in this chapter, and perhaps the most enduringly significant American legal realist, saw legal realism's focus as on lawyers' craft techniques and sociological observation of judicial behaviour, but not on jurisprudence as a study of legal values (Twining 2012, 575).

the seriousness of realism's links to *social science*. Although some realists did engage in empirical research, they rarely drew on social theory. In general, realism declared the importance of behavioural study of legal processes but hardly engaged in any extensive way with sociology.

Pound's sociological jurisprudence managed to avoid both of these lines of criticism. It was intended as juristic theory in the fullest sense, with a clear appreciation of the importance of a value focus in the jurist's work. And, at least initially, it explicitly sought an alliance with nascent sociology as an academic theoretically oriented discipline. It promised to link jurisprudence and social science, doing so entirely on the jurist's terms. The result would be sociological jurisprudence (not sociology of law).

Sociological jurisprudence as an enterprise still promises this link today (Cotterrell 2018), but Pound's own work fell short despite its initial ambition, mainly because he lost interest quickly in the ongoing development of the social sciences. He left it to others to pursue the ambition of a jurisprudence that would remain continually aware of evolving sociological research and theory and use these resources ambitiously for its own purposes.

Pathways to Collaboration

Ultimately of greatest historical interest here is the work of jurists who have tried to develop social theory of their own integrated into their juristic projects, or who have taken ideas from sociology into their juristic theory as a key component. Here, just a few examples can be given.

Ehrlich, here as in so much else, can be regarded as the true pioneer. Not only did he contribute to jurisprudence as a scholar wishing to safeguard and promote the idea of law in the polity which, as a jurist, he was committed to serve, but he also created his own 'homespun' sociology as a by-product of that committed juristic practice. So, perhaps more than any other of the European pioneers of social scientific studies of law, he can properly be regarded as simultaneously a sociological jurist and a sociologist of law. His work faces, almost equally, towards jurisprudence, on one side, and social science, on the other (Vogl 2009).

Hauriou and Duguit

As noted earlier, Santi Romano firmly distanced himself from sociology, seeing his work as a contribution only to jurisprudence. Yet, a sense of changing empirical social reality hangs over his writings, and the idea that sociology might usurp the jurist's prerogatives is surely never far from his consciousness as he develops his ideas in *The Legal Order*. Maurice Hauriou (1856–1929), a law professor at Toulouse University, thought that his own ideas had 'parallel effect' to Romano's (Gray 2010, 36), but 'all of Hauriou's analyses were impregnated with sociology' and he claimed that while 'a little [engagement with] sociology leads away from law, a lot leads back to it' (Audren and Milet 2008, viii).

In fact, Hauriou's idea of the institution, which he came to see as the most basic frame within which legal ideas exist and develop, is explicitly sociological. By contrast, Romano insisted, perhaps awkwardly and certainly defensively, that the institution is an entirely juristic idea, not a sociological one, even though it is the framework of all social life.[9] As a jurist, Romano seemed to want to subsume sociology into jurisprudence – to swallow it juristically – so that the jurist still monopolises all legally relevant knowledge even if this is knowledge of the vibrancy and profusion of the social world.

Hauriou writes: 'Groups or social systems will conduct themselves like living organisms provided they, like organisms, are organised' (Broderick 1970, 133). In his view, the primary phenomena of a social organisation are (i) a directing, unifying idea or purpose, (ii) an organ or organs providing government for it, (iii) a separation of organs and powers creating a balance that can stabilise the organisation around its directing idea, and (iv) an element of popular acceptance and consent from the people active in it 'but also for all those who live within the social milieu' (Ibid, 134). When these elements are established and flourish, what results is an *institution*. 'To sum up, the form of the institution, which is its durable element, consists in a system of balances of powers and of consents constructed around an idea' (Ibid, 135).

One such institution is the state, but there can be numerous others. Institutions exist despite changes in their membership, and they can be of any size and exist for any purpose. They are the basis of law because law structures institutions. Crucially, for Hauriou, as for Romano, law has its very existence in this vast array of social institutions. But, for Hauriou, law's function is to regulate an institution; law is not, as for Romano, the institution itself. The legal centrality of the state is displaced. But Hauriou is clearer than Romano about the place of the state and state law: the state is one kind of institution among many, but it can provide a regulatory umbrella for others; and it governs other institutions, rather than individuals 'because institutions are more important than [individuals] . . . to the duration of the social order' which is 'a system endowed with a slow and uniform movement' (Ibid, 132, 136).

What Hauriou offers is an outline social theory; a way of conceptualising how social order is arranged, how society can be envisaged as a system, how individuals are linked (as members within institutions) in stable social relations, how organisations are structured, how social change typically occurs. And law now appears as something emerging directly out of social organisation. But ultimately, state law remains central (none of Romano's seeming

9 See Chapter 9, pp. 136–7.

theoretical ambivalence here); the state provides the ultimate, essential, overall regulatory framework for society's institutional diversity and complexity (Ibid, 138).

Hauriou's theory of institutions can be understood, in part, as a reaction against other (more dominating) sociological ideas of his time, especially those associated with Durkheim's sociology. While Durkheim privileged 'society' or the 'social' as sociology's special concern, Hauriou's ostensible focus is mainly on the individual, and the individual's experience of living in relation to others. He sees the subjective purposes that individuals pursue as the real creative forces in society. Law is a dynamic force of individual action (expressed in rights) continually crystalising into stabilising rules. It has both subjective and objective aspects: on the one hand, law frees creative energy producing innovation and movement; on the other, it ensures stable structures that fix social life in predictable patterns. The concept of the institution allows these two aspects of law to co-exist: 'An institution is an idea of a work or enterprise that is realised and endures juridically in a social milieu', it has objective existence but also embodies energy and creativity: 'Institutions are born, live and die juridically' (Ibid, 99, 100).

The aim of the theory seems always to be to explain how law finds its place in all of social life, how it can best stabilise social relations and be a framework for individual initiative. This is not a distanced social scientific stance, but a jurist's committed one. The idea of the institution serves juristic purposes. But Hauriou's curiosity about the social world is harnessed to expand the jurist's horizon. The balance of subjective rights and objective law, familiar in continental European juristic thought, is maintained but, in trying to analyse this balance, Hauriou devises a social theory. Jurisprudence and a very personal social theory are brought together.

In France in Hauriou's time, Durkheim's sociology dominated much of social science and many jurists felt the need to take a position in relation to this. Hauriou's affirmation of juristic concern for the individual (which he thought Durkheim under-emphasised) and his rejection of anything that could be associated with socialism was one response. But the reaction of Hauriou's compatriot and almost exact contemporary, Léon Duguit (1859–1928), was entirely different. Duguit, a highly influential professor of public law at Bordeaux University, did not develop his own social theory, like Hauriou, nor did he reject sociology. Instead, he explicitly borrowed directly from Durkheimian sociology for his own juristic purposes (Duguit 1921a).

Durkheim (1984) had seen solidarity as the essential unifying component of modern societies. Organic solidarity relies on the interdependence of numerous different functions created by the ever-increasing division of labour; that is, by the growing specialisation of socially useful tasks in which people could be employed, and the necessary interrelation and harmonisation of these tasks. Mechanical solidarity, by contrast, arises from shared ideas, attitudes, and beliefs. Every society, Durkheim claimed, required some combination of both kinds of solidarity, but the former would dominate in large, complex, modern societies.

Duguit (1921a) adopted Durkheim's idea of solidarity, treating it as the essential key to explaining the basis of law's authority. While Hauriou saw law as rooted in the institutions of social life, and thus not solely the product of the state or within the state's control, Duguit, as a constitutional lawyer, was centrally concerned with the extent of the state's authority to create and impose law. The thrust of his juristic thought was to deny the unfettered authority of the state in relation to law and to relocate ultimate legal authority (exercised through the state) in society – or, more precisely, in the need for social solidarity. Law would depend for its authority primarily on its contribution to building and maintaining this solidarity (the integration and cohesion of society). Whereas orthodox jurisprudence typically rooted the authority of law in the concept of the sovereignty of the state, Duguit (1921b) denied this sovereignty as a meaningful foundation of the state's law-making monopoly. The state's creation and management of law would need to be judged not by the idea of state sovereignty but by the imperative placed on law (and the state) to build and sustain solidarity.

It is interesting to compare Hauriou and Duguit because their approaches to sociology are so radically different. Do they represent contrasting pathways from jurisprudence toward sociology that remain instructive today? If so, which may be more profitable *as an approach*, whatever may be the assessment of these jurists' substantive ideas about law? Hauriou, feeling a need to create his own sociology for juristic purposes, actively contributes to social theory as a by-product of his jurisprudence. In this, he can be regarded as pursuing a path parallel to Ehrlich's. By contrast, Duguit simply takes a foundational idea of his public law directly from Durkheim's sociology, but his own work makes no contribution at all to sociology.

Durkheimian sociology is much concerned with studying social conditions that facilitate or undermine solidarity, as well as its types and locations, and how far it is a normal or abnormal condition of modern societies. These matters do not concern Duguit. He does not participate in sociological inquiry. And, as a jurist, he recognises only 'objective' law – the positive law that stabilises and structures society – rather than 'subjective' individual rights (which are so important in Hauriou's thought). It may be that Durkheim's early work also prioritises the social rather than the individual life, but this is not true of his sociology as a whole, which has been properly characterised as emphasising a value system of moral individualism.[10]

10 See Chapter 3, pp. 54–5.

Karl Llewellyn

The work of both Hauriou and Duguit remains prominent in the history of continental European juristic thought but is hardly known today in the Anglophone common law world. If we seek common law jurists of the past who have actively contributed to sociology and have seen this contribution as fundamental for their jurisprudential concerns, only one figure clearly stands out. This is the American Karl Llewellyn (1893–1962). He has been called 'the most fertile and inventive legal scholar of his generation . . . the most romantic of legal realists' and 'the most down-to-earth of legal theorists' (Twining 2012, xxv).

'Down to earth' could mean suspicious of philosophical abstraction; 'romantic' could suggest a concern, beyond everyday legal practice, for a vision as to what a legal system might aim for; 'fertile and inventive' might imply unusual intellectual curiosity and the capacity to pursue it. All of these are accurate characterisations of Llewellyn, a larger-than-life figure in juristic thought and social science whose full accomplishment cannot be pinned down in a few sentences.[11] What is important here about him is the combination of (i) his distinctive view of jurisprudence, (ii) his attempt to build a social science of law grounded in careful study of sociology and anthropology, and (iii) his effort to integrate jurisprudence and his largely self-created sociology of law.

Llewellyn's definition of jurisprudence is almost wantonly imprecise, inviting the ready scorn of contemporary professional legal philosophers: 'Jurisprudence means to me: any careful and sustained thinking about any phase of things legal, if the thinking seeks to reach beyond the practical solution of an immediate problem in hand. Jurisprudence thus includes any type at all of honest and thoughtful generalization in the field of the legal' (quoted in Twining 2012, 172). So, it might embrace everything from the most abstract legal philosophy to the seasoned reflections of lawyers on their practical craft. But Llewellyn had little sympathy for any idea of jurisprudence as 'a quaint, intricate, esoteric game, remote from contemporary life and understood by few beyond the handful of people who actually play it . . . [H]e believed that even the most humble [legal] practitioner could benefit both professionally and personally from having an articulate and coherent working theory' (Twining 2012, 173).

This is not unrelated to the view of jurisprudence, distinguished from contemporary legal philosophy, which this book tries to defend (see also Cotterrell 2018). Llewellyn effectively disowned, as irrelevant for lawyers, the freestanding abstractions of legal philosophy. In his down-to-earth, folksy language he

11 Twining 2012 is a magisterial survey of Llewellyn's work and offers a unique portrait of a highly complex and multifaceted scholar.

presented juristic values as merely '"fighting faiths"', bolstered by "the best reason we can muster"', and he sought 'roughly workable' concepts and a 'horse-sense' approach to legal ideas (Twining 2012, 173).

This juristic outlook reveals the sharpest possible (and deliberate) divide from the professional orientations of many contemporary Anglophone legal philosophers. At the same time, it allows an opening in jurisprudence for any knowledge that can contribute to what Llewellyn would have praised as juristic common sense. He read Ehrlich and Weber, who may have been the strongest sociological influences on him, and gradually developed a view that, in line with strong currents of theory in sociology of law, emphasised that law need not be seen as invariably monopolised by the state.

It seems likely that Llewellyn was much influenced by the key idea of Ehrlich's sociology of law: the idea that at least some social norms entirely outside the control and even knowledge of state legal agencies could have as much or more practical authority over individuals as state law itself could. But Llewellyn went further and developed a theory of law's social and political functions that could apply irrespective of whether or not law was created or recognised by the state. Like other American legal realists, his special focus in modern state law was on the work of courts. So, when he came to study law in societies without a state, this translated into asking especially how 'trouble cases' – disputes and conflicts – were dealt with in society.

One side of Llewellyn is as a sophisticated doctrinal scholar of modern American contract and commercial law (and the primary drafter of the US Uniform Commercial Code); another side is as a dedicated socio-legal researcher. Not satisfied only to speculate about the working of non-state law, he set out to study it empirically. Collaborating with an anthropologist, E. Adamson Hoebel (who did almost all the fieldwork), Llewellyn documented traditional tribal practices of Cheyenne Indians, producing what is essentially a casebook of Cheyenne trouble-case resolution (Llewellyn and Hoebel 1941). He generalised the insights so gained, in what became known as the law-jobs theory, a checklist of the functions law must perform in any society large or small if that society is to survive (Ibid, ch11; Twining 2012, 175–84).

Law must (i) deal with trouble cases; (ii) preventively channel conduct and expectations, and also re-channel these to adjust to change; (iii) allocate authority and establish procedures for its exercise; (iv) provide overall direction and incentive for the social group; and (v) develop 'juristic method', that is, mature skill in handling and reconciling the other law-jobs. It is not necessary to elaborate on the law-jobs here: what is important to note is Llewellyn's socio-legal ambition in devising (and testing) a functional model of law for use in any context.

This is emphatically not an essentialist philosophy of law – not a concept for all times and places, still less a definition of law. It is a working tool to guide empirical research in observing what Llewellyn calls law-government, provisionally identifying what it may be useful, sociologically (and juristically), to treat as legal phenomena, judged as such in terms not of their form but their function. The law-jobs idea maintains the realist focus on how law works, not what law as an abstract idea 'in essence' is.

The law-jobs concept is not an elaborate contribution to sociology, but a jurist's effort to find a way to think of law that frees it from juristic assumptions about the inevitable centrality of the state in the legal world. So, it stands in the same tradition as Ehrlich's idea of living law, Hauriou's social theory of the institution, Petrażycki's concept of unofficial law, much anthropological writing on law in non-state societies, and Selznick's (1969) effort to explore an idea of legality in modern socio-economic environments (especially those of industrial relations in the workplace) that may often be outside the reach of state law.

What of Llewellyn's work as *jurisprudence*? It clearly fits his own very open definition of the term. But if, as this book argues, jurisprudence should be seen as a theoretical resource to serve the jurist's commitment to the wellbeing of the idea of law as a complex affair of values, does Llewellyn's legal realism qualify? I suggested that doubts can exist as to whether American legal realism in general is jurisprudence in this sense (cf. Schlegel 1995, 2–3). Llewellyn, however, is an outlier in the realist mainstream, despite his centrality as a leader in it as a movement. He well recognised the importance of juristic values. He had cautious sympathy for natural law thought and understood the multi-faceted nature of justice as a value in law (Twining 2012, 185–8). Far from being a narrow legal technician, or an uncommitted social scientist, Llewellyn showed a unique diversity of concerns and inventiveness as a committed jurist.

The Memory of Pioneers

In the parallel histories of jurisprudence and sociology which this chapter has sampled, Llewellyn and a few other very individual scholars can be seen as having pointed to possibilities for imaginative explorations across the divides of academic disciplines. In all cases, their work, set in the context of their times and viewed more generally, should receive fuller recognition for its ambition. As the next chapter seeks to show, the scope of parallel contemporary concerns of jurisprudence and social science is now substantial. On a range of issues, collaboration and interaction is possible and necessary. The ideas discussed in the present chapter are pioneer contributions – early projects in bridge building – that deserve to be remembered as scholarship continues to develop.

12

CONTEMPORARY INTERACTIONS

Legal Theory and Social Theory

This chapter compares current research foci of jurisprudence and social theory and possibilities for interaction across them. By social theory is meant here, as in previous chapters, theoretical study of the nature of 'the social' (social phenomena in general) or 'society'. So, leaving aside the glimpses of intellectual history in the previous chapter, what links exist between these fields today? Despite all differences in their research traditions, how far do their interests and concerns converge or overlap today?

Legal theory is a term of several meanings. It has been claimed that it 'is merely a subset of a wider activity known as social theory' (Van Zandt 1989, 34). Certainly, insofar as law is a social phenomenon, inquiry about it is inquiry about an aspect of the social, and so surely a topic for social theory. When law is studied theoretically using the methods and theories of social science, the enterprise is often called socio-legal theory, or is seen as the theoretical aspects of sociology of law or socio-legal studies. Legal theory in this sense is explanatory social scientific theory.

But jurists usually characterise legal theory differently. For them it is mainly a matter of understanding the nature of law in its conceptual structures and modes of reasoning or evaluation, rather than in the contingent patterns of social action, social relations, and social institutions studied by social scientists. Legal theory as *juristic* theory or jurisprudence (the concern of this chapter) aims to systematise law, critique its workings, and reveal its failings and potential to make it operate in more valuable ways.

Social theory as a category also reveals its complexities. How does it differ from social philosophy, or from jurisprudence? Is social theory specifically *sociological* theory – the theoretical components of the discipline of sociology? Today, its core remains in sociological methods and traditions, but it is usually

DOI: 10.4324/9781003340324-16

considered to extend further (Delanty 2023, 411–2), so that some philosophers and literary and psychoanalytic theorists are recognised as contributing to it (Elliott and Turner 2001). Nevertheless, it is best seen as having essential sociological characteristics even if its interests and methods extend beyond those of sociology as an academic discipline. Above all, social theory needs to be (i) *empirically* oriented, (ii) focused on the nature of *social* phenomena, and (iii) attuned to *variation and diversity* in these phenomena across time and place. Insofar as intellectual projects adopt such a perspective they relate to social theory, whatever disciplinary allegiances, if any, they claim.

This chapter explores points of contact today between jurisprudence and social theory. But each of these fields today is diverse and it is hard to generalise across them, so the focus here is on a few clusters of issues – ones that, although understood or studied in different ways by legal scholars and social scientists, are clearly of contemporary significance for both.

Despite claims about early sociology's hostility to law, noted in the previous chapter, it has been claimed that social theory actually emerged out of juristic thought, gradually separating itself from it, and this process extended over centuries (Kelley 1990). In a long historical view, it has even been claimed that 'law formed the conceptual archetype and even substratum of sociological thought' and 'furnished most of its vocabulary' (Ibid, 275), a claim that might find a modern echo in relation to aspects of Max Weber's sociology (Turner and Factor 1994). But links between jurisprudence and social theory loosened as sociology made rigorous empirical research central to its disciplinary identity, while legal scholarship remained largely wedded to conceptual and normative analyses. So, it could be said by the 1990s that jurisprudence 'is a field . . . today largely unrecognized by sociologists' (Scheppele 1994, 383). More recently, however, with change in the scope of both social theory and of legal theory, new possibilities for interaction – even mutual learning – have arisen.

Both fields are concerned, though in different ways, with large structures of social life, with social institutions and the generality and diversity of social relations. To some degree jurisprudence and social theory potentially compete in generalising about, and intellectually organising, the social world (Cotterrell 2006a, 2–3). In what follows a series of five themes is used to provide a basis for comparisons.

Theme 1: Legal Individualism

How far should the individual be seen as central in social and legal analysis? This is a useful starting point because most modern legal thought organises its analyses around assumed characteristics of the individual as a reasoning being, accepting personal responsibilities and liabilities, making choices, and asserting rights. And in recent social theory this outlook is also adopted in the work of James Coleman (1990).

Individuals, pursuing their interests and controlling resources in doing so, are for Coleman the basic units for social analysis. Through individuals' mutual exchanges and unilateral transfers, they build social relations that can persist over time. But 'individuals do not act independently, goals are not independently arrived at, and interests are not wholly selfish' (Coleman 1990, 301). So, cooperation and the creation of social institutions and structures follow. Law frames individuals' interactions and what results from them. Authority is conferred when individuals transfer control over their actions to others.

Coleman's interest in organisational structures leads to an emphasis on *corporate* actors, the overwhelming dominance of which in contemporary life is a 'massive social change' creating 'a new social world' (Coleman 1992, 279). But, crucially, such actors 'merit existence only insofar as they further the ends of natural persons' (Marsden 2005, 16) and must be controlled to ensure this. Despite the pervasiveness of corporations and massive organisational structures, the individual, for Coleman, remains the bedrock of the social. Corporations must be made accountable to individuals they affect. Law, in Coleman's social theory, serves individualism.

This stance is sharply at odds with other social theory that displaces the individual from such a central place in analysis. But it partly mirrors modern legal thought. Individual responsibility remains the central case in law, especially when intention or motive must be examined. Rational choice decisions, usually presuming ultimately human motivation, are a postulate of much economic analysis of law, which has been influential in juristic thought. But legal theory avoids many complications of assessing the unique individuality of human beings by using the concept of legal person which constructs actors in law in abstract terms (even if individuals are often the carriers of this abstract legal personality).

As in pre-modern times, so today, the person in law is in not limited to the individual. So legal theory has been able to keep a focus on the human individual as central to law's concerns but not be confined conceptually in doing so.[1] At one time the nature of corporate personality (as in the limited liability business corporation) was a major issue for legal theorists (Hallis 1930). Did the corporation really have a personality recognised by law? Or was this only a fiction to refer to an association of individuals? Today these issues are no longer pressing. Corporate personality is a pervasive feature of legal life, just as Coleman rightly sees corporate actors as pervading social life.

The concept of rights, crucially important for Coleman as a legal expression of individual autonomy, became an object of attack in critical legal studies (CLS), partly insofar as it symbolised the separation of individuals from each

1 For example, as moves are being made to expand legal personality to support rights of inanimate nature. See Chapter 13.

other (like legal fences built around them), and so from any strong sense of community (Gabel 1984). But this CLS stance soon ran into opposition. Critical race theorists insisted that rights had to remain important in legal and social life, at least for their occasional practical utility despite their frequent frustration in practice (Williams 1991; Matsuda 1996, ch6). If legal individualism deterred wider legal concerns with solidarity and community, it at least gave some chance for minority groups to assert claims on an equivalent basis to the majority, relying on the promise (even if frequently broken) of equality before the law – the rights of individuals seen as formally equal persons.

From a contrasting ideological standpoint, pervasive neo-liberal thought, represented in juristic analysis (Grewal and Purdy 2014), also emphasises legal individualism, but for crucially different reasons. If liberal law sees the individual as the ultimate *moral component of society*, neo-liberal law stresses 'stable and well-protected property rights, enforcement of private contracts' and 'a particular ideal of entrepreneurial liberty, not visions of society' (Blalock 2014, 84). Entrepreneurs are often corporate actors, but the underlying model is still the autonomous, self-focused, atomistic individual. Law, in this juristic vision, holds the ring in individuals' chosen transactional activities.

Much social theory, however, does not privilege the position of the individual in the social. Niklas Luhmann's influential systems theory initially puzzled many legal theorists by insisting that all social analysis must be of systems of communication and 'not individuals, social groups . . .' (King and Schütz 1994, 262–3). Law, for Luhmann (2004), is one kind of social communication system revolving self-referentially, in all its normative discursive analyses, solely around one issue: whether a set of circumstances is 'legal' or 'illegal'. Law's discourse continues whatever individuals do; its normative pronouncements exist whether or not people follow them. Legal discourse assesses circumstances entirely in its own interpretive terms. In Luhmann's austere vision, it declares normative positions that may be observed (or ignored) by other social systems (for example, of economy, polity, or science). But all social analysis is in terms of the operations of systems, not individual motivations.

Other social theory takes a less absolute, more oblique view of the individual. For example, Bruno Latour claimed that actors participating in social life may be individuals but can also be non-human entities. For example, not only sailors but also winds and ocean currents may determine trade routes and, in Latour's (2010) ethnographic study of France's highest administrative court, the Conseil D'État, the court, and its law exist not just in individuals and their practices, but in files, dossiers, technologies, and the organisation of the court building. Individuals are partly displaced because law is 'a network of people and of things' (Levi and Valverde 2008, 806) acting on, limiting, and enabling each other. One might think also of the actions of traffic lights, or the algorithms that control high frequency trading of investments.

This suggests that a major issue for law is how far it can keep up with rapid technological change – something only weakly addressed in most current legal theory. And presumably, any natural phenomenon is an actor for Latour, or what he calls an 'actant' if 'it has no figuration yet' (Latour 2005, 54–5, 71). Certainly, climate change and global pandemics should be reminders that legal and social theories underestimate nature as an active force at their peril.[2]

Against Latour, it might be insisted that only *people* really act socially (Cotterell 2011) even if, to paraphrase Marx, they do so not under conditions of their own choosing. But juristic thought has, from pre-modern times, been able to envisage non-human entities – animals, funds, corporate entities of all kinds, even sacred idols[3] – as actors of legal significance. To this extent Luhmann is right that legal discourse interprets social reality for itself, in its own ways. Western juristic thought is beginning to accommodate the idea that non-human natural entities (animals, rivers, mountains etc.) should in some way be considered actors in law – legal subjects. This is a matter to return to in the following chapter.

Theme 2: Law's Autonomy and Identity

Another cluster of issues linking legal and social theory concerns the distinctiveness (or otherwise) of law as a social phenomenon. Remarkably, a basic question in much legal philosophy is still 'what is law?', a widespread (but never fulfilled) assumption being that some conclusive answer can be given independently of sociological inquiries. So, law is thought to have an elusive philosophical essence not dependent on social context. Most sociologists of law tend to treat such an approach as either misguided or irrelevant: law should be explored in its vast variety of forms, locations, and effects rather than as a timeless essence. From the beginnings of modern sociology of law, more than a century ago, it was recognised that generalisations about law must be based on observation of concrete regulatory phenomena; one can work with serviceable models of 'the legal' for research purposes.

Conceptualising the idea of law is not, however, misguided for juristic purposes. Jurists need to be able to identify what will count as *legal* ideas for practical purposes, distinguishing them from the non-legal (such as social, technical, or administrative regulation, and moral, political, or other kinds of reasoning). And lawyers need to be able to assess the juristic significance of such forms of regulation as 'soft law', standards, rankings, and indicators which today have

2 See further, Chapter 13, pp. 212–3.

3 *Pramatha Nath Mullick* v *Pradyumna Kumar Mullick* (1925) LR 52 Ind. App. 245 (Privy Council).

great importance, co-existing or often competing with law, even replacing it in some contexts (Nelken 2015; Di Robilant 2006). However closely linked law is in practice with other (political, economic, scientific, etc.) features of the social, most lawyers assume some distinctive identity of law. They try to see it as a coherent body of ideas and practices, however diverse its doctrinal fields may be. Indeed, in some European contexts, the idea of a pure 'legal science', developed by jurists in their self-contained professional world, is taken for granted; law's autonomy as an intellectual universe goes largely unchallenged (Samuel 2009, 440–2).

One reason why the influence of Luhmann's social theory has grown in legal theory, especially in some continental European contexts, is that it clearly recognises this kind of autonomy of the legal but theorises it in much more sophisticated terms than does most juristic theory. Law as a communication system or discourse is, for Luhmann, cognitively open but operationally (or normatively) closed (King and Schütz 1994, 302–5); that is, it readily receives information from any source, but understands this in its *own* ways to fulfil its *own* distinct function.

This function of law is not to control or steer society, to engage in or reflect politics, to structure the economy, to mirror scientific findings, or to support morality; it is solely to pronounce what is 'legal' or 'illegal' and thereby provide normative judgments that can be observed by other social systems (economy, polity, science, etc.). These systems will read (or ignore) law's normative judgments using *their* own criteria: for example, economic efficiency or relevance to policy goals.

As noted earlier, individuals are absent from this picture, but Luhmann's theory well mirrors the typical abstraction of legal thought and its frequent intellectual isolation, despite law's vital social significance. Luhmann's theory has often been called a social theoretical reworking of Hans Kelsen's legal philosophy (Bertilsson 2006, 112). Both theorists present law as a self-contained, self-reproducing discourse: Kelsen did so to try to protect law from politicisation, while Luhmann wanted to emphasise law's inability to control directly other spheres of social life in ways that lawmakers may intend. But it has been mainly left to Luhmann's followers to explore how law can sometimes productively interact with other social systems in society, by developing *alongside* them, despite its normative closure (Febbrajo and Harste 2013).

The price paid for Luhmann's portrayal of legal discourse is the absence of human agency: issues about responsibility, values, and human aspirations for law disappear. The closest correlate of this in legal theory is contemporary legal positivism's separation of conceptual issues about law from moral judgments, or from other issues about law's social or political contexts. Other kinds of legal theory move in different directions. After legal realism established the importance of thinking of law in relation to politics and policy, the chief progeny of realism (economic analysis of law and critical legal studies) followed this. And once people are re-admitted to the picture, law looks very different from Luhmann's image.

Thus, against Luhmann, the sociologist Pierre Bourdieu sees law as a field of human action. The 'juridical field' is one social field among many.[4] Like others, it is populated by people (primarily legal professionals) who compete and jockey for position in it but unite to present and defend the field in its external relations. Internally it may be disunited and conflictual but externally it tends to show a united front. What structures the field is especially the habitus (the commonly assumed ways of acting, thinking, experiencing the field, and relating to situations) shared by members in it.

Sometimes Bourdieu (1987, 831) talks of existing in the juridical field, like other fields, as knowing how to play a game. Law's autonomy is highly relative: law is close to politics and the state, and political and legal personnel and relationships overlap. Law's autonomy is not (as with Luhmann) in modes of discourse but in its distinctive *practices*, which involve rules but are ultimately more important than rules and not necessarily confined by them. An analogy in legal theory with this view exists in certain kinds of legal realism, most notably Lundstedt's theory, considered in Chapter 10, which treats law as a kind of social machinery. This 'legal machinery' consists, like Bourdieu's juridical field, less in rules than in practices and understandings but, as has been seen, for Lundstedt these must engage *citizens'* psychological dispositions no less than those of legal professionals.

Theme 3: Law and Power

Law's relation to power is often left vague in legal theory. Power hardly figures as a topic in mainstream contemporary legal philosophy except in the claim that the concept of law depends on the existence of rules *conferring powers* on citizens and officials (Hart 1994). This approach entirely displaced the earlier notion (Austin 1885, 177) that the exercise of sovereign power was modern law's essence. The idea that law *reflects* power relations in society survives strongly in juristic theory only in critical legal studies and associated critical theory such as feminist legal theory and critical race theory. In them, power is a central concern and law is readily seen as its agent – as in the power of majorities over minorities, but also the power that law sometimes promises, to minorities and women, of rights to an equal place in society or recognition of distinct identities and life conditions.

The idea of sovereignty is still prominent – if much contested – in legal fields such as constitutional and international law (Bartelson 2006; Loughlin and Tierney 2018). But it has been argued that this idea in juristic thought

4 See Chapter 2, p. 29.

is no longer attached to any political theory of sovereignty that could sustain it (Herzog 2020). And power itself has not been much analysed as a general concept in contemporary juristic theory. This is probably why Michel Foucault's social theory has much influenced recent critical legal thought.

Foucault offers resources for analysing not only the changing nature of power itself, but also its relation to law and to the traditional linking of law to sovereignty. Indeed, it has been said that Foucault was interested in law only 'to the point that it helps him propose his very particular understanding of power' (Wickham 2013, 218). And because he rethought power in a way that marginalised the sovereign coercive power of the state, he 'expelled' law (which he associated with this sovereign power) from his theory (Hunt 1992). Power in modern society is, for Foucault, primarily *not* this sovereign legal coercion. The task of power is 'to qualify, measure, appraise, and hierarchize, rather than display itself in its murderous splendour' (Foucault 1978, 144). Modern power 'is not only preventative, it is also creative or . . . productive' (Tadros 1998, 77–8). It is the way in which everything gets done in society. This view can then be developed in one of two directions.

One is towards *displacing attention from law*, because the means of social government '*instead of being laws*, now come to be a range of multiform tactics' (Foucault 1991, 95; my emphasis); these are administrative regulations and the many kinds of *discipline* imposed by social institutions, leading to socially mandated self-discipline. The modern form of power is 'bio-power' (1978, 140) – the management and direction of human bodies – pervading life in all its personal and social aspects, and perhaps, according to some followers of Foucault, now even extending beyond national jurisdictions (Hardt and Negri 2000, 23–4).

Another, different direction of analysis follows Foucault's seemingly inconsistent remark that modern '*law* operates more and more as a norm' (1978, 144, my emphasis), as a social mechanism, and less as juridical sovereign power. In other words, *law remains important* but in new ways. Perhaps it now mainly exists to guide social and personal understandings about conduct. Bio-power, harnessed to law, is socially pervasive – empowering but, more importantly, also enveloping and confining individuals in the social.

Such a vision of power working in innumerable ways through law's devices of influence and control corresponds with many aspects of the way lawyers today see it. But Foucault's influence has been regretted for blunting critiques of law's sheer violence. The legal scholar Robin West asserts that Foucault's claim of 'the omnipresence of power . . . eventually emasculated the moral critique' of law (quoted in Blalock 2014, 82). So, other social theorists like Bourdieu, rejecting Foucault, have kept a focus on law's link to politics and the state, how it 'consecrates the established order' (Bourdieu 1987, 838) or is only 'disguised force' (Bertilsson 2006, 110).

Debates about what exactly law means for Foucault partly mirror issues in contemporary legal theory. Law is almost always seen juristically in terms of hierarchies of authority. But must these be understood as structures of sovereignty, or can they be organised in more fluid rule networks (Ost and Van der Kerchove 2002) or institutional interactions (Culver and Giudici 2010)? Is law slowly detaching itself from the tutelage of the sovereign state, as international legal institutions flourish and seem to acquire greater autonomy from individual states (Besson 2009)? Can overarching constitutional structures exist without being tied to any sovereign state (Teubner 2012; Sweet 2009)? And what happens to hierarchies of authority in new forms of transnational law that readily facilitate private socio-economic relations across state boundaries (Cotterrell 2018, 122–39)? Where does authority lie and what is its source? All of these are pressing juristic issues today.

The most disturbing effort to attach Foucault's idea of bio-power to law is found in the work of the political philosopher Giorgio Agamben. If bio-power extending through all aspects of human life were to be linked to law's coercive sovereign power (as in Agamben's work), this raises the question: where does law's regulatory power and reach stop? What degree of control of life is open to law (Agamben 1998, 120)? In totalitarian regimes no region of life is excluded from the reach of sovereign power, and if this power is not separated, as perhaps Foucault envisaged, from bio-power, but rather *integrated* with it, there is no limit to the potential for sovereign power to control life – or indeed to deny life. For Agamben, the concentration camp is the paradigmatic location in which all value of life is denied, yet this *non-life* or, as he terms it, 'bare life', still remains governed by sovereign power. In the camp, human life is removed from all legal protection, yet is somehow still within the horizon of law.

The message of this for legal and social theory is that the horrors of wholly unrestrained bio-power that is exerted over human life by sovereign legal coercion (as in the Holocaust) are not a grotesque aberration to be consigned to history (see also Bauman 1989). In a 'state of exception', law acts dictatorially and exceptionally, with emergency powers, to preserve its overall regulatory hegemony – a use of law defended, for example, by the jurist Carl Schmitt (2011) in the Weimar Republic in the 1920s. But this state of exception can, Agamben (2005) suggests, become *normality* for some people in modern legal regimes that, with the vast intrusiveness of bio-power, can use minute forms of surveillance, control, and oppression.

Today, as he notes (1998, 133–4), refugees can risk being seen legally merely as bare life. Perhaps other categories can exist too, among the destitute, forgotten, and reviled, all those treated as utterly alien, beyond society's membership or protection. In this radical extension of Foucault's thought, law's power to exclude people socially while including them in its jurisdiction, is portrayed in a salutary way for both legal and social theory. For the former what is essential is to see that juridical attention today must extend to those people seemingly entirely outside law's concern in practice, but whose bare life is still lived in its sight.

Theme 4: Law as an Integrative Mechanism

If Agamben focuses on the excluded, much social theory asks, by contrast, how far society might be seen as an inclusive, *integrated* whole. Implicitly, this is a concern for legal theory too. The idea of unity in law, considered earlier, tends to presuppose a unified realm of social life, envisaged in terms of interconnections of legal relations represented in integrated patterns of legal doctrine. Juristic theory typically assumes that the social can be understood in terms of rationally ordered, interconnected regulatory patterns. But some legal theory has seen conflict, not integration, as the organising principle of social life. For example, Marxist theory of class conflict has informed both legal and social theory.

However, Marxism never made a fundamental impact on the mainstream of Western legal thought, and critical legal theory has rarely been content to see fundamental social divisions just in terms of economic class conflict (cf. Mutua 2008). Instead, it has organised itself around a variety of differentiations of the social – for example, by gender, race, ethnicity, or sexual orientation – primarily when these differentiations have been represented in legal theory by scholars who belong to the populations directly affected and can share or empathise with their socio-legal experience.

Since the members or allies of the economically weakest classes have rarely occupied positions from which they could powerfully shape legal scholarship, their voices have rarely been heard in legal theory. This is why Marxism, speaking to the interests of the dispossessed, has rarely gained any firm foothold in Western juristic thought, whatever its impact in social theory. Critical legal theory is mainly a coalition of many minority perspectives, each with its own constituency. But the concerns of the poor are typically reflected only in special legal fields (poverty law, welfare law, etc.), and not at all in general movements in contemporary legal theory.

If social theorists have usually portrayed the social as complex in its differentiation, they have equally often presented law, in a long theoretical tradition, as a means of social integration. A central theme of Durkheim's sociology was that law is such a means; it symbolises the possible forms of social solidarity and has the task of sustaining them (Cotterrell 1999, 2022). In this perspective, law is an affair of values, closely linked to morality as a unifying social force.

Durkheimian sociology has often been seen as mistaking law's aspirations for its social reality, drastically underplaying the phenomena of social power, as considered earlier. But the tendency to try to see law as a means of social integration is predictable whenever social theory is influenced by legal theory, given law's typical juristic presentation as a unity and as an overall, co-ordinating, and mediating regulatory structure of social life.

Talcott Parsons and his followers identified law as an integrative system in society, which linked all other aspects of the social (Bredemeier 1962). Today, a sophisticated expression of this tendency in social theory is found in Jeffrey Alexander's magnum opus, *The Civil Sphere* (2006). Comparably with Parsons' concept of the societal community (Parsons (1977, 182–214), Alexander's 'civil sphere' is an arena of solidarity, 'a sphere or subsystem of society that is analytically and, to various degrees, empirically separated from the spheres of political, economic, family, and religious life' (Alexander 2006, 53). It is the locus of general, society-wide solidarity, cutting across all local, particularised allegiances. It characterises civil society, of which 'law can be very a highly significant boundary mechanism', giving or refusing 'legal membership in an overarching civil sphere' (Ibid, 153).

Alexander considers how giving and refusing this membership has been done in the United States, especially as regards civil rights. Law is one mechanism, among others, for maintaining boundaries of the civil sphere, determining inclusion in or exclusion from it. Demands for entry come from sectional constituencies and particularistic interests. But, to gain entry, sectional demands must be translated into generalised interests that can be accommodated in the civil sphere. Law's task seems, in part, to be to build solidarity in this sphere. But history also shows it excluding population groups from it. Either way, for Alexander, law is a key institutional support of the civil sphere.

Alexander's civil sphere is comparable in some respects with Jürgen Habermas' 'lifeworld'. Habermas (1986) originally saw law as facing in two directions: on the one hand, co-ordinating social systems such as economy, polity, science, and technology; on the other, protecting the lifeworld – the realm of people's moral experience in everyday social interactions; the place where a general, overarching solidarity in society might be built. The lifeworld can be unified, Habermas argues, only by a communicative rationality in which all can participate. In his later work (1996), he has insisted unambiguously that law's function is to serve the lifeworld, keeping open possibilities of rational interpersonal communication and so the hope of bridging citizens' diverse perspectives in complex, pluralistic, modern societies. In this picture, law is clearly an agent of social integration, operating through communication and facilitating rational communication. It gets its ultimate legitimacy (essentially its moral justification) from the lifeworld, for which it provides regulation (Deflem 2013, 84, 85).

In Habermas' approach, not only are necessary links between law and morality affirmed but law is given special status as a focus of allegiance in modern pluralistic societies. Unifying values are hard to find in complex modern societies when the experience of different social groups can be so radically varied. Maybe, then, law itself, in its most visible, overarching form as a constitution, can be the focus of common allegiance. So, Habermas (1996, 500) has promoted the idea of 'constitutional patriotism' – a shared belief in constitutionality – to characterise such a socially and politically unifying role of law. A critical view might be that this, like so much earlier thinking on law's integrative functions, expresses aspirations more than realities. Despite jurisprudence's tendency to assume the unity of the legal (and perhaps the social), it has, in its most socially aware forms, had to recognise the differentiation, even fragmentation, of both the legal and the social.

Feminist theory shows this movement clearly. Early liberal feminism held to the idea of equality as the value necessary to overcome gender discriminations. But subsequently, radical feminism assumed that difference and inequality are inbuilt in the 'male' character of legal thought; and cultural feminism argued that differences in gendered experience should be given constructive recognition in law. Eventually, the legal scholar Kimberle Crenshaw (1989) propounded the idea of 'intersectionality' to emphasise how gender, race, and other kinds of discrimination often interact and provide mutual reinforcement.

With such complexities, 'simple' categories of 'women' or 'race' can come to seem too undifferentiated to recognise the complex varieties of experience (black or gay female, trans male, etc.) of population groups demanding an adequate presence in social and legal thought. Attempts to categorise social diversity in ways that do not recognise its full complexity risk 'essentialism' – the postulating of fixed unities (of women's experience, black experience, etc.) that may not exist. In this rapid evolution of theoretical positions, the end point could be to lose the very categories of differentiation and discrimination ('woman', 'black', etc.) on which critical legal theory had initially been based. Perhaps the only clear way forward is to retrace some steps – to reinstate the basic demand for *human equality* as the guiding value for law, and to focus on the most general forms of social categorisation and exclusion as key, pragmatic, initial targets for legal reform.

Social theory might benefit from the experience of critical legal theory in trying to confront social discriminations and inequalities, if only because practically oriented juristic thought has always had to consider how theory can address case-by-case problems. While some forms of both social and legal theory present themselves as value-free, or unconcerned with moral evaluation, it is hard to address the complex differentiation of the social without examining the possibility of some unifying social values. Hence the relatively recent recovery of the old idea of a sociology of morality (Hitlin and Vaisey 2010), a field that Durkheim pioneered.

As noted earlier,[5] Durkheim insisted that the only possible unifying moral basis for complex modern societies, and for law that served their need for

5 See Chapter 3.

solidarity, would be universal respect for every individual as equal in human worth. The basis of this value system would be found not in philosophy but in *sociology* – by asking what kind of general identification with others in a society remains possible for individuals in that society when they differ fundamentally in social experience and interests (Cotterrell 1999, 112–5). So, it is often said that belief in human rights (embodying much of Durkheim's value system of moral individualism) is now the only possible unifying 'religion' in Western societies (Cole 2012; Féron 2014).

Efforts to link legal and social theory in terms of values have also been made from the perspective of natural law thought which, in its classical forms, locates ultimate legal values in a natural condition of human existence, or a universal human reason. Natural law thought has been marginalised in most contemporary juristic theory, dominated by positivism or assumptions of the relativity of values. However, it has recently been claimed that natural law is a necessary foundation of social theory, insofar as social theory assumes certain universal attributes of humanity that make possible comparison of social experience in different times and places.

The argument is that social theory, when it considers human subjectivity and values, works with 'implicit notions of human nature' inherited from natural law thought (Chernilo 2013, 15). Whatever is to be made of this argument, natural law has actually occasionally been invoked in modern social theory, notably (and controversially) by Philip Selznick (1961) to argue that values are immanent in social institutions including law.[6] And Roscoe Pound (1958, 63–5), pioneering sociological jurisprudence, showed sympathy for natural law although he thought that law's ultimate values could be generalised from positive law itself. But most legal or social theory, if it seeks law's values, is likely to do so not in natural law terms but by reflecting on historical legal experience. In any case, the effort to theorise law's place in integrating societies will surely remain a point of contact between jurisprudence and social theory.

Theme 5: Law in and beyond the State

One final theme, suggesting common concerns of jurisprudence and social theory, is the frequent assumption, underlying both types of theory, that the widest locus for their analyses is 'society', in the specific sense of the politically organised society of the nation state. Society and law are typically assumed, ultimately, to exist under the political umbrella of the state. In sociology this assumption has been called methodological nationalism (Beck and Sznaider 2006). In juristic thought it underlies the ideas that all law is created or

6 See Chapter 11, pp. 170–1.

authorised by the state, and that the state sets the boundaries of law's jurisdiction, mainly on the basis of its territorial claims.

In both social theory and legal theory, many developments now challenge methodological or jurisdictional nationalism – some of which have been noted in earlier chapters. Theories of globalisation, of world society or system (Luhmann 1982), of post-colonialism (Go 2016), and of de-centred transnational empire (Hardt and Negri 2000) are among those that impact social theory. In legal theory, the impact of legal and regulatory developments beyond or across state boundaries is forcing change in juristic thinking. The growth of transnational law – regulation governing cross-national socio-economic relations involving private actors – has been mentioned earlier. Difficult issues arise for jurisprudence (Cotterrell 2018, 103–39). What counts as 'law', as contrasted with other kinds of regulation (and how far does this distinction still matter)? Where does the boundary, if any, now lie between public and private regulation? Where does regulatory authority lie? How are questions of legal authority to be managed when different regulatory regimes overlap, compete, or are indeterminately related to each other?

From a social theoretical perspective many of these issues can be reframed as questions about how social relations, or 'society', are being organised beyond national society. Indeed, the utility of the concept of society has often been challenged (Bauman 2002) and proposals are made to rethink the social in terms of *communities* not necessarily limited within national society (Djelic and Quack 2010). Perhaps, jurisprudence can help social theory because of lawyers' focus on the particularity of regulatory problems, and the case-by-case processing of disputes. The problem of how different legal regimes can operate in the same social space has long been a focus of practical juristic analysis – especially in relation to (i) federal legal systems, (ii) colonial and postcolonial systems (where state law may have to co-exist with indigenous customary law), and (iii) conditions, widespread globally, where systems of state law and religious law co-exist, each with autonomous sources of its authority.

Theories of legal pluralism discussed in earlier chapters address such matters. As Western societies become increasingly multicultural, and different groups seek law that reflects their cultural distinctiveness, legal pluralism is a significant interest for jurists who recognise that the idea of the modern Western state's monopoly of law is often no longer adequate for legal theory (Roughan and Halpin 2017). Juristic thought has long been concerned with the way in which conflicts between laws originating in different systems can be managed. The old legal field of conflict of laws, traditionally concerned with deciding which law should apply when laws of different state legal systems are invoked in the same case, is being re-theorised in efforts to build a new 'conflicts law' that might address a wider panorama of legal pluralism (Michaels 2020).

The effort to rethink legal concepts for transnational use continues apace. Global legal pluralism is now a familiar concept, as noted in Chapter 1, and the idea of 'global administrative law' explores principles of administrative justice and procedure that could operate effectively beyond the context of states (Kingsbury 2009). The concept of 'societal constitutionalism' especially developed by Gunther Teubner (2012) draws on Luhmann's systems theory to envisage a plurality of social spheres, not necessarily limited within national boundaries, ordering themselves on the basis of constitutional structures that would encourage responsibility and accountability within and beyond these spheres.

The variety of these and other developments in theory is extensive. A ferment in legal and constitutional theory has been inspired by the increasing transnational and international reach of law. It is this legal development, above all, that gives new relevance to the idea of sociological jurisprudence, attuned to juristic values but drawing on new social scientific research exploring how the idea of 'society' is being transformed by the ongoing wide development of transnational social relations, institutions, and forces (Cotterrell 2018).

Conclusion

This chapter has focused on a few issues currently important in both juristic theory and social theory. They may indicate the most pressing problems about contemporary law that can suggest unifying foci for jurisprudence and social theory. They indicate points of contact that may be a basis for cooperation in research. But the ultimate objectives of jurisprudence and social theory remain different. If jurisprudence is committed to serving the idea of law as a potentially valuable social institution (a commitment often demanding criticism of the failings of existing law), it cannot be a wholly disinterested study (Cotterrell 2018, 32–57). But social theory has no such *necessary* commitment to the wellbeing of the idea of law. Its key task is to increase understanding of the social world, using the methods of social science. Critical evaluation of existing law can sometimes be a product of social theory. But, as social science, social theory's essential commitment is only to uncommitted, dispassionate examination of its subject-matter. Its key task is to analyse the nature of social life.[7]

Nevertheless, as social theory has become less monopolised by the scientific disciplinary protocols of academic sociology its interests have sometimes come closer to those of juristic theory. In any case, it often provides ideas of juristic relevance. Law is a part of social experience. Life enters the dry, abstract doctrines of law through the inputs of social inquiry. Correspondingly, social science will fail to see important dimensions of the study of social life if it

7 Delanty (2023, 416) speaks of this as 'taking responsibility for the present . . . understanding choices and courses of action' presented by social reality.

underestimates the social significance of juristic thought which animates much of the practical regulation on which social organisation depends.

From the intersections of legal and social theory considered in this chapter some suggestions might be made as to where current priorities for theoretical inquiries about law may lie. The question of the place of the individual in social thought, and before the law, remains to haunt socio-legal inquiry.

The exclusion of the individual in a picture of the social in terms of systems (as in Luhmann's thought) might seem reminiscent of Weber's (1930, 181–2) idea of an 'iron cage' of impersonal regulation enclosing individuals; and Foucault's idea of bio-power suggests a disciplinary confinement of personal life even in what appear to be conditions of freedom and empowerment. Correspondingly, Coleman's social theoretical individualism has been criticised for under-emphasising the powerful constraints that social structures and forces impose on individual rational choice (Alexander 1992).

In jurisprudence and sociology of law, a long tradition of thought criticises the often excessive 'distance' of individual citizens from state power and its legal expressions. Ehrlich (1936) stressed the remoteness of lawmakers from citizens. For many decades, legal sociologists have empirically studied citizens' knowledge and opinions about law (Schultz 2023), and today this tradition is continued in studies of popular legal consciousness, and of legal cultures (attitudes to and experience of law) of citizens and legal professionals (Halliday 2019; Nelken 2020). In jurisprudence, Lon Fuller (1969) emphasised moral and technical failures – in effect a regulatory fraud on citizens – arising from insensitive, ignorant law-making.

These issues are aspects of the previously noted problem of excessive moral distance[8] that plagues much of contemporary law. It is hard to see how law can operate as an integrative mechanism in society without this problem being addressed in theoretical studies of law. It underlies many of the most important issues – for example about populism, democracy, authoritarianism, and liberty – on the current agenda of political inquiry.

8 See Chapter 6, p. 88.

13

LINKED FUTURES

Jurisprudence and Socio-Legal Studies

The aim of this final chapter is to look to the future. That involves drawing together various strands of research with which this book has been concerned, In Part I an attempt was made to sketch key parts of the terrain of socio-legal inquiry – focusing on theoretical aspects. That terrain includes the century-long heritage of sociology of law, with its strong links to an idea of sociology as a theoretically and empirically oriented social scientific enterprise. The terrain also includes the diverse activities now called socio-legal studies (SLS) or 'law and society' research. I argued that SLS draws from many intellectual fields, but its focus is always on law, and its key alignment is mainly with the methods of the social sciences.

In the book's second part, the aim was to illustrate a particular idea of jurisprudence. The intention was to show jurisprudence as an outward-facing enterprise geared to the responsibilities and concerns of jurists – theoretically minded lawyers committed to serving an idea of law as a socially valuable practice. Jurisprudential theories are rooted in the social and political conditions of the times in which they are developed, even if jurists do not always admit this. Juristic theory reflects those social and political realities (and must be understood in relation to them), but its relevance may not be confined by them. Jurisprudence, as illustrated in the ideas of Petrażycki, Ehrlich, Romano, and Lundstedt, and much other and later theory, reflects, at least indirectly, social variation and historical change. If it rarely invokes sociological ideas, it often presents insights relevant to socio-legal inquiry. So, it can suggest the possibility of conversations between juristic and social scientific thought. Chapter 12 offered some documentation of that possibility as it exists at the present time.

But what possibilities might be predicted for the future? Major challenges exist for both jurisprudence and socio-legal inquiry. These need to be clarified

DOI: 10.4324/9781003340324-17

before suggestions can be made for ongoing cross-influence between these research fields. For jurisprudence, the key challenge is, simply, to be *accepted as relevant* – as having something truly important and timely to say to lawyers and perhaps to citizens more widely – in conditions in which the tasks of law are changing at an ever-increasing rate and the social and political conditions in which they are to be performed are being radically transformed. These changing tasks and conditions will be discussed subsequently. The challenge for mainstream jurisprudence is to recognise and address them, but a pre-requisite for this is to discard some typical attitudes and assumptions in its current practice that blind many juristic theorists to urgent priorities.

For socio-legal inquiry, in its diverse forms as sociology of law and SLS, the challenges are no less fundamental. But they can be more easily stated than can those for jurisprudence, and perhaps are more manageable, so it seems appropriate to deal with them first here. It can be said that, in terms of the comparisons and meeting points that this book has aimed to explore, the main challenge for SLS is not in the kinds of topics it can address or its methods of addressing them but in the identity of the research field itself and the way that identity is shaped.

The Identity of Socio-Legal Studies

SLS is rich in empirical and policy-oriented research and is often very sensitive to social theory bearing on its particular projects. But, just as sociology of law can be related to a long heritage of theoretical development stretching back to Durkheim, Weber, Marx, Ehrlich, Gurvitch, and others, SLS too could benefit from a stronger attention in much of its research production to the rich and long development of the literature of social theory. Why is this important? I suggest it is because social theory can be thought of as the unifying theory of social science.

Whether SLS sees itself in the tradition of sociology or not, and whether or not it explicitly locates all its activities inside social science, it will benefit if it can insist on sufficient autonomy as a field of studies to embrace the great diversity of types of research pursued in it. I have argued that the safest and perhaps ultimately most intellectually comfortable home for SLS is in research-intensive university law schools.[1] But juristic studies in law schools are not a sufficiently secure base for SLS in *epistemological* terms – not sufficient to fix its identity as a field of knowledge. A stronger association with social theory for SLS would provide an external reference point for all the kinds of knowledge of law as a social phenomenon that SLS produces. This would not isolate it

1 See Chapter 5.

from the law school but bring something into that environment that cannot otherwise generally be found there.

Probably every research field needs theoretical reference points of its own; a tradition of theoretical resources to appeal to and draw upon to establish epistemological foundations for its projects. Jurisprudence, as presently conceived, cannot provide this. And it is no part of this book's argument that jurisprudence could somehow morph into social theory. Certainly, it can benefit by drawing on social theory and empirical social research, but that is for the enrichment of jurisprudence and juristic practice (a matter to discuss later in this chapter). SLS would lose much if its only general theoretical point of reference was in jurisprudence. However closely integrated (in teaching and research), SLS eventually becomes in the law school world, especially in Anglophone common law contexts, it needs – for its intellectual security and richness, and its inbuilt identity – a mooring, beyond juristic thought, in social theory.

Why not appeal to literary theory, economic theory, feminist theory (as a specific kind of social theory), psychoanalytic theory etc. to provide these benefits? Any of these are possibilities, and each has been advocated and built into important regions of SLS practice. But social theory is the theory of the social *at large* in all its aspects, the theory that attempts to address in general terms the whole realm of social relations and structures of social life. It promises much more than it has ever been able to deliver but what it does offer is (i) an always ambitious scope to make sense of the whole range of components of the social and their interaction – which law in its modern forms also addresses (Cotterrell 2006a, 1–3) and (ii) an equally ambitious comparative and historical vision – no other kind of theory attempts an overview of social existence as infinitely empirically varied and necessarily always in a process of change.

This goes along with another desideratum: a more deliberate and ubiquitous consciousness, in SLS as a field, of the historical traditions of its own development. Aspects of this were touched upon in Chapter 2. History and theory go together in many of the most productive and enlightening approaches to social science (just as they do in the most rewarding perspectives on jurisprudence). Chapter 5 suggested the need for greater awareness in SLS of the intellectual history of social research on law. It might be thought that empirical SLS research does not need any historical perspective, and often this is true. But sensitivity to theory as an epistemological basis of SLS probably should go along with some sensitivity to the history of social theory (and of jurisprudence). Perhaps it is somewhat tragic that the great figures who have built insightful social theories of law in the past are now often forgotten, their work little known and much neglected, or assumed to have little or nothing to say to today's world of socio-legal research. The ideas of the past have to be treated with caution, contextualised in their time and place, and discounted in the light of historical change that has transformed the socio-economic and political environment in which they were developed. But that does not mean that the great works of the past are never worth scouring for insights for the present.

Two closely related obstacles appear, like persistent ghosts, in the way of strengthening the theoretical foundations of SLS. They have been noted at various points in previous chapters. One might be called 'Allen's jibe'; the other, 'Kelsen's subversion'. When C. K. Allen (1964, 32) called Ehrlich's sociology of law 'megalomaniac jurisprudence' he was making the powerful, simple point that Ehrlich's failure to make clear the scope of his concept of law risked confusion about what legal studies could cover; yet Ehrlich freely used the term 'law' to encompass many kinds of regulation and normativity beyond familiar juristic ideas of law. Putting it differently: when must we stop talking about law as an idea and recognise that we are merely describing the many kinds of normative expectations and obligations that pervade social life (cf. Merry 1988)? Allen's jibe pointed to the obvious inadequacies of Ehrlich's effort to specify the nature of law in a way that would distinguish it from other social norms.

Closely related is Kelsen's subversion of the whole idea of an autonomous sociology of law. As noted earlier, he claimed that sociology of law would need to rely on juristic thought to provide it with a concept of law before it could begin to study *legal* phenomena (Kelsen 1945, 177). Jurisprudence would be needed to give sociology of law its subject-matter – to define the scope of the legal. Without this, sociology of law would become just general sociology, a study of the social at large. It would have to be left to the lawyers (or legal philosophers) to decide what, 'in essence', law is, as a distinctive part of the social. Sociology of law could only be parasitic on juristic theory. Kelsen's earliest version of this critique was his claim that Ehrlich failed to distinguish the normative from the factual ('ought' from 'is'). For many other critics, the matter could be summarised as a confusion of custom (the *factual* reality of habitual social practices) from law (the official *normative* specification of rights and duties).

It is surprising that this weak line of criticism of sociology of law has survived for so long. Ultimately it is a criticism specific to Ehrlich's failure to indicate a concept of 'living law' clearly enough to meet juristic needs. As Chapter 8 argued, Ehrlich really had no defence against this claim that his efforts to mark the 'legal' from the 'social' were inadequate *from the perspective of jurisprudence*. But, for sociology of law, this critique misses the point. Ehrlich was in the unusual situation (perhaps difficult for orthodox jurists to accept) of wishing to wear two entirely distinct intellectual hats – one of them, that of a jurist serving an imperial state legal system; the other that of a sociologist observing patterns of effective regulation and authority in social life.

For a sociologist it was unnecessary to offer a juristically operable concept of law; what was needed was a panorama of effective social regulation. The rules recognised juristically as law would be only a part of this picture, and those rules could be identified in the practices of lawyers. Thus, the problem of identifying law is either (i) to be solved pragmatically for the purposes of sociological research, or (ii) to be left to lawyers to solve for juristic purposes. As a sociologist Ehrlich could take the former approach; as a jurist he could take the latter.

Today, both Allen's jibe and Kelsen's subversion are easily countered. As already discussed in Chapter 2, sociology of law can create its own concept (or working model) of law for the purposes of research. Such a concept will typically pay careful attention to concepts of law developed in jurisprudence (because such concepts, if they influence legal practice, are social phenomena in themselves and so are within the range of social scientific concerns). But sociology of law – and SLS – need not be in any way confined by juristic ideas. Socio-legal inquiry can set its own agendas. Often, it will be appropriate to adopt lawyers' everyday understandings of what counts intellectually and normatively as law. But SLS, like sociology of law, does not always have to adopt such understandings. If appropriate to its inquiries, it can develop its own conceptions, taking account of but not confined by juristic understandings.

To the extent that SLS does become interested in developing its own concept of law for its own purposes, it moves closer to the theoretical outlooks of sociology of law, and towards a concern with social theory. Conversely, to the extent that it stays close to (or just adopts) lawyers' typical assumptions about the nature and scope of law, it maintains a strong potential relationship with juristic legal studies. SLS is a 'broad church' and can face in either direction. Its character varies depending on which of them it favours. One way to characterise SLS despite the immense diversity of the work it includes is to see it as an intellectual spectrum, one end of which lies in the juridical, the other in the realm of social theory.

The Identity of Jurisprudence

As regards jurisprudence, I suggested before that the key challenge it faces for the future is to be accepted as relevant – to be seen as having something truly important and timely to say to lawyers, and perhaps to citizens at large. Philip Selznick (1959, 117) thought that sociology's most important ideas eventually become part of general knowledge. It is hard to say that this absorption into general knowledge is common in jurisprudence. Its currently mainstream theoretical inquiries can seem ever more esoteric. The kinds of jurisprudence discussed in previous chapters can all be read as having something important to say about life as experienced by citizens and addressed in the practice of lawyers. But, in the contemporary Anglophone context of legal theory that appeals to philosophy for its intellectual and professional validation, methods, and criteria of interest, the question of relevance beyond an extremely small audience becomes an important one. Ronald Dworkin complained about this situation as regards contemporary positivist legal theory. But insofar as jurisprudence has been treated as synonymous with contemporary legal philosophy the question of relevance (or irrelevance) can be addressed to it generally.

A main reason for distinguishing jurisprudence from contemporary legal philosophy is to provide a basis for reasserting the relevance and importance of jurisprudence as a necessary resource of theory for jurists. As such it is theory to aid them in their practical work of shaping, interpreting, and critiquing existing law to affirm the idea of law in general as something socially valuable – recognisable as socially valuable by citizens, and respected as such by governments (Cotterrell 2018). While law can be studied from many points of view, the point of view of jurisprudence – that is, the not dispassionate but committed viewpoint of the jurist – is different from the viewpoint of philosophy, which has its own protocols, literary traditions, foci of debate, and topics of interest. Essentially jurisprudence must offer theory for legal practitioners and scholars pursuing juristic responsibilities for the wellbeing of the idea of law.

Any juristic idea of law is necessarily contested, but it is contested around the value-oriented needs of making law work well *in practice*, not around the demands of rigour in philosophical conceptualisation. Jurisprudence can draw from philosophy, as from any intellectual discipline or field of practice. But its aims are different from those pursued in professionalised philosophy. And a confusion of jurisprudence and contemporary philosophy of law enfeebles any claims of jurisprudence to relevance for the practice and experience of law.

This restates, in different words, ideas that appear earlier in this book, but it is necessary to emphasise them. However valuable contemporary legal philosophy may be, as philosophy, it holds out no prospect for collaboration with SLS nor, despite a longstanding common interest in theory, with sociology of law. Indeed, despite innovations in so-called naturalised jurisprudence (Leiter 2007), some calls to infuse sociological insight into philosophy (Collins 1988), and much interesting literature in the philosophy of science and of social science, the divide between sociology and contemporary Anglophone philosophy remains unbridgeable (Delanty 2023, 412). Nor is there any serious desire to bridge it.

We have noted in previous chapters that the term legal philosophy was often used in the past for studies that, in this book's terms, can be called jurisprudence, and that did make efforts to reach out to or make use of ideas from sociology. But philosophy, as understood by legal scholars then, may have appeared less professionally self-conscious and disciplinarily well-demarcated than it now is. In any case, the situation seems very different today. So, in considering prospects for the future development of jurisprudence, and for new interactions with SLS and sociology of law, it is necessary to set aside legal philosophy as generally understood today. That does not imply making any judgment about its worth as philosophy, a matter with which this book is not concerned. But this setting aside of something which has, for half a century and more, been seen as integral to jurisprudence is not easy to do.

The Hart-Phenomenon

The Hungarian scholar Csaba Varga (2005) described, as the 'Hart-Phenomenon', the remarkable impact of one book, published as an introductory student text, in shaping attitudes and approaches to legal theory in the Anglophone world and eventually far beyond it. H. L. A. Hart's *The Concept of Law* (1994) has had little presence in previous chapters, despite its great international influence in legal philosophy. My explanation (undoubtedly controversial) is that this famous book should *not* be treated primarily as a work of jurisprudence in the sense I have proposed – as an enterprise aimed solely at serving and promoting the juristic practice of law as a socially valuable idea.

In other writing, Hart and some of his leading followers discussed moral and political issues in ways that are undoubtedly juristically relevant. But *The Concept of Law* is not addressed to such issues. It presents itself as a dispassionate, uncommitted analysis of the subject of its title. It has no special commitment to law's wellbeing. Hart saw himself as a philosopher rather than a lawyer, his main expertise and allegiances were in academic philosophy, and he sometimes showed impatience with any idea of jurisprudence as other than an inquiry in philosophy. He found little worthwhile to discuss in sociology, and adopted an approach that, rooted in linguistic philosophy, tended to value conceptual analysis as an end in itself.

These assertions will not be documented here. They have often been made and elaborated elsewhere (e.g. Lacey 2005, 151, 160, 229; Campbell 1988; Varga 2005, 87; Simpson 2011, 34–55). And there is no intention in this book to engage in a fruitless polemic against inquiries in legal philosophy that should be assessed on their own terms. Properly understood, as philosophy rather than jurisprudence, these inquiries exist in an intellectual field beyond the subject-matter of this book. So, the only direct significance here of the 'Hart-phenomenon' is its impact on future possibilities for productive relations between jurisprudence and SLS.

If there is such an impact it arises mainly from the typical assumption in much contemporary legal philosophy of the overriding value of seeking *essential* meanings of legal concepts; that is, meanings that can be held to be valid irrespective of any rooting of conceptual inquiries in particular empirically identified contexts. Joseph Raz claimed that legal philosophy seeks the 'essential' as regards the nature of law, whereas sociology of law – as sociology – focuses on the historically and locally contingent; that is, on what attributes law possesses in specific social contexts.[2] But this can be a misleading distinction. In fact,

2 See Chapter 5, p. 69.

social theory always seeks to generalise as far as possible beyond the narrowly local. It aims for wide applicability. But it is true that it can never aspire to timelessness or universality. It must always be rooted in empirical context, however wide its intended reach. Insofar as social theory reflects a sociological outlook it assumes the idea of comparative and historical social *variation* (rather than any idea of the essential, the timeless, or the universal) (Cotterrell and Selznick 2004, 296).

Irrespective of whether a search for essential meaning of concepts is philosophically valuable – a matter not relevant for debate here – jurisprudence has to address the concerns of jurists working in particular legal systems, social environments, and political regimes, and conditions. Seeking the wellbeing of the idea of law in the circumstances of legal practice, jurisprudence is necessarily concerned with the contingent and variable in law. Its task is to produce theoretical knowledge relevant to local circumstances, even though it can be hoped that such knowledge may find relevance and applicability beyond the contexts in which its ideas were originally produced. So, Chapter 10 illustrated conditions in which theory clearly rooted in local contexts is sometimes also able to transcend them.

Raz' comment may entail an assumption that legal theory can only address the essential, rather than the contingent. If so, it fails to recognise that a focus on social variation does not prevent the production of insightful theories of law within social theory. But it is correct to point to a clear contrast in outlook between philosophical essentialism and sociologically oriented theories of law. These theories, like those in jurisprudence, are always to be seen as grounded in a cultural and historical context, however far reaching their generalisations claim to be.

Hart admitted to 'an excessive distrust' of sociology (Lacey 2005, 162), but it is possible, even likely, that some of Weber's sociological ideas influenced him (Ibid, 230–1) as they certainly influenced philosophical writings that he linked to some of his ideas (Winch 1958, 45–50, 111–20; cf. Hart 1994, 289). To his later regret, Hart (1994, vi) called *The Concept of Law* an essay in descriptive sociology. In doing so he revealed a not untypical view in philosophy, that statements about the social can be labelled 'sociological' without any reference to sociology (cf. Lacey 2005, 229). Yet Hart thought that Roscoe Pound's explicit juristic appeals to sociological ideas showed 'inexcusable analytical imprecision' (Ibid, 181).

The intellectual environment in which Hart's legal philosophy existed seemed to create an unbridgeable gulf separating it from the outlooks of social science. In such an environment, his book, far more philosophically acute than the Anglophone jurisprudence preceding it, led many thoughtful legal scholars to his accessible kind of philosophy when they sought theoretical insight, rather than to the unmediated complexities of social theory. Requiring no prior knowledge of philosophy on the part of the reader

The Concept of Law promised an attractive theoretical sophistication in legal studies, but its long-term effect was to drive jurisprudence into a philosophical backwater, deterring juristic engagement with contingent and timely socio-legal problems with which the most important kinds of social theory wrestled.

Changed Conditions

More than half a century since *The Concept of Law* was first published, conditions are different. In principle, Anglophone jurisprudence has far more resources to draw on than it did then. Much literature now addresses moral and political philosophical issues related to law. But mainstream jurisprudence is still dominated by contemporary legal philosophy, especially in its positivist forms. These approaches struggle to make adequate intellectual space for practical moral and political concerns which should be central to jurisprudence. Thus, the divide between mainstream jurisprudence and social science is maintained.

Some ways in which circumstances have changed in recent decades, both for jurisprudence and for social scientific studies of law, were signalled in Chapter 12. But these were expressed mainly in terms of juxtaposition and comparison of intellectual fields (rather than of their communication or intersections). However, taking a long (historically informed) view and projecting that view towards the future, it is possible to see several ways in which these fields intersect.

For example, it is possible to learn from a long tradition of jurisprudence borrowing from social science or even contributing to social theory as an extension of its inquiries. Previous chapters have referred to: (i) Duguit, borrowing from Durkheim's sociology to inform a theory of public law; (ii) Hauriou, creating his own social theory of the institution to explore the bases of jurisprudence in the characteristics of social organisation; (iii) Ehrlich, driven to build a homespun sociology in order to try to make state law relevant to its conditions of existence; (iv) Pound, using a sociological idea of social control to frame a theory of law's functions; and (v) Llewellyn devising his 'law-jobs' theory to extend realist understanding of law in action. Numerous other examples could be given.

There has been less intellectual traffic the other way. It seems that sociology has rarely borrowed directly from jurisprudence in modern times. In general, social theory has kept its aims clearly separated from those of jurists. For example, despite the great interest in law which Weber (1968) and Niklas Luhmann (2004) showed, both firmly insisted on separating social inquiry, as dispassionate science, from juristic analysis. Philip Selznick (1961) is a rare exception, explicitly aligning his sociology in its later phases with jurisprudence. And Donald Black, perhaps uniquely in modern times, claimed (at least rhetorically) that sociology might replace juristic approaches, at least in the courtroom.[3]

In future, there is no reason why jurists cannot use social scientific insights for their own purposes as they have done in the past. The idea of a sociological jurisprudence certainly does not need to be confined to a memory of Roscoe Pound's ideas. There is much evidence that the idea of such a jurisprudence is alive and well, and being realised, and many possibilities for the enriching of jurisprudential thought through social science exist (Cotterrell 2018, 2020; Teubner 2011; Fischman 2013). There is no reason to deny the fact-value dichotomy (the need to distinguish observational studies of social phenomena from normative inquiries about law and morality) which so much concerned Kelsen (1945). Empirical social inquiry can sometimes show matters about which normative judgments have to be made. It can also reveal conditions that determine whether and when normative issues seem meaningful and pertinent. And it can study the effects (or lack of effects) of normative decisions in practice. In changing socio-economic and political circumstances all these contributions of social research bearing on normative issues assume ever-increasing, fundamental importance. Sociological inquiry and normative evaluation are distinct. But the former can inform the latter in many ways.

One can ask what developments are currently occurring to promote actively the interaction of juristic theory and SLS, to make this seem not merely desirable but imperative. Only a few pointers will be noted here, all relating to themes widely discussed in literature elsewhere. In concluding this book, three such themes are chosen from many other indications of change. They suggest priorities likely to seem more urgent over time and that indicate an obvious need for juristic thought and social theory to communicate with each other. Lawyers and SLS scholars may need to note, more widely, concerns that now occupy social theorists. Equally, social scientists may need to recognise, more clearly, law's centrality in shaping aspects of socio-economic stability and change, and the institutional frameworks of politics.

Three Themes for the Present and Future

The Differentiation of the Social

The first of these themes was discussed in some of its aspects extensively in earlier chapters. This is the theme of *increased sensitivity to the differentiation of the social*. In Chapters 3 and 4 this was considered in terms of relations of law and culture. More generally, what is entailed is a growing recognition of the immense complexity and diversity of the human populations that typically

3 See Chapter 11, pp. 170–1.

make up modern Western societies. In juristic thought a 'jurisprudence of difference' has come into being, inspired by different social constituencies having different stakes in law and pushing their priorities and experiences forward to bring about legal change. As representatives of these constituencies have entered academia and legal practice, jurisprudence – at least beyond its traditional mainstream – has had to recognise that law and legal ideas are far from uniform in meaning and significance across society at large.

Various movements have carried diversity – often resisted but ultimately inevitable – into juristic thought. Until relatively recently these movements could have been treated as parallel but distinct from each other: feminism, critical race theory, LGBTQ+ rights campaigning, disability rights advocacy, the claims of organised religious constituencies, and so on. But now, these movements must be seen as linked symptoms of what has become an ever-widening political recognition of the vast complexity (perhaps fragmentation) of the social – a kind of centrifugal force of perceived difference, often based in historical and ongoing injustices.

If, in juristic thought, modern law is typically assumed to provide an overall, basic normative structure for political society governed by state law, how can jurisprudence adequately manage the diversity of contemporary society within the image of a single, integrated legal system? If jurisprudence is, in some of its fundamental aspects, concerned with the idea of law as a structure of ultimate legal values, the value most pertinent here is justice. If justice is popularly understood as fairness in social relations, an appropriate balance, how is fair balancing to be achieved when the claims and interests of groups become so diverse, and communal networks are differentiated in ways that the state may struggle even to comprehend?

Social science cannot solve this juristic problem. But SLS examines many aspects of the differentiation of the social that bear on legal processes. And social theory can give a wider, overall view of the extent and character of this differentiation, especially through its perspectives on power in society and the integration of the social, as considered in the previous chapter. The abstractions of social theory need to be tempered by attention to particularities – that is, the detail of social relations and interactions. And these particularities are the everyday concern of judicial decision-making and case-law. Social theory might learn from legal experience – law's 'method of detail' – in regulating social relations. And jurisprudence can learn from the panoramas of social change that social theory seeks to reveal. SLS, here as elsewhere, can stand between jurisprudence and social theory, contributing to and drawing from both.

But there is one aspect of the differentiation of the social – indeed, its fragmentation – that is too rarely discussed in jurisprudence and in most projects of socio-legal inquiry. This is the seemingly ever-growing, vast divide in many Western societies between 'haves' and 'have-nots' – the very rich and the economically marginalised who are 'just getting by' or failing to do so and wracked by fear of destitution. There is no prominent organised constituency permanently representing the poor, the homeless, and the destitute in the academic debates of the jurisprudence of difference. The economic differentiation of the social is a largely forgotten item missing from the agenda of interaction between jurisprudence and social science.

Law and State

A second theme has also been signalled in previous chapters. It is that of the *radical rethinking of the modern relationship between law and state*. It might also be called the theme of the transnational. Aspects of this rethinking are (i) the expansion of public international law into many new fields, (ii) the ambition of this law increasingly to address or influence private actors (individuals and corporations), and (iii) the growth of transnational law; that is, law regulating socio-economic relations involving private actors that cross nation state borders (Cotterrell 2018, 103–55). All of this has been associated with the political and socio-economic processes that have been labelled globalisation (Hendry 2021).

It might seem, however, that the age of globalisation has quickly passed. The reassertion of nationalism – sometimes associated with the intensification of populist movements to 'take back control' of government and country, and to reassert national legal autonomy in the face of transnational pressures – has become a dominant fashion in contemporary politics in many countries.[4] Has the advance of transnational law, like that of globalisation, come to an end? The question is important because, if the answer is yes, perhaps the established modern relation of law and state has not changed fundamentally. Jurists, habitually focused on state law as the only ultimately significant law (international law often being seen as a consensually authorised extension of the law of states), might breathe a sigh of relief that the complexities of the location of transnational authority and the legal character of transnational law need not concern them.

Yet, as long as the maintenance of international peace is a priority, the 'transnational' is unlikely to atrophy or cease to expand its legal reach. Like international law governing the relations of states, transnational law governing cross-border dealings of private actors has expanded mainly for economic reasons, to promote and facilitate trade. As such, it is a legal means of transnationally promoting instrumental relations of community. Among the four types of community discussed earlier in this book,[5] instrumental (primarily

4 See Chapter 9, pp. 141–3.
5 See Chapters 1 and 3.

economic) community is generally the weakest, but law protecting it can be relatively strong (Cotterrell 2008, ch2; 2006a, 121–6). So, municipal contract and commercial law are typically well-defined, extensively developed and widely used. The same may be true of international economic law, which may be the most practically effective and widely operative kind of international law today. Correspondingly, the most extensively developed transnational law serves economic (trade, investment, financial) purposes. So, criticism of transnational law often associates its development with the economic interests of global commercial and financial elites, unconnected with and unresponsive to the interests of ordinary citizens in the political societies affected by transnationalism.

However, the alternative to effective transnational law and international economic law is likely to be unrestrained, globally anarchic competition between states, and – at the extreme – the risk of war between them. If jurisprudence is concerned to promote and protect an idea of law in terms of ultimate values of justice, security, and solidarity, as I have proposed,[6] its focus cannot only be on law within the jurist's own political society (Taekema 2019, 513–19). The juristic value that seems most central here is solidarity – across and between transnational and international populations. Juristic concerns extend transnationally, but it is not easy to address these in practice. Among the practical challenges for transnational jurists are those of persuasively identifying sources of legal authority beyond the nation state, working out how to negotiate competing authority claims arising from different sources, and assessing the kinds of regulation (public and private; state and non-state; international and national) that can, in certain contexts and for certain purposes, be treated juristically as law.

This is a formidable theoretical and practical agenda. But it is possible that ultimately world peace could depend on accepting and progressing it partly through transnational juristic collaboration. Here, jurisprudence needs the aid of SLS and social theory. What kinds of entities can create regulation that jurists might need to recognise in practice as law? How is law produced in communal networks, which may exist within nation state political societies or may be transnational (for example of networks of traders, bankers, industrial producers, or religious believers)? In what circumstances is regulation that operates transnationally accepted as legitimate?

Ultimately these are not philosophical but empirical questions: about the character and quality of social organisation, the structuring of communal networks, the dispositions and motivations of network members, and the operation of power in and between networks. They are questions for nation states as communal networks, and for communal networks within and beyond nation

6 See Chapter 6, pp. 82–3, 85; and see Cotterrell 2018, ch3.

states. It is likely that transnational jurisprudence in future will depend increasingly on social science to suggest answers to such questions about the conditions under which legal regulation becomes possible, is created, and operates. SLS should have a major role to play in its bridging capacity. And the extension of legal regulation in communal networks beyond state territorial jurisdiction may give new incentives for social theory to rethink the idea of the social in new contexts.

Society and Nature

The third and final theme to be noted here may be the most important. But it is less well-developed than the previous two in both jurisprudence and SLS; in sociology, too, it lacks the prominence it deserves (Koehrsen et al. 2020). It is the theme of *evolving relations between society and nature.* Juristically, it seems to concern most centrally the value of security, among the three ultimate juristic values that I have earlier derived from Radbruch's thought.[7] The threat of ecological catastrophe which seems ever more imminent is a threat to all human security. Radbruch's value of security was concerned with security through law, as in the rule of law, and certainty and predictability in interpreting and applying law. But dramatic and violent climate change creating increasingly hostile and precarious environments for human existence, threatens all security in the most fundamental way. It encourages massive movements of population, the inundation of cities, coasts and small island nations, the desertification of agricultural land, and the vast destruction of human and wildlife habitats.

Environmental law, both municipal and international, is aimed at protecting nature from human depredation or repairing human damage to nature. But vastly important as it is, it is just one juristic specialisation, sometimes marginalised (Tarlock 2004, 217), and usually only one optional subject in the law school curriculum (Bouwer et al. 2023). It aims to serve human interests by protecting nature in a way compatible with those interests. So, it typically gives rights for humans to assert to secure their environment of co-existence. But human interests are variable and their relation to nature (as natural resources) can be different for different populations. While humans may squabble and disagree about access to natural resources, nature increasingly burns and drowns.

However, some contemporary ecological thinking displaces the centre of attention from humanity to nature itself; to animals, mountains, lakes and rivers; or to humanity as part of nature, not in confrontation with it. Should rivers, lakes, and mountains have rights? In various contexts this attribution of rights to inanimate phenomena has occurred. Through legally appointed

7 See also the discussion of Lundstedt's view of security in Chapter 10.

human guardians, rivers can litigate, asserting claims to their own preservation and security. Such an approach is surely no panacea. As in orthodox environmental law, nature gains protection only through human agents (O'Donnell 2018), and complex political, religious, and other issues can arise in asserting rights of nature (Brunet 2023). But where inanimate nature appears to be given enforceable legal rights, it is put in the centre of legal attention as an actor, a person in law, and not relegated to being an object of legal attention (or inattention).

This may be the echo in contemporary juristic thought of very old, premodern ideas of nature; ideas of humanity as a part of nature (and not necessarily possessing claims to prosper that are more urgent and fundamental than the claims of nature to survive); ideas that recognise that human survival is impossible unless nature as a whole survives. For jurisprudence, it implies a possible displacement of a deep cultural assumption of modern law: that of the inevitable centrality of individual human beings as the focus of all legal thought.

Recognising rights of nature in law may be a last chance to shift juristic thought away from the relentless and reckless pursuit of human interests, towards a stewardship of the earth that ought to be a central focus of jurisprudence's idea of law. Juristic thought, SLS, and social theory can face in the same direction on this matter. Social theory, by incorporating ecological thought about the conditions of sustainable social life, and SLS with its established concern with the effectiveness of environmental law have much to offer. For jurisprudence, a key issue is how to reconcile a focus on individual rights, which has properly evolved into an ever-wider concern for human rights, with new-old ideas about the scope of legal personhood; ideas, rooted in past centuries and non-Western contexts, that might be harnessed today to help to reset legally, at the eleventh hour, humanity's relationship to the natural world.[8]

8 The three themes considered in the last part of this chapter are further elaborated and differently documented in Cotterrell 2023b.

REFERENCES

Aasen, H. S., Gloppen, S., Magnussen, A.-M. and Nilssen, E. eds. (2014), *Juridification and Social Citizenship in the Welfare State*. Cheltenham: Edward Elgar.

Agamben, G. (1998), *Homo Sacer: Sovereign Power and Bare Life*, transl. D. Heller-Roazen. Stanford: Stanford University Press.

———. (2005), *State of Exception*, transl. K. Attell. Chicago: University of Chicago Press.

Ahmed, F. and Krayem, G. (2021), *Understanding Sharia Processes: Women's Experiences of Family Disputes*. Oxford: Hart.

Ailon, G. (2019), '"No One To Trust": The Cultural Embedding of Atomism in Financial Markets', 70 *British Journal of Sociology* 927–47.

Alexander, J. C. (1992), 'Shaky Foundations: The Presuppositions and Internal Contradictions of James Coleman's *Foundations of Social Theory*', 21 *Theory and Society* 203–17.

———. (2006), *The Civil Sphere*. New York: Oxford University Press.

Allen, C. K. (1964), *Law in the Making*, 7th ed. Oxford: Oxford University Press.

Andrini, S. and Arnaud, A.-J. ed. (1995), *Jean Carbonnier, Renato Treves et la sociologie du droit: Archéologie d'un discipline*. Paris: L.G.D.J.

Arnaud, A.-J. (1995), 'Legal Pluralism and the Building of Europe', in H. Petersen and H. Zahle eds, *Legal Polycentricity: Consequences of Pluralism in Law*, pp. 149–69. Aldershot: Dartmouth.

Aron, R. (1965), *Main Currents of Sociological Thought*, vol. 1, transl. R. Howard and H. Weaver. London: Weidenfeld and Nicolson.

Arvind, T. T. (2012), 'Beyond "Right" and "Duty": Lundstedt's Theory of Obligations', in D. Nolan and A. Robertson eds, *Rights and Private Law*, pp. 151–81. Oxford: Hart.

———. (2013), 'Vilhelm Lundstedt and the Social Function of Legislation', 1 *Theory and Practice of Legislation* 33–57.

Ashiagbor, D., Kotiswaran, P. and Perry-Kessaris, A. eds. (2013), *Towards an Economic Sociology of Law*. Oxford: Wiley-Blackwell.

Audren, F. and Milet, M. (2008), 'Préface: Maurice Hauriou Sociologue: Entre Sociologie Catholique et Physique Sociale', in M. Hauriou, *Écrits sociologiques*, pp. v–lvii. Paris: Dalloz.

Austin, J. (1885), *Lectures on Jurisprudence*, 5th ed. Clark, NJ: Lawbook Exchange reprint, 2005.

Awrey, D., Blair, W. and Kershaw, D. (2013), 'Between Law and Markets: Is There a Role for Culture and Ethics in Financial Regulation?', 38 *Delaware Journal of Corporate Law* 191–245.

Babb, H. W. (1937), 'Petrazhitskii: Science of Legal Policy and Theory of Law', 17 *Boston University Law Review* 793–829.

———. (1938), 'Petrazhitskii: Theory of Law', 18 *Boston University Law Review* 511–78.

Bader, V. (2009), 'Legal Pluralism and Differentiated Morality: Shari'a in Ontario?', in R. Grillo et al. eds, *Legal Practice and Cultural Diversity*, pp. 49–72. Abingdon: Routledge.

Banakar, R. (1998), 'The Identity Crisis of a "Stepchild": Reflections on the Paradigmatic Deficiencies of Sociology of Law', 21(81) *Retfaerd* 3–21.

———. (2002), 'Sociological Jurisprudence', in R. Banakar and M. Travers eds, *An Introduction to Law and Social Theory*, 1st ed, 33–49. Oxford: Hart.

———. (2003), *Merging Law and Sociology: Beyond the Dichotomies in Socio-Legal Research*. Glienicke, Berlin: Galda + Wilch Verlag.

———. (2016), 'Law, Policy and Social Control amidst Flux', in K. Dahlstrand ed, *Festskrift till Karsten Åstrom*, pp. 47–74. Lund: Jurist förlaget I Lund.

Banakas, E. (2002), 'The Contribution of Comparative Law to the Harmonization of European Private Law', in A. Harding and E. Örücü eds, *Comparative Law in the 21st Century*, pp. 179–91. The Hague: Kluwer.

Bano, S. (2012), *Muslim Women and Shari'ah Councils: Transcending the Boundaries of Community and Law*. London: Palgrave Macmillan.

Barber, N. W. (2006), 'Legal Pluralism and the European Union', 12 *European Law Journal* 306–29.

Barberis, M. (2013), 'Santi Romano, Neoinstitutionalism and Legal Pluralism', 21 *National Italian American Bar Association Law Journal* 27–35.

Bartelson, J. (2006), 'The Concept of Sovereignty Revisited', 17 *European Journal of International Law* 463–74.

Bauman, Z. (1989), *Modernity and the Holocaust*. Cambridge: Polity.

———. (2002), *Society Under Siege*. Cambridge: Polity.

Beck, U. and Sznaider, N. (2006), 'Unpacking Cosmopolitanism for the Social Sciences: A Research Agenda', 57 *British Journal of Sociology* 1–22.

Becker, H. S. (1967), 'Whose Side Are We On?', 14 *Social Problems* 239–47.

Benewick, R. (1992), 'Gaetano Mosca 1858–1941', in R. Benewick and P. Green eds, *Routledge Dictionary of Twentieth Century Thinkers*, pp. 165–6. London: Routledge.

Bentley, A. F. (1908), *The Process of Government: A Study of Social Pressures*. New Brunswick, NJ: Transaction reprint, 1995.

Berman, P. S. (2002), 'The Globalization of Jurisdiction', 151 *University of Pennsylvania Law Review* 311–546.

———. (2012), *Global Legal Pluralism: A Jurisprudence of Law beyond Borders*. New York: Cambridge University Press.

Berolzheimer, F. (1912), *The World's Legal Philosophies*, transl. R. S. Jastrow. Clark, NJ: Lawbook Exchange reprint, 2004.

Bertilsson, T. M. (2006), 'On the Accumulation of Cosmopolitan Capital: A Comment on Bourdieu and Law', 29(3) *Retfaerd* 108–15.

Besson, S. (2009), 'The Authority of International Law: Lifting the State Veil', 31 *Sydney Law Review* 343–80.

Bjarup, J. (2005), 'The Philosophy of Scandinavian Legal Realism', 18 *Ratio Juris* 1–15.

Black, D. (1976), *The Behavior of Law*. New York: Academic Press.

———. (1989), *Sociological Justice*. New York: Oxford University Press.

Blalock, C. (2014), 'Neoliberalism and the Crisis of Legal Theory', 77 *Law and Contemporary Problems* 71–104.

Bourdieu, P. (1987), 'The Force of Law: Toward a Sociology of the Juridical Field', 38 *Hastings Law Journal* 814–53.

Bouwer, K. et al. (2023), 'Climate Change isn't Optional': Climate Change in the Core Law Curriculum', 43(2) *Legal Studies* 240–58.

Bowen, J. R. (2016), *On British Islam: Religion, Law, and Everyday Practice in Shari'a Councils*. Princeton: Princeton University Press.

Bredemeier, H. C. (1962), 'Law as an Integrative Mechanism', in W. M. Evan ed, *Law and Sociology: Exploratory Essays*, pp. 73–88. New York: Free Press.

Broderick, A. ed. (1970), *The French Institutionalists: Maurice Hauriou; Georges Renard; Joseph T. Delos*, transl. M. Welling. Cambridge, MA: Harvard University Press.

Brown, J. (2008), 'Williams Tries to Defuse Row over Sharia Law but Refuses to Apologise', *The Independent*, February 12th. www.independent.co.uk/news/uk/home-news/williams-tries-to-defuse-row-over-sharia-law-but-refuses-to-apologise-781009.html

Brubaker, R. (1984), *The Limits of Rationality: An Essay on the Social and Moral Thought of Max Weber*. London: Allen & Unwin.

Brunet, P. (2023), 'Rights of Nature and New Communities: Toward an Animist Legal Ontology?', in W. Gephart and D. Witte eds, *Communities and the(ir) Law*, pp. 279–92. Frankfurt am Main: Vittorio Klostermann.

Calliess, G.-P. and Zumbansen, P. (2010), *Rough Consensus and Running Code: A Theory of Transnational Private Law*. Oxford: Hart.

Campbell, A. H. (1958), 'Book Review', 21 *Modern Law Review* 566–9.

Campbell, C. M. (1988), 'The Career of the Concept', in P. Leith and P. Ingram eds, *The Jurisprudence of Orthodoxy: Queen's University Essays on H. L. A. Hart*, pp. 1–25. London: Routledge.

Caranta, R. (2009), 'The Fall from Fundamentalism in Italian Administrative Law', in M. Ruffert ed, *The Public-private Law Divide: Potential for Transformation?*, pp. 99–121. London: British Institute of International and Comparative Law.

Carbonnier, J. (2001), *Flexible droit: Pour une sociologie du droit sans rigueur*, 10th ed. Paris: L.G.D.J.

Cardozo, B. N. (1921), *The Nature of the Judicial Process*. New Haven: Yale University Press.

Cassese, A. (1999), 'A Follow-Up: Forcible Humanitarian Countermeasures and *Opinio Necessitatis*', 10 *European Journal of International Law* 791–9.

Chappe, R., Semmler, W. and Nell, E. (2013), 'The U.S. Financial Culture of Risk', 20 *Constellations* 422–41.

Chernilo, D. (2013), *The Natural Law Foundations of Modern Social Theory: A Quest for Universalism*. Cambridge: Cambridge University Press.
Citrin, J. and Sides, J. (2008), 'Immigration and the Imagined Community in Europe and the United States', 56 *Political Studies* 33–56.
Cole, W. M. (2012), 'A Civil Religion for World Society: The Direct and Diffuse Effects of Human Rights Treaties, 1981–2007', 27 *Sociological Forum* 937–60.
Coleman, J. L. (2002), 'Methodology', in J. Coleman and S. Shapiro eds, *Oxford Handbook of Jurisprudence and Philosophy of Law*, pp. 311–51. Oxford: Oxford University Press.
Coleman, J. S. (1990), *Foundations of Social Theory*. Cambridge, MA: Harvard University Press.
———. (1992), 'The Problematics of Social Theory: Four Reviews of *Foundations of Social Theory*', 21 *Theory and Society* 263–83.
Collins, R. (1988), 'For a Sociological Philosophy', 17 *Theory and Society* 669–702.
Conley, J. M. and O'Barr, W. M. (2002), 'Back to the Trobriands: The Enduring Influence of Malinowski's *Crime and Custom in Savage Society*', 27 *Law & Social Inquiry* 847–74.
Conte, E. (2023), 'Legal Pluralism from History to Theory and Back: Otto von Gierke, Santi Romano, and Francesco Calasso on Medieval Institutions', *Law and History Review* 1–12.
Cotterrell, R. (1995), *Law's Community: Legal Theory in Sociological Perspective*. Oxford: Oxford University Press.
———. (1997), 'Establishing Sociology of Law in Sweden', 23 *Socio-Legal Newsletter* 4.
———. (1999), *Émile Durkheim: Law in a Moral Domain*. Stanford: Stanford University Press.
———. (2003), *The Politics of Jurisprudence: A Critical Introduction to Legal Philosophy*, 2nd ed. Oxford: Oxford University Press.
———. (2006a), *Law, Culture and Society: Legal Ideas in the Mirror of Social Theory*. Abingdon: Routledge.
———. (2006b) 'Per Stjernquist 1912–2005', 48 *Socio-Legal Newsletter* 9.
———. (2008), *Living Law: Studies in Legal and Social Theory*. Abingdon: Routledge.
———. (2009), 'Spectres of Transnationalism: Changing Terrains of Sociology of Law', 36 *Journal of Law & Society* 481–500.
———. (2011), 'Ant's Eye-view of Law', 11 *Journal of Classical Sociology* 506–10.
———. (2012) 'Comparative Sociology of Law', in D. Clark ed, *Comparative Law and Society*, pp. 39–60. Cheltenham: Edward Elgar.
———. (2013), 'Northern Lights: From Swedish Realism to Sociology of Law', 40 *Journal of Law and Society* 657–69.
———. (2018), *Sociological Jurisprudence: Juristic Thought and Social Inquiry*. Abingdon: Routledge.
———. (2019), 'Access to Justice, Moral Distance and Changing Demands on Law', 36 *Windsor Yearbook of Access to Justice* 193–209.
———. (2020), 'Sociological Jurisprudence: Tradition and Prospects', in J. Přibáň ed, *Research Handbook of the Sociology of Law*, pp. 19–30. Cheltenham: Edward Elgar.
———. (2021), 'Selznick's Concepts of Culture and Community', in P. van Seters ed, *The Anthem Companion to Philip Selznick*, pp. 149–67. London: Anthem Press.
———. (2022), 'Law and Justice in Durkheim's Sociology', in G. Fitzi and N. Marcucci eds, *Anthem Companion to Émile Durkheim*, pp. 131–53. London: Anthem Press.

———. (2023a), 'Law and Community in Multicultural Society', in W. Gephart and D. Witte eds, *Communities and the(ir) Law*, pp. 65–84. Frankfurt am Main: Vittorio Klostermann.

———. (2023b) 'A Socio-Legal Quest: From Jurisprudence to Sociology of Law and Back Again', 50 *Journal of Law and Society* 3–16.

———. and Selznick, P. (2004), 'Selznick Interviewed', 31 *Journal of Law and Society* 291–317.

Crenshaw, K. (1989), 'Demarginalizing the Intersection of Race and Sex: A Black Feminist Critique of Antidiscrimination Doctrine, Feminist Theory and Antiracist Politics', *University of Chicago Legal Forum* 138–67.

Croce, M. (2017), 'Afterword', in S. Romano, *The Legal Order*, pp. 111–28. Abingdon: Routledge.

———. (2021), 'Juridification as Politics: An Institutional View', 47 *Philosophy & Social Criticism* 1025–42.

Culver, K. C. and Giudici, M. (2010), *Legality's Borders: An Essay in General Jurisprudence*. New York: Oxford University Press.

Curran, V. G. (1998), 'Cultural Immersion, Difference and Categories in US Comparative Law', 46 *American Journal of Comparative Law* 43–92.

Dalberg-Larsen, J. (2000), *The Unity of Law: An Illusion? On Legal Pluralism in Theory and Practice*. Berlin: Galda & Wilch.

Deegan, M. J. (1988), *Jane Addams and the Men of the Chicago School, 1892–1918*. London: Routledge reprint, 2017.

Deflem, M. (2008), *Sociology of Law: Visions of a Scholarly Tradition*. Cambridge: Cambridge University Press.

———. (2013), 'The Legal Theory of Jürgen Habermas: Between the Philosophy and the Sociology of Law', in R. Banakar and M. Travers eds, *Law and Social Theory*, pp. 75–90. Oxford: Hart.

Del Vecchio, G. (1953), *Philosophy of Law*, transl. T. O. Martin. Washington, DC: Catholic University of America Press.

Delanty, G. (2023), 'Social Theory: Legacies and Future Directions – An Interview (by D. Chernilo and A. Mascareño)', 26 *European Journal of Social Theory* 408–23.

Di Robilant, A. (2006), 'Genealogies of Soft Law', 54 *American Journal of Comparative Law* 499–554.

Djelic, M.-L. and Quack, S. eds. (2010), *Transnational Communities: Shaping Global Economic Governance*. Cambridge: Cambridge University Press.

Doo, L.-W. (1973), 'Dispute Settlement in Chinese-American Communities', 21 *American Journal of Comparative Law* 627–56.

Duguit, L. (1921a), 'Social Solidarity', in A. Fouillée, J. Charmont, L. Duguit and R. Demogue, *Modern French Legal Philosophy*, transl. J. P. Chamberlain and E. F. Scott, pp. 258–84. Boston: Boston Book Co.

———. (1921b), *Law in the Modern State*, transl. F. and H. J. Laski. London: Allen & Unwin.

Dunn, F. S. (1926), 'Book Review', 26 *Columbia Law Review* 1050–1.

Durkheim, É. (1957), *Professional Ethics and Civic Morals*, transl. C. Brookfield. London: Routledge & Kegan Paul.

———. (1984), *The Division of Labour in Society*, transl. W. D. Halls. London: Macmillan.

Dworkin, R. M. (1986), *Law's Empire*. Oxford: Hart reprint, 1998.

———. (2006), *Justice in Robes*. Cambridge, MA: Harvard University Press.

Edelman, L. B. and Stryker, R. (2005), 'A Sociological Approach to Law and the Economy', in N. J. Smelser and R. Swedberg eds, *Handbook of Economic Sociology*, 2nd ed, pp. 527–51. Princeton: Princeton University Press.

Ehrlich, E. (1917a), 'Judicial Freedom of Decision: Its Principles and Objects', in J. H. Wigmore et al. eds, *Science of Legal Method: Select Essays by Various Authors*, transl. E. Bruncken and L. B. Register, pp. 47–84. Boston: Boston Book Co.

———. (1917b), *The National Problems in Austria*. The Hague: M. Nijhoff.

———. (1936), *Fundamental Principles of the Sociology of Law*, transl. W. L. Moll. New Brunswick: Transaction reprint, 2002.

Eisenberg, T. (2011), 'The Origins, Nature, and Promise of Empirical Legal Studies and a Response to Concerns', *University of Illinois Law Review* 1713–38.

Elliott, A. and Turner, B. S. eds. (2001), *Profiles in Contemporary Social Theory*. London: Sage.

Evald, J. (2014), *Alf Ross: A Life*. Copenhagen: DJØF.

Febbrajo, A. and Harste, G. eds. (2013), *Law and Intersystemic Communication: Understanding 'Structural Coupling'*. London: Routledge.

Féron, H. (2014), 'Human Rights and Faith: A "World-Wide Secular Religion"?', 7 *Ethics & Global Politics* 181–200.

Ferrari, A. and Pastorelli, S. eds. (2013), *The Burqa Affair Across Europe: Between Public and Private Space*. Abingdon: Routledge.

Ferrari, V. ed. (1990), *Developing Sociology of Law: A World-Wide Documentary Enquiry*. Milano: Giuffrè.

Fillafer, F. L. (2022), 'Imperial Diversity, Fractured Sovereignty, and Legal Universals: Hans Kelsen and Eugen Ehrlich in their Habsburg Context', 19 *Modern Intellectual History* 421–43.

Finkin, M. W. (2010), 'Some Further Thoughts on the Usefulness of Comparativism in the Law of Employee Privacy', 14 *Employee Rights & Employment Policy Journal* 11–53.

Fioravanti, M. (2016), 'L'ordinamento giuridico', in S. Dauchy et al. eds, *The Formation and Transmission of Western Legal Culture: 150 Books that Made the Law in the Age of Printing*, pp. 442–4. Cham: Springer.

Fischman, J. B. (2013), 'Reuniting "Is" and "Ought" in Empirical Legal Scholarship', 162 *University of Pennsylvania Law Review* 117–68.

Fittipaldi, E. (2012), *Everyday Legal Ontology: A Psychological and Linguistic Investigation within the Framework of Leon Petrażycki's Theory of Law*. Milano: Edizioni Universitarie di Lettere Economia Diritto.

———. and Treviño, J. eds. (2023), *Leon Petrażycki: Law, Emotions, Society*. London: Routledge.

Foblets, M. C. and Renteln, A. D. eds. (2009), *Multicultural Jurisprudence: Comparative Perspectives on the Cultural Defence*. Oxford: Hart.

Fontanelli, F. (2011), 'Santi Romano and *L'ordinamento giuridico*: The Relevance of a Forgotten Masterpiece for Contemporary International, Transnational and Global Legal Relations', 2 *Transnational Legal Theory* 67–117.

Ford, J. B., Richard, M. P. and Talbutt, P. C. eds. (1996), *Sorokin and Civilization: A Centennial Assessment*. New Brunswick, NJ: Transaction.

Foucault, M. (1978), *The History of Sexuality. Vol. 1 An Introduction*, transl. R Hurley. London: Penguin reprint, 1990.

———. (1991), 'Governmentality', in G. Burchell, C. Gordon and P. Miller eds, *The Foucault Effect: Studies in Governmentality*, pp. 87–104. London: Harvester Wheatsheaf.

Fourneret, J. (2006), 'France: Banning Legal Pluralism by Passing a Law', 29 *Hastings International and Comparative Law Review* 233–49.

Francescakis, P. (1975), 'Introduction à l'édition francaise', in S. Romano, *L'ordre juridique*, 2nd ed, transl. L. Francois and P. Gothot, pp. v–xix. Paris: Dalloz reprint, 2002.

Freeman, M. D. A. (2014), *Lloyd's Introduction to Jurisprudence*, 9th ed. London: Sweet & Maxwell.

Friedman, G. S. and Whitman, J. Q. (2003), 'The European Transformation of Harassment Law: Discrimination versus Dignity', 9 *Columbia Journal of European Law* 241–74.

Friedman, L. M. (1994), 'Is There a Modern Legal Culture?', 7 *Ratio Juris* 117–31.

———. (1997), 'The Concept of Legal Culture: A Reply', in D. Nelken ed, *Comparing Legal Cultures*, pp. 33–9. Abingdon: Routledge.

Friedmann, W. (1967), *Legal Theory*, 5th ed. New York: Columbia University Press.

Fuller, L. L. (1969), *The Morality of Law*, revised ed. New Haven: Yale University Press.

Gabel, P. (1984), 'The Phenomenology of Rights Consciousness and the Pact of the Withdrawn Selves', 62 *Texas Law Review* 1563–99.

Gecas, V. (2008), 'The Ebb and Flow of Sociological Interest in Values', 23 *Sociological Forum* 344–50.

Geertz, C. (1983), *Local Knowledge: Further Essays in Interpretive Anthropology*. New York: Basic Books.

Gella, A. (1977), 'An Unrecognized Social Theorist – Petrażycki', 22 *Polish Review* 76–9.

Gény, F. (1925), 'The Critical System (Idealistic and Formal) of R. Stammler', in R. Stammler, *The Theory of Justice*, pp. 493–552. New York: Macmillan.

Gilad, S. (2014), 'Beyond Endogeneity: How Firms and Regulators Co-Construct the Meaning of Regulation', 36 *Law & Policy* 134–64.

Gitlin, T. (1995), *The Twilight of Common Dreams: Why America is Wracked by Culture Wars*. New York: Henry Holt.

Go, J. (2016), *Postcolonial Thought and Social Theory*. Oxford: Oxford University Press.

Goldberg, C. (2000), 'A Law of Their Own: Native Challenges to American Law', 25 *Law & Social Inquiry* 263–84.

Goldthorpe, J. (1996), 'The Quantitative Analysis of Large-Scale Data Sets and Rational Action Theory: For a Sociological Alliance', 12 *European Sociological Review* 109–26.

Gorecki, J. (1975a), 'Social Engineering through Law', in J. Gorecki ed, *Sociology and Jurisprudence of Leon Petrażycki*, pp. 115–32. Urbana, IL: University of Illinois Press.

———. ed. (1975b), *Sociology and Jurisprudence of Leon Petrażycki*. Urbana, IL: University of Illinois Press.

Gray, C. B. (2010), *The Methodology of Maurice Hauriou: Legal, Sociological, Philosophical*. Amsterdam: Rodopi.

Grewal, D. S. and Purdy, J. (2014), 'Introduction: Law and Neoliberalism', 77 *Law and Contemporary Problems* 1–23.

Griffiths, J. (2006), 'The Idea of Sociology of Law and its Relation to Law and to Sociology', in M. Freeman ed, *Law and Sociology*, pp. 49–68. Oxford: Oxford University Press.

Grillo, R., Ballard, R., Ferrari, A., Hoekema, A., Maussen, M. and Shah, P. eds. (2009), *Legal Practice and Cultural Diversity*. Abingdon: Routledge.

Grødeland, Å. B. and Miller, W. L. (2015), *European Legal Cultures in Transition*. Cambridge: Cambridge University Press.

Gurvitch, G. (1931), *Le temps present et l'idée du droit social*. Paris: J. Vrin.

———. (1932), *L'idée du droit social – Notion et système du droit social: Histoire doctrinale depuis le 17e siècle jusqu'à la fin du 19e siècle*. Aalen: Scientia Verlag reprint, 1972.

———. (1935), *L'expérience juridique et la philosophie pluraliste du droit*. Paris: A. Pedone.

———. (1947), *Sociology of Law*. London: Routledge & Kegan Paul.

Habermas, J. (1986), 'Law as Medium and Law as Institution', in G. Teubner ed, *Dilemmas of Law in the Welfare State*, pp. 203–20. Berlin/New York: Walter de Gruyter.

———. (1996), *Between Facts and Norms: Contributions to a Discourse Theory of Law and Democracy*, transl. W. Rehg. Cambridge MA: MIT Press.

Halliday, S. (2019), 'After Hegemony: The Varieties of Legal Consciousness Research', 28 *Social and Legal Studies* 859–78.

Hallis, F. (1930), *Corporate Personality: A Study in Jurisprudence*. Aalen: Scientia Verlag reprint, 1978.

Hardt, M. and Negri, A. (2000), *Empire*. Cambridge, MA: Harvard University Press.

Hart, H. L. A. (1983), *Essays on Jurisprudence and Philosophy*. Oxford: Oxford University Press.

———. (1994), *The Concept of Law*, 2nd ed with new postscript. Oxford: Oxford University Press.

Heise, M. (2002), 'The Past, Present, and Future of Empirical Legal Scholarship: Judicial Decision Making and the New Empiricism', *University of Illinois Law Review* 819–50.

Helleringer, G. and Purnhagen, K. eds. (2014), *Towards a European Legal Culture*. Baden-Baden: C. H. Beck/Hart/Nomos.

Hellner, J. (1958), 'Legal Philosophy in the Analysis of Tort Problems', 2 *Scandinavian Studies in Law* 149–76.

Hendry, J. (2021), 'One Umbrella or Two? Comparative (Socio-)Legal Studies in Light of Globalisation', 16 *Journal of Comparative Law* 531–47.

Hertogh, M. (2004), 'A "European" Conception of Legal Consciousness: Rediscovering Eugen Ehrlich', 31 *Journal of Law and Society* 457–81.

Herzog, D. (2020), *Sovereignty RIP*. New Haven: Yale University Press.

Hirsch, M. (2015), *Invitation to the Sociology of International Law*. Oxford: Oxford University Press.

Hitlin, S. and Vaisey, S. eds. (2010), *Handbook of the Sociology of Morality*. New York: Springer.

Honoré, A. M. (1973), 'Groups, Laws and Obedience', in A. W. B. Simpson ed, *Oxford Essays in Jurisprudence*, 2nd ser, pp. 1–21. Oxford: Oxford University Press.

Hopman, M. J. (2022), 'Wait, What Are We Fighting about? Kelsen, Ehrlich and the Reconciliation of Normative Jurisprudence and Sociology of Law', 54 *Legal Pluralism and Critical Social Analysis* 155–75.

Hull, N. E. H. (1997), *Roscoe Pound and Karl Llewellyn: Searching for an American Jurisprudence*. Chicago: University of Chicago Press.

Hunt, A. (1992), 'Foucault's Expulsion of Law: Toward a Retrieval', 17 *Law and Social Inquiry* 1–38.

Husserl, G. (1938), 'Book Review', 5 *University of Chicago Law Review* 330–40.

Jhering, R. V. (1913), *Law as a Means to an End*, transl. I. Husik. Union, NJ: Lawbook Exchange reprint, 1999.

———. (1915), *The Struggle for Law*, transl. J. J. Lalor. Chicago: Callaghan.

Joerges, C. (2011), 'A New Type of Conflicts Law as the Legal Paradigm of the Post-national Constellation', in C. Joerges and J. Falke eds, *Karl Polanyi, Globalisation and the Potential of Law in Transnational Markets*, pp. 465–501. Oxford: Hart.

Johnston, B. V. (1998), 'Introduction', in P. A. Sorokin, *On the Practice of Sociology*, pp. 1–55. Chicago: University of Chicago Press.

Jones, H. W. (1958), 'Book Review', 58 *Columbia Law Review* 755–9.

Kelley, D. R. (1990), *The Human Measure: Social Thought in the Western Legal Tradition*. Cambridge, MA: Harvard University Press.

Kelsen, H. (1945), *General Theory of Law and State*, transl. A. Wedberg. New York: Russell & Russell reprint, 1961.

King, M. and Schütz, A. (1994), 'The Ambitious Modesty of Niklas Luhmann', 21 *Journal of Law and Society* 261–87.

Kingsbury, B. (2009), 'The Concept of "Law" in Global Administrative Law', 20 *European Journal of International Law* 23–57.

Kirchgaessner, S. (2016), 'Food Theft is No Crime for the Hungry, Italian Court Rules', *The Guardian*, May 4th. https://codacons.it/food-theft-is-no-crime-for-the-hungry-italian-court-rules/

Koehrsen, J. et al. (2020), 'Climate Change in Sociology: Still Silent or Resonating?', 68 *Current Sociology* 738–60.

Kojder, A. (1999), 'Adam Podgórecki's Vita Activa', 2(126) *Polish Sociological Review* 323–30.

———. (2006), 'Leon Petrażycki's Socio-legal Ideas and Their Contemporary Continuation', 6 *Journal of Classical Sociology* 333–58.

Kotarbiński, T. (1975), 'The Concept of Adequate Theory', in J. Gorecki ed, *Sociology and Jurisprudence of Leon Petrażycki*, pp. 17–21. Urbana, IL: University of Illinois Press.

Krisch, N. (2005), 'International Law in Times of Hegemony: Unequal Power and the Shaping of the International Legal Order', 16 *European Journal of International Law* 369–408.

Kurczewski, J. (2001), 'Sociology of Law in Poland', 32 *American Sociologist* 85–98.

La Torre, M. (1999), 'Legal Pluralism as an Evolutionary Achievement of Community Law', 12 *Ratio Juris* 182–95.

Lacey, N. (2005), *The Nightmare and the Noble Dream: A Life of H. L. A. Hart*. Oxford: Oxford University Press.

Lande, J. (1975), 'The Sociology of Petrażycki', in J. Gorecki ed, *Sociology and Jurisprudence of Leon Petrażycki*, pp. 23–37. Urbana, IL: University of Illinois Press.

Lando, O. (1997), 'Why Codify the European Law of Contract?', 5 *European Review of Private Law* 525–36.

———. (1999), 'Optional or Mandatory Europeanisation of Contract Law', in S. Feiden and C. U. Schmid eds, *Evolutionary Perspectives and Projects on Harmonisation of Private Law in the EU*. EUI Working Paper LAW 99/7, pp. 11–29. Florence: European University Institute.

———. (2001), 'Comparative Law and Lawmaking', 75 *Tulane Law Review* 1015–32.

Lasson, A. (1914), 'Kohler's Philosophy of Law', in J. Kohler, *Philosophy of Law*, transl. A. Albrecht, pp. 319–32. South Hackensack, NJ: Rothman reprint, 1969.
Latour, B. (2005), *Reassembling the Social: An Introduction to Actor-Network-Theory*. Oxford: Oxford University Press.
———. (2010), *The Making of Law: An Ethnography of the Conseil d'État*, transl. M. Brilman and A. Pottage. Cambridge: Polity.
Lee, J. (2021), 'The Legacy of Robert K. Merton: On Theories of the Middle Range', 36 *Sociological Forum* 515–9.
Legrand, P. (1996), 'European Legal Systems are not Converging', 45 *International and Comparative Law Quarterly* 52–81.
———. (2006), 'Antivonbar', 1 *Journal of Comparative Law* 13–40.
Leiter, B. (2007), *Naturalizing Jurisprudence: Essays on American Legal Realism and Naturalism in Legal Philosophy*. Oxford: Oxford University Press.
Levi, R. and Valverde, M. (2008), 'Studying Law by Association: Bruno Latour Goes to the Conseil d'État', 33 *Law and Social Inquiry* 805–25.
Levy, E. (1950), 'The Reception of Highly Developed Legal Systems by Peoples of Different Cultures', 25 *Washington Law Review* 233–45.
Likhovski, A. (2003), 'Czernowitz, Lincoln, Jerusalem, and the Comparative History of American Jurisprudence', 4 *Theoretical Inquiries in Law* 621–57.
Lindsey, E. (1926), 'Book Review', 74 *University of Pennsylvania Law Review* 520–1.
Littlefield, N. O. (1967), 'Eugen Ehrlich's Fundamental Principles of the Sociology of Law', 19 *Maine Law Review* 1–27.
Ljungman, S. (1955), 'Vilhelm Lundstedt 11.9.1882–20.8.1955', 68 *Tidsskrift for Rettsvitenskap* 352–60.
Llewellyn, K. N. and Hoebel, E. A. (1941), *The Cheyenne Way: Conflict and Case Law in Primitive Jurisprudence*. Norman: University of Oklahoma Press.
Loughlin, M. and Tierney, S. (2018), 'The Shibboleth of Sovereignty', 81 *Modern Law Review* 989–1016.
Luhmann N. (1982), 'The World Society as a Social System', 8 *International Journal of General Systems* 131–8.
———. (2004), *Law as a Social System*, transl. K. A. Ziegert. Oxford: Oxford University Press.
Lundstedt, A. V. (1925), *Superstition or Rationality in Action for Peace? Arguments against Founding a World Peace on the Common Sense of Justice – A Criticism of Jurisprudence*. London: Longmans, Green.
———. (1933), 'The Responsibility of Legal Science for the Fate of Man and Nations', 10 *New York University Law Quarterly Review* 326–40.
———. (1956), *Legal Thinking Revised: My Views on Law*. Stockholm: Almqvist & Wiksell.
Lyotard, J.-F. (1984), *The Postmodern Condition: A Report on Knowledge*, transl. G. Bennington and B. Massumi. Manchester: Manchester University Press.
Magee, B. (1998), *Confessions of a Philosopher: A Journey through Western Philosophy*. London: Orion.
Malinowski, B. (1926), *Crime and Custom in Savage Society*. London: Routledge & Kegan Paul.
Marsden, P. V. (2005), 'The Sociology of James S. Coleman', 31 *Annual Review of Sociology* 1–24.
Martinez, L. P. (1994), 'Taxes, Morals, and Legitimacy', *Brigham Young University Law Review* 521–69.

Massell, G. J. (1968), 'Law as an Instrument of Revolutionary Change in a Traditional Milieu: The Case of Soviet Central Asia', 2 *Law & Society Review* 179–228.
Matsuda, M. J. (1996), *Where Is Your Body? And Other Essays on Race, Gender and the Law*. Boston: Beacon Press.
May, T. (2015), *A Stronger Britain, Built on Our Values*. London: Home Office. https://www.gov.uk/government/speeches/a-stronger-britain-built-on-our-values
Meisel, J. H. (1962), *The Myth of the Ruling Class: Gaetano Mosca and the Elite*. Ann Arbor: University of Michigan Press.
Merry, S. E. (1988), 'Legal Pluralism', 22 *Law & Society Review* 869–96.
Mezey, N. (2001), 'Law as Culture', 13 *Yale Journal of Law & the Humanities* 35–67.
Michaels, R. (2016), 'Does Brexit Spell the Death of Transnational Law?', 17 *German Law Journal* 51–61.
———. (2020), 'Global Legal Pluralism and Conflict of Laws', in P. S. Berman ed, *Oxford Handbook of Global Legal Pluralism*, pp. 629–48. New York: Oxford University Press.
Miles, A. (2015), 'The (Re)genesis of Values: Examining the Importance of Values for Action', 80 *American Sociological Review* 680–704.
Mills, C. W. (1959), *The Sociological Imagination*. Harmondsworth: Penguin reprint, 1970.
Mindus, P. (2009), *A Real Mind: The Life and Work of Axel Hägerström*. Dordrecht: Springer.
Molin, K. (1982–4), 'A. Vilhelm Lundstedt', 24 *Svenskt biografiskt lexikon* 376.
Moorhead, R. and Hinchly, V. (2015), 'Professional Minimalism? The Ethical Consciousness of Commercial Lawyers', 42 *Journal of Law and Society* 387–412.
Mortimer, C. (2015), 'Fundraising Appeal for Woman Fined £330 for Stealing 75p Mars Bar Reaches Nearly £14k', *The Independent*, August 18th. www.independent.co.uk/news/uk/home-news/fundraising-appeal-for-woman-fined-ps330-for-stealing-75p-mars-bar-reaches-nearly-ps14k-10459372.html
Mosca, G. (1939), *The Ruling Class*, transl. H. D. Kahn. New York: McGraw-Hill.
Motyka, K. (2006), 'Law and Sociology: The Petrażyckian Perspective', in M. Freeman ed, *Law and Sociology*, pp. 119–40. Oxford: Oxford University Press.
———. (2007), *Leon Petrażycki: Challenge to Legal Orthodoxy*. Lublin: Towarzystwo Naukowe Katolickiego Uniwersitetu Jana Pawła II.
Müller, J. W. (2008), 'A General Theory of Constitutional Patriotism', 6 *International Journal of Constitutional Law* 72–95.
Munro, C. R. (1981), 'The Swedish Missionary: Vilhelm Lundstedt', *Juridical Review* 55–77.
Murphy, R. (1988), *Social Closure: The Theory of Monopolization and Exclusion*. Oxford: Oxford University Press.
Mussolini, B. (2000a), 'Foundations and Doctrine of Fascism', in J. T. Schnapp ed, *A Primer of Italian Fascism*, pp. 46–71. Lincoln: University of Nebraska Press.
———. (2000b), 'Address to the National Corporative Council', in J. T. Schnapp ed, *A Primer of Italian Fascism*, pp. 154–64. Lincoln: University of Nebraska Press.
Mutua, A. (2008), 'Introducing ClassCrits: From Class Blindness to a Critical Legal Analysis of Economic Inequality', 56 *Buffalo Law Review* 859–913.
Nash, G. B., Crabtree, C. and Dunn, R. E. (1997), *History on Trial: Culture Wars and the Teaching of the Past*. New York: Knopf.
Nelken, D. (1984), 'Law in Action or Living Law? Back to the Beginning in Sociology of Law', 4 *Legal Studies* 157–74.

———. (2003), 'Beyond Compare? Criticizing "The American Way of Law"', 28 *Law & Social Inquiry* 799–831.
———. (2009), 'Ehrlich's Legacies: Back to the Future in the Sociology of Law?', in M. Hertogh ed, *Living Law: Reconsidering Eugen Ehrlich*, pp. 237–72. Oxford: Hart.
———. (2010), *Comparative Criminal Justice: Making Sense of Difference*. London: Sage.
———. (2015), 'The Changing Roles of Social Indicators: From Explanation to Governance', in V. Mitsilegas, P. Alldridge and L. Cheliotis eds, *Globalisation, Criminal Law and Criminal Justice*, pp. 25–43. Oxford: Hart.
———. (2020), 'Sociology of Legal Culture', in J. Přibáň ed, *Research Handbook on the Sociology of Law*, pp. 136–49. Cheltenham: Edward Elgar.
Neumann, F. L. (1937), 'Book Review', 43 *American Journal of Sociology* 351–3.
Noreau, P. and Arnaud. A.-J. (1998), 'The Sociology of Law in France: Trends and Paradigms', 25 *Journal of Law and Society* 258–83.
Northrop, F. S. C. (1959), *The Complexity of Legal and Ethical Experience: Studies in the Method of Normative Subjects*. Boston: Little, Brown.
O'Donnell, E. (2018), *Legal Rights for Rivers: Competition, Collaboration and Water Governance*. Abingdon: Routledge.
Olivecrona, K. (1939), *Law as Fact*, 1st ed. Copenhagen: Einar Munksgaard.
———. (1948), 'Is a Sociological Explanation of Law Possible?', 14 *Theoria* 167–207.
———. (1959), 'The Legal Theories of Axel Hägerström and Vilhelm Lundstedt', 3 *Scandinavian Studies in Law* 125–50.
———. (1971), *Law as Fact*, 2nd ed. London: Stevens.
Olsen, J. (2008), 'Danish Papers Reprint Cartoon of Muhammad', *The Guardian*, February 14th. www.theguardian.com/world/2008/feb/14/muhammadcartoons.islam
Ordower, H. (2010), 'The Culture of Tax Avoidance', 55 *Saint Louis University Law Journal* 47–128.
Orfield, L. B. (1956), 'A Survey of Scandinavian Legal Philosophy, Part II', *Wisconsin Law Review* 585–624.
Orwell, G. (2004), *Why I Write*. London: Penguin.
Ost, F. and Van de Kerchove, M. (2002), *De la pyramide au réseau? Pour une théorie dialectique du droit*. Brussels: Publications des Facultés universitaires Saint-Louis.
Pałecki, K. (1984), 'Leon Petrażycki: Sociology and Legal Sciences', in P. Sztompka ed, *Masters of Polish Sociology*, pp. 133–58. Wrocław: Polska Akademia Nauk.
Parsons, T. (1977), *The Evolution of Societies*. Englewood Cliffs: Prentice-Hall.
Paton, G. W. (1972), *A Textbook of Jurisprudence*, 4th ed. Oxford: Oxford University Press.
Peczenik, A. (1975), 'Leon Petrażycki and the Post-Realistic Jurisprudence', in J. Gorecki ed, *Sociology and Jurisprudence of Leon Petrażycki*, pp. 83–105. Urbana, IL: University of Illinois Press.
Petrażycki, L. (1955), *Law and Morality*, transl. H. W. Babb. Cambridge, MA: Harvard University Press.
Petrusson, U. and Glavå, M. (2008), 'Law in a Global Knowledge Economy: Following the Path of Scandinavian Sociolegal Theory', 53 *Scandinavian Studies in Law* 94–133.
Pianingiani, G. and Chan, S. (2016), 'Can the Homeless and Hungry Steal Food? Maybe, an Italian Court Says', *New York Times*, May 3rd. www.nytimes.com/2016/05/04/world/europe/food-theft-in-italy-may-not-be-a-crime-court-rules.html

Piggott, R. (2008), 'Turkey in Radical Revision of Islamic Texts', *BBC News*, February 26th. http://news.bbc.co.uk/1/hi/world/europe/7264903.stm

Podgórecki, A. (1980), 'Unrecognised Father of Sociology of Law: Leon Petrażycki – Reflections Based on Jan Gorecki's *Sociology and Jurisprudence of Leon Petrażycki*', 15 *Law & Society Review* 183–202.

Pospisil, L. J. (1971), *Anthropology of Law: A Comparative Theory*. New York: Harper and Row.

Pound, R. (1911), 'The Scope and Purpose of Sociological Jurisprudence II', 25 *Harvard Law Review* 140–68.

———. (1912), 'The Scope and Purpose of Sociological Jurisprudence III', 25 *Harvard Law Review* 489–516.

———. (1917), 'The Limits of Effective Legal Action', 27 *International Journal of Ethics* 150–67.

———. (1942), *Social Control through Law*. New Haven: Yale University Press.

———. (1943), 'Sociology of Law and Sociological Jurisprudence', 5 *University of Toronto Law Journal* 1–20.

———. (1958), *The Ideal Element in Law*. Indianapolis: Liberty Fund reprint, 2002.

Prebble, Z. M. and Prebble, J. (2010), 'The Morality of Tax Avoidance', 43 *Creighton Law Review* 693–745.

Purcell jr., E. A. (1973), *The Crisis of Democratic Theory: Scientific Naturalism and the Problem of Value*. Lexington: University Press of Kentucky.

Quinney, R. (1980), *Class, State, and Crime*, 2nd ed. New York: Longman.

Radbruch, G. (1950), 'Legal Philosophy', in *The Legal Philosophies of Lask, Radbruch and Dabin*, transl. K. Wilk, pp. 43–224. Cambridge, MA: Harvard University Press.

Randall, H. J. (1926), 'Book Review', 42 *Law Quarterly Review* 420–1.

Rawls, J. (1958), 'Book Review', 44 *Cornell Law Quarterly* 169.

Raz, J. (2009), *The Authority of Law: Essays on Law and Morality*, 2nd ed. Oxford: Oxford University Press.

Rehbinder, M. (1972), 'The Development and Present State of Fact Research in Law in the United States', 24 *Journal of Legal Education* 567–89.

———. (1978), 'Neues über Leben und Werk von Eugen Ehrlich', in F. Kaulbach and W. Krawietz eds, *Recht und Gesellschaft: Festschrift für Helmut Schelsky zum 65. Geburtstag*, pp. 403–18. Berlin: Duncker & Humblot.

———. (1986), *Die Begründung der Rechtssoziologie durch Eugen Ehrlich*, 2nd ed. Berlin: Duncker & Humblot.

Rheinstein, M. (1979), *Collected Works, Volume 1: Jurisprudence and Sociology, Comparative Law and Common Law (USA)*. Tübingen: J. C. B. Mohr (Paul Siebeck).

Richard, G. (1892), *L'origine de l'idée de droit*. Paris: Thorin et fils.

Romano, S. (2015), 'L'état moderne et sa crise', in *Jus politicum: Revue de droit politique*, no. 14, transl. D. Soldini. http://juspoliticum.com/article/L'Etat-moderne-et-sa-crise-968.html

———. (2017), *The Legal Order*, transl. M. Croce. Abingdon: Routledge.

Rose, N. (1996), 'The Death of the Social? Re-figuring the Territory of Government', 25 *Economy and Society* 327–56.

Rosenfeld, M. (2007), 'Habermas' Call for Cosmopolitan Constitutional Patriotism in an Age of Global Terror: A Pluralist Appraisal', 14 *Constellations* 159–81.

Ross, A. (1974), *On Law and Justice*. London: Stevens & Sons.

Ross, E. A. (1901), *Social Control: A Survey of the Foundations of Order*. New York: Macmillan.

Roughan, N. and Halpin, A. eds. (2017), *In Pursuit of Pluralist Jurisprudence*. Cambridge: Cambridge University Press.
Rudzinski, A. W. (1976), 'Petrażycki's Significance for Contemporary Legal and Moral Theory', 21 *American Journal of Jurisprudence* 107–30.
Ruggiu, I. (2019), *Culture and the Judiciary: The Anthropologist Judge*, transl. J. Daw. Abingdon: Routledge.
Rydström, J. (2003), *Sinners and Citizens: Bestiality and Homosexuality in Sweden, 1880–1950*. Chicago: University of Chicago Press.
Saguy, A. C. and Stuart, F. (2008), 'Culture and Law: Beyond a Paradigm of Cause and Effect', 619 *Annals of the American Academy of Political and Social Science* 149–64.
Samuel, G. (2003), *Epistemology and Method in Law*. Abingdon: Routledge.
———. (2009), 'Interdisciplinarity and the Authority Paradigm: Should Law Be Taken Seriously by Scientists and Social Scientists?', 36 *Journal of Law and Society* 431–59.
Sandulli, A. (2009), 'Santi Romano and the Perception of the Public Law Complexity', transl. M. L. Mariniello, 1 *Italian Journal of Public Law* 1–38.
Sarat, A. and Silbey, S. (1988), 'The Pull of the Policy Audience', 10 *Law & Policy* 97–166.
Schall, C. E. (2012), '(Social) Democracy in the Blood? Civic and Ethnic Idioms of Nation and the Consolidation of Swedish Social Democratic Power, 1928–1932', 25 *Journal of Historical Sociology* 440–74.
Scheppele, K. L. (1994), 'Legal Theory and Social Theory', 20 *Annual Review of Sociology* 383–406.
Schiff, D. (1981), 'N. S. Timasheff's Sociology of Law', 44 *Modern Law Review* 400–21.
Schlegel, J. H. (1995), *American Legal Realism and Empirical Social Science*. Chapel Hill: University of North Carolina Press.
Schmidt, F. (1978), 'The Uppsala School of Legal Thinking', 22 *Scandinavian Studies in Law* 149–75.
Schmitt, C. (2011), 'The Dictatorship of the Reich President According to Art 48 of the Reich Constitution', transl. E. Kennedy, 18 *Constellations* 299–323.
Schultz, U. (2023), 'Knowledge and Opinion about Law: The Importance of Law-related Education', in H. Hydén, R. Cotterrell, D. Nelken and U. Schultz eds, *Combining the Legal and the Social in Sociology of Law: An Homage to Reza Banakar*, pp. 161–72. Oxford: Hart.
Segerstedt, T. T. (1949), 'A Research into the General Sense of Justice', (with G. Karlsson and B. G. Rundblad), 15 *Theoria* 323–38.
Sejersted, F. (2011), *The Age of Social Democracy: Norway and Sweden in the Twentieth Century*. Princeton: Princeton University Press.
Selznick, P. (1959), 'The Sociology of Law', in R. K. Merton, L. Broom and L. S. Cottrell eds, *Sociology Today, Vol 1: Problems and Prospects*, pp. 115–27. New York: Basic Books.
———. (1961), 'Sociology and Natural Law', 6 *Natural Law Forum* 84–108.
———. (1969), *Law, Society, and Industrial Justice*, with P. Nonet and H. M. Vollmer. New York: Russell Sage.
———. (1992), *The Moral Commonwealth: Social Theory and the Promise of Community*. Berkeley: University of California Press.
———. (2008), *A Humanist Science: Values and Ideals in Social Inquiry*. Stanford: Stanford University Press.
Siems, M. (2022), *Comparative Law*. Cambridge: Cambridge University Press.
Silbey, S. S. (2013), 'What Makes a Social Science of Law? Doubling the Social in Socio-Legal Studies'. in D. Feenan ed, *Exploring the 'Socio' of Socio-Legal Studies*, pp. 20–36. Basingstoke: Palgrave Macmillan.

Simmel. G. (1971), 'The Stranger', transl. D. N. Levine, in D. N. Levine ed, *Georg Simmel on Individuality and Social Forms*, pp. 143–9. Chicago: University of Chicago Press.

Simon, J. (1999), 'Law after Society', 24 *Law & Social Inquiry* 143–94.

Simpson, A. (2019), 'Establishing a Disciplining Financial Disposition in the City of London: Resilience, Speed and Intelligence', 53 *Sociology* 1061–76.

Simpson, A. W. B. (2011), *Reflections on* The Concept of Law. Oxford: Oxford University Press.

Singer, J. W. (1988), 'Legal Realism Now', 76 *California Law Review* 465–544.

Skinner, Q. (1969), 'Meaning and Understanding in the History of Ideas', 8 *History and Theory* 3–53.

Soldini, D. (2015), 'Santi Romano, penseur pluraliste et étatiste', *Jus politicum: Revue de droit politique* 14. http://juspoliticum.com/uploads/5704f95a12565-jp14_soldini.pdf

Sorokin, P. (1928), *Contemporary Sociological Theories*. New York: Harper.

———. (1947), 'The Organized Group (Institution) and Law-Norms', in P. Sayre ed, *Interpretations of Legal Philosophies: Essays in Honor of Roscoe Pound*, pp. 668–95. New York: Oxford University Press.

———. (1950), *Leaves from a Russian Diary – and Thirty Years After*. Boston: Beacon Press.

———. (1956), 'Book Review', 69 *Harvard Law Review* 1150–57.

Spaak, T. (2014), *A Critical Appraisal of Karl Olivecrona's Legal Philosophy*. Heidelberg: Springer.

———. (2017), 'Realism about the Nature of Law', 30 *Ratio Juris* 75–104.

Spates, J. L. (1983), 'The Sociology of Values', 9 *Annual Review of Sociology* 27–49.

Stammler, R. (1925), *The Theory of Justice*, transl. I. Husik. New York: Macmillan.

Stjernquist, P. (2000), *Organized Cooperation Facing Law: An Anthropological Study*. Stockholm: Almqvist & Wiksell.

Stone, J. (1966), *Social Dimensions of Law and Justice*. Sydney: Maitland.

Strang, J. (2009a), 'The Scandinavian Value Nihilists and the Crisis of Democracy in the 1930s and 40s', 19(1) *Nordeuropaforum* 37–63.

———. (2009b), 'Two Generations of Scandinavian Legal Realists', 32(1) *Retfaerd* 62–82.

Strathern, M. (1985), 'Discovering "Social Control"', 12 *Journal of Law and Society* 111–34.

Sumner, W. G. (1906), *Folkways: A Study of the Sociological Importance of Usages, Manners, Customs, Mores, and Morals*. New York: New American Library reprint, 1960.

Sundberg, J. (1986), 'Scandinavian Unrealism', 9 *Rechtstheorie Beiheft* 305–21.

Sundell, J.-O. (2005), 'Vilhelm Lundstedt: A Biographical Sketch', 48 *Scandinavian Studies in Law* 465–78.

Swedberg, R. (2003), 'The Case for an Economic Sociology of Law', 32 *Theory and Society* 1–37.

———. (2005), 'Can There Be a Sociological Concept of Interest?', 34 *Theory and Society* 359–90.

Sweet, A. S. (2009), 'Constitutionalism, Legal Pluralism, and International Regimes', 16 *Indiana Journal of Global Legal Studies* 621–45.

Tadros, V. (1998), 'Between Governance and Discipline: The Law and Michel Foucault', 18 *Oxford Journal of Legal Studies* 75–103.

Taekema, S. (2019), 'How to Be a Transnational Jurist: Reflections on Cotterrell's *Sociological Jurisprudence*', 32(4) *Ratio Juris* 509–20.

Tait, R. (2008), 'Three Arrested in Denmark over Plot to Kill Muhammad Cartoonist', *The Guardian*, February 13th. www.theguardian.com/world/2008/feb/13/muhammedcartoonrow

Tamanaha, B. Z. (2006), *Law as a Means to an End: Threat to the Rule of Law*. Cambridge: Cambridge University Press.

———. (2007), 'How an Instrumental View of Law Corrodes the Rule of Law', 56 *DePaul Law Review* 469–505.

Tarlock, A. D. (2004), 'Is There a There There in Environmental Law?', 19 *Journal of Land Use & Environmental Law* 213–54.

Tas, L. (2014), *Legal Pluralism in Action: Dispute Resolution and the Kurdish Peace Committee*. Abingdon: Routledge.

Taylor, P. (2017), 'Brexit: When Taking Back Control Means Giving Up Control', *Politico*, September 12th. www.politico.eu/article/brexit-taking-back-control-united-kingdom-giving-up-control/

Teubner, G. ed. (1987), *Juridification of Social Spheres: A Comparative Analysis in the Areas of Labor, Corporate, Antitrust and Social Welfare Law*. Berlin: Walter de Gruyter.

———. (2011), 'Sociological Jurisprudence – Impossible but Necessary: The Case of Contractual Networks', in R. W. Gordon and M. J. Horwitz eds, *Law, Society, and History: Themes in the Legal Sociology and Legal History of Lawrence M. Friedman*, pp. 367–94. Cambridge: Cambridge University Press.

———. (2012), *Constitutional Fragments: Societal Constitutionalism and Globalization*. Oxford: Oxford University Press.

Timasheff, N. S. (1937), 'Book Review', 2 *American Sociological Review* 120–4.

———. (1939), *An Introduction to the Sociology of Law*. Westport: Greenwood Press reprint, 1974.

———. (1955), 'Introduction', in L. Petrażycki ed, *Law and Morality*, pp. xvii–xxxviii. Cambridge, MA: Harvard University Press.

Travis, A. (2016), 'Legal Fears Stall New Laws to Tackle Extremism', *The Guardian*, May 4th.

Traynor, I. (2008), 'Turkey Strives for 21st Century Form of Islam', *The Guardian*, February 27th. www.theguardian.com/world/2008/feb/27/turkey.islam

Trägårdh, L. (2002), 'Crisis and the Politics of National Community: Germany and Sweden, 1933/1994', in N. Witoszek and L. Trägårdh eds, *Culture and Crisis: The Case of Germany and Sweden*, pp. 75–109. New York: Berghahn.

Treves, R. (1985), 'Hans Kelsen et la sociologie du droit', 1 *Droit et Société* 15–21.

———. (1995), *Sociologie du droit*, transl. W. Baranès and O. Simsek. Paris: Presses Universitaires de France.

———. and Van Loon, J. F. G. eds. (1968), *Norms and Actions: National Reports on Sociology of Law*. Hague: Martinus Nijhoff.

Treviño, A. J. ed. (2008), *Talcott Parsons on Law and the Legal System*. Newcastle: Cambridge Scholars Publishing.

———. (2013), 'Sociological Jurisprudence', in R. Banakar and M. Travers eds, *An Introduction to Law and Social Theory*, 2nd ed, pp. 35–51. Oxford: Hart.

Turner, B. S. (2007), 'Managing Religions: State Responses to Religious Diversity', 1 *Contemporary Islam* 123–37.

Turner, S. P. and Factor, R. A. (1994), *Max Weber: The Lawyer as Social Thinker*. London: Routledge.

Twining, W. (1978), 'The Great Juristic Bazaar', 14 *Journal of the Society of Public Teachers of Law* (n. s.) 185–200.

———. (2012), *Karl Llewellyn and the Realist Movement*, 2nd ed. Cambridge: Cambridge University Press.

Van Den Steen, E. (2010), 'On the Origin of Shared Beliefs (and Corporate Culture)', 41 *RAND Journal of Economics* 617–48.

Van Dyke, V. (1962), 'Values and Interests', 56 *American Political Science Review* 567–76.

Van Klink, B. (2008), 'Facts and Norms: The Unfinished Debate Between Eugen Ehrlich and Kans Kelsen', in M. Hertogh ed, *Living Law: Reconsidering Eugen Ehrlich*, pp. 127–55. Oxford: Hart.

Van Zandt, D. E. (1989), 'The Relevance of Social Theory to Legal Theory', 83 *Northwestern University Law Review* 10–37.

Varella, M. D. (2013), 'Central Aspects of the Debate on Complexity and Fragmentation of International Law', 27 *Emory International Law Review* 1–22.

Varga, C. (2005), 'The "Hart-Phenomenon"', 91 *Archiv für Rechts- und Sozialphilosophie* 83–95.

Vinogradoff, P. (1920), 'The Crisis of Modern Jurisprudence', in *The Collected Papers of Paul Vinogradoff, vol. 2: Jurisprudence*, pp. 215–25. London: Wildy reprint, 1964.

Vinx, L. (2018), 'Santi Romano Against the State?', 11 *Ethics & Global Politics* 1–12.

Vogl, S. (2009), 'Eugen Ehrlich's Linking of Sociology and Jurisprudence and the Reception of his Work in Japan', in M. Hertogh ed, *Living Law: Reconsidering Eugen Ehrlich*, pp. 95–233. Oxford: Hart.

Vogt, W. P. (1982), 'Obligation and Right: The Durkheimians and the Sociology of Law', in P. Besnard ed, *The Sociological Domain: The Durkheimians and the Founding of French Sociology*, pp. 177–98. Cambridge: Cambridge University Press.

Von Bar, C. and Lando, O. (2002), 'Communication on European Contract Law: Joint Response of the Commission on European Contract Law and the Study Group on a European Civil Code', 10 *European Review of Private Law* 183–248.

Wacks, R. (2012), *Understanding Jurisprudence: An Introduction to Legal Theory*, 3rd ed. Oxford: Oxford University Press.

Wagner, R. (1975), 'Fakultäten, Lehrkörper und Rektoren der "Francisco-Josephina"', in R. Wagner ed, *Alma Mater Francisco Josephina: Die deutschsprachige Nationalitäten-Universität in Czernowitz*, pp. 122–32. München: Verlag Hans Meschendörfer.

Walicki, A. (1967), *Legal Philosophies of Russian Liberalism*. Notre Dame: University of Notre Dame Press reprint, 1992.

Weber, M. (1930), *The Protestant Ethic and the Spirit of Capitalism*, transl. T. Parsons. London: Unwin reprint, 1985.

———. (1948), *From Max Weber: Essays in Sociology*, transl. H. Gerth and C. W. Mills. London: Routledge & Kegan Paul.

———. (1949), *Methodology of Social Sciences*, transl. E. A. Shils and H. A. Finch. New Brunswick: Transaction reprint, 2011.

———. (1968), *Economy and Society: An Outline of Interpretive Sociology*, transl. E. Fischoff et al. Berkeley: University of California Press reprint, 1978.

Weiler, B. (2002), 'E Pluribus Unum? The Kakanian Intellectual and the Question of Cultural Pluralism', Paper for Conference at St Anthony's College, Oxford, May 24–26. https://docslib.org/doc/5783464/the-kakanian-intellectual-and-the-question-of-cultural-pluralism

Welk, W. G. (1938), *Fascist Economic Policy: An Analysis of Italy's Economic Experiment*. Cambridge, MA: Harvard University Press.

Werfel, F. (1937), *Twilight of a World*, transl. H. T. Lowe-Porter. London: Jarrolds.

Whitman, J. Q. (2000), 'Enforcing Civility and Respect: Three Societies', 109 *Yale Law Journal* 1279–398.

———. (2004), 'Two Western Cultures of Privacy: Dignity versus Liberty', 113 *Yale Law Journal* 1151–221.

———. (2005), *Harsh Justice: Criminal Punishment and the Widening Divide Between America and Europe.* New York: Oxford University Press.

Wicenty, D. (2018), 'The Experience of Oppression and the Price of Nonconformity: A Brief Biography of Adam Podgórecki', 70 *Studies in East European thought* 61–81.

Wickham, G. (2013), 'Foucault and Law', in R. Banakar and M. Travers eds, *Law and Social Theory*, 2nd ed, pp. 217–32. Oxford: Hart.

Wieacker, F. (1990), 'Foundations of European Legal Culture', 38 *American Journal of Comparative Law* 1–29.

Wigmore, J. H. et al eds. (1917), *Science of Legal Method: Select Essays by Various Authors*, transl. E. Bruncken and L. B. Register. Boston: Boston Book Co.

Williams, C. (2022), *An Economic Sociology of Law Reimagined: Beyond Embeddedness.* Abingdon: Routledge.

Williams, P. J. (1991), *The Alchemy of Race and Rights.* Cambridge, MA: Harvard University Press.

Williams, R. (2008), 'Civil and Religious Law in England: A Religious Perspective', 10 *Ecclesiastical Law Journal* 262–82.

Winch, P. (1958), *The Idea of a Social Science and Its Relation to Philosophy.* London: Routledge & Kegan Paul.

Witteveen, W. J. (2005), 'Turning to Communication in the Study of Legislation', in N. Zeegers, W. Witteveen and B. van Klink eds, *Social and Symbolic Effects of Legislation Under the Rule of Law*, pp. 17–44. Lewiston: Edwin Mellen.

Woodman, G. R. (1997), 'Legal Pluralism and the Search for Justice', 40 *Journal of African Law* 152–67.

———. (1998), 'Ideological Combat and Social Observation: Recent Debate about Legal Pluralism', 42 *Journal of Legal Pluralism and Unofficial Law* 21–59.

Wuthnow, R. (2008), 'The Sociological Study of Values', 23 *Sociological Forum* 333–43.

Young, I. M. (2002), *Inclusion and Democracy.* Oxford: Oxford University Press.

Zamboni, M. (2002), 'Law and Legal Politics: Vilhelm Lundstedt and the Law-Maker Function', 6 *Associations* 35–61.

———. (2008), *Law and Politics: A Dilemma for Contemporary Legal Theory.* Berlin: Springer-Verlag.

Zanetti, G. (2011), 'Italian Normative Pluralism: What is Unique about the Future of Italy', 2(1) *California Italian Studies.* https://escholarship.org/uc/item/16c8282p

Zetterberg, K. (1980–1), 'K. A. Rickard Lindström', 23 *Svenskt biografiskt lexikon* 649.

Ziegert, K. A. (1979), 'The Sociology Behind Eugen Ehrlich's Sociology of Law', 7 *International Journal of the Sociology of Law* 225–73.

Zimmermann, R. (1996), 'Savigny's Legacy: Legal History, Comparative Law, and the Emergence of a European Legal Science', 112 *Law Quarterly Review* 576–605.

Zweig, S. (2009), *The World of Yesterday: Memoirs of a European*, transl. A. Bell. London: Pushkin Press.

Zweigert, K. and Kötz, H. (1998), *An Introduction to Comparative Law*, 3rd ed. Oxford: Oxford University Press.

INDEX

Milton Keynes UK
Ingram Content Group UK Ltd.
UKHW020348210224
438206UK00014B/82

9 781032 374635